'*Neurodiversity and Mental Health* offers a comprehensive and thought-provoking exploration of the intersection between neurodivergence and mental wellbeing. Bringing together leading voices from research, clinical practice, and lived experience, this volume critically examines how neurodiversity is understood, represented, and supported across diverse contexts. The book unpacks the evolving concept of neurodiversity and traces its origins and contemporary relevance in academic, healthcare, and social spheres.

Chapters address key barriers and enablers in accessing appropriate healthcare, shedding light on systemic inequalities and the importance of inclusive, person-centred approaches. The complex relationship between neurodivergence and mental health is examined in particular depth.

The book also explores the educational landscape, analysing how schools and universities can foster environments that celebrate cognitive diversity. A final section offers global perspectives, emphasising cultural, social, and policy variations in how neurodiversity is perceived and supported worldwide. One size does not fit all.

This essential text is an invaluable resource for students, clinicians, educators, policymakers, and anyone interested in advancing equity and understanding in the fields of neurodiversity and mental health.'

Brendan Kelly, *Professor of Psychiatry, Trinity College Dublin*

'This timely and comprehensive book brings together diverse voices to explore the intersection of neurodivergence and mental health. Drawing on both lived experience and research, it highlights how conditions like ADHD, autism, and DCD are often misunderstood, especially when co-occurring with anxiety or depression. It challenges outdated narratives and addresses the impact of stigma and systemic exclusion. This is a valuable resource for creating more inclusive, neurodiversity-affirming mental health care across the lifespan.'

Professor Amanda Kirby, *Emeritus Professor, University of South Wales*

Neurodiversity and Mental Health

Neurodiversity and Mental Health presents an evidenced-based and theoretically informed guide on effective, impactful strategies for collaborative advancement in the area of neurodiversity and mental health in terms of healthcare services and other social and political institutions.

Moving beyond generic approaches and assumptions about neurodivergence, the contributors demonstrate strategic priorities that optimise outcomes for co-occurring mental health challenges and neurodivergence. The book synthesises the prevailing ideas, sets the cultural and scientific context, and provides a useful resource for individuals and services to signpost necessary changes. Drawing together the international literature on co-occurring mental illness and neurodivergence, it pinpoints exemplars of best practice and provides a roadmap for further research and service innovation.

Neurodiversity and Mental Health will be essential reading for any practitioner, student, or scholar seeking to understand how mental health challenges and neurodiversity co-occur, and how to ensure optimal outcomes for patients.

Etain Quigley, PhD, is Lecturer in Law at Maynooth University, specialising in neurodiversity, mental health, youth justice, and criminology. She has held Irish Research Council awards, worked on FP7 and H2020 projects, and serves on Mental Health Tribunals. She is also a co-founding editor of *Neurodiversity*.

Andrew Eddy is the co-founder of the Neurodiversity Hub community of practice, working with universities and employers to facilitate neurodivergent higher education students become more work-ready and increase their employment opportunities. Andrew is retired but continues his interest in neurodiversity and advocating for more inclusive workplaces and learning spaces.

Timothy Frawley, PhD, is Associate Professor in Mental Health Nursing at UCD. A registered psychiatric nurse and educator, he has held leadership roles in curriculum development, governance, and research. His work focuses on neurodiversity, nursing governance, and service user involvement.

Charlotte Valeur is an investment banker, FTSE Chair, published author, and professor in governance and leadership, with a wealth of board experience across many sectors. A lifelong human rights advocate, Charlotte is driven to play her part in creating an inclusive society, advocating for equality and inclusion for all. To this effect, she also founded the global Institute of Neurodiversity ION in 2021.

Blánaid Gavin, PhD, is a child and adolescent psychiatrist who has worked clinically with children and teenagers for over 20 years. She is particularly interested in expanding understanding in relation to child and adolescent mental health. To this end, she has been involved in teaching and research focused on optimising outcomes for young people. She specialises in the area of ADHD.

Neurodiversity: International Perspectives on Theory Policy and Practice

Series Editors
Etain Quigley, Andrew Eddy, Timothy Frawley, Charlotte Valeur, and Blánaid Gavin

About the Series

This five-book series explores neurodiversity across important and interconnected domains – mental health, higher education, the criminal justice system, gender, and relationships. The series grew from a series of annual international online conferences organised by University College Dublin, Maynooth University, ADHD Ireland, ION and the Neurodiversity Hub. The conference sparked significant interest and dialogue, leading to a series of follow-up masterclasses, and eventually, this book series.

At its core, this series seeks to push beyond traditional academic boundaries by creating a platform for neurodivergent and neuro-mixed voices to share research, lived experience, and critical reflections. Contributors were invited for their scholarly expertise, but also for their capacity to bring authentic, engaged, and at times challenging perspectives to the forefront. The resulting volumes reflect an inclusive and dialogic approach that takes on complexity, fosters respectful disagreement, and centres empowerment for those often marginalised by dominant systems and narratives.

The books are underpinned by a neurodiversity-affirmative framework, which seeks to move away from deficit-based thinking and clinical labelling, and instead recognises and values neurological variation as part of human diversity. While clinical terminology (such as "Autism Spectrum Disorder" or "ADHD") is used where chosen by authors, the editorial team encouraged contributors to adopt affirming, identity-respecting language and to situate their work within the broader goals of inclusivity and transformation.

Each book in this series focuses on a distinct yet overlapping domain in which neurodivergent individuals often experience systemic barriers, exclusion, and misunderstanding. These volumes seek to shift the paradigm:

- from assimilation to authentic inclusion;
- from pathologisation to validation;
- from silencing to co-production of knowledge.

The first book addresses the critical link between neurodiversity and mental health, where masking, marginalisation, and social exclusion can lead to significant distress. The second book turns its attention to higher education, interrogating how inclusive practices can be implemented and reimagined through neurodivergent-led scholarship. Future volumes will examine how neurodiversity intersects with the criminal justice system, with gendered experiences, and within the context of interpersonal relationships, bringing fresh perspectives to policy, practice, and daily life.

The editorial approach has been both rigorous and reflexive. Contributors were encouraged to draw on both empirical research and theoretical frameworks, while also writing in a style and structure that best reflected their message. In doing so, this series fosters an academic space that honours diversity not only in neurological profile but also in scholarly voice.

This series is grounded in the principle of "nothing about us without us." It champions a rights-based, community-led approach to knowledge and advocacy, promoting systemic change through informed dialogue and shared vision. It aims not only to advance academic and policy discourse, but to support a growing movement that reclaims space, agency, and dignity for neurodivergent individuals around the world.

This series is, unapologetically, part of a wider paradigm shift – one that affirms neurodivergent lives, challenges institutional norms, and creates space for critical and collaborative transformation.

Books in this Series

Neurodiversity and Mental Health
Edited by Etain Quigley, Andrew Eddy, Timothy Frawley, Charlotte Valeur, and Blánaid Gavin

For more information about this series, please visit: https://www.routledge.com/

Neurodiversity and Mental Health

Edited by Etain Quigley, Andrew Eddy, Timothy Frawley, Charlotte Valeur, and Blánaid Gavin

Routledge
Taylor & Francis Group

LONDON AND NEW YORK

Designed cover image: Getty Images

First published 2026
by Routledge
4 Park Square, Milton Park, Abingdon, Oxon OX14 4RN

and by Routledge
605 Third Avenue, New York, NY 10158

Routledge is an imprint of the Taylor & Francis Group, an informa business

British Library Cataloguing-in-Publication Data
A catalogue record for this book is available from the British Library

ISBN: 978-1-032-80201-5 (hbk)
ISBN: 978-1-032-80198-8 (pbk)
ISBN: 978-1-003-49594-9 (ebk)

DOI: 10.4324/9781003495949

Typeset in Times New Roman
by Apex CoVantage, LLC

Contents

Contributors

Etain Quigley is Lecturer in Law at Maynooth University, Ireland. She teaches and conducts research in the areas of neurodiversity, mental health, youth justice, and criminological theory and has been appointed and reappointed to sit on mental health tribunals for over a decade. Dr Quigley completed her PhD and postdoctoral work at University College Dublin, Ireland. She was successful in her application for the Irish Research Council Government of Ireland Postdoctoral Scholarship. She was also successful in receiving a Teaching and Learning Fellowship and two Irish Research Council New Foundations awards. Moreover, she has worked on an Fp7 and an H2020 research project. Finally, she is a co-founding editor of the Sage journal *Neurodiversity*.

Dimitrios Adamis is Consultant Psychiatrist at Sligo Mental Health Services and a part-time consultant in the ADHD specialist clinic for adults in north-west of Ireland. He has led several research studies on two attentional disorders: delirium in older adults and ADHD in adulthood. His current focus is on adult ADHD. He collaborates with a number of centres, including University of Limerick and Galway, University College Dublin, Institute of Psychiatry in London, and Academic Medical Center, Amsterdam, in The Netherlands. He is Honorary Professor in Galway and Limerick Universities. He has authored and co-authored approximately 150 peer-review papers and 15 book chapters.

Charlotte Boatman is a PhD student in Neurodevelopmental Sciences at the Institute of Psychiatry, Psychology, and Neuroscience, King's College London. She has a BSc and MSc in Psychology and Cognitive Neuropsychology and a background working in the latter field both clinically and in research. Her current research interests involve using co-production and participatory practices to enhance the field. More specifically, she focuses on autistic burnout, its predictors and consequences, anxiety, and support and treatment for these experiences.

Hugo D. Critchley studied Physiology and Medicine at the University of Liverpool, undertook a DPhil in Psychological Studies at Oxford, and trained in psychiatry/neuropsychiatry in parallel with research jobs at KCL Institute of Psychiatry and UCL Institute of Neurology. From research in autism at Kings

(1996–1998), he developed a clinical neuroscience research programme at UCL focused on understanding the bidirectional mind–brain–body interaction. At UCLH, Hugo was a consultant neuropsychiatrist for the National Tourette Syndrome Clinic (2003–2006), before moving to Brighton and Sussex Medical School (Universities of Brighton and Sussex) as foundation Chair of Psychiatry. In Sussex, he developed an imaging and psychiatry research group and led (until 2022) a new Department of Clinical Neuroscience. Hugo co-developed a cross-diagnostic adult Neurodevelopmental Service at Sussex Partnership NHS Foundation Trust in 2006, where he continues to work clinically. Hugo chaired the Academic Faculty of the Royal College of Psychiatrists from 2019 to 2022.

Mary Doherty ("Mary") is Clinical Associate Professor at UCD School of Medicine, University College Dublin. For most of my life, I had no idea that I was autistic, although I knew I was different to others from a very early age. Life finally made sense when I was identified as autistic in my 40s, and I also received a diagnosis of ADHD a couple of years later. I would also fit the criteria for Tourette's, although it's never been formally diagnosed, and therefore I consider myself to be multiply neurodivergent. I am the mother of two wonderful neurodivergent young people. I always wanted to be a doctor, and I trained as an anaesthetist.

Sarah Douglas is an autism/ND academic research study advisor who has contributed to much-needed areas of research such as education, self-harm, suicidality, anxiety, IPV, and sexual assault. She is Autistic Representative for the AIMS-2-TRIALS research consortium, a core member of the Respect for Neurodevelopment Network, and Honorary Research Associate at Bristol University. Sarah is also a member of the Autism and ID Advisory Group for SARSAS, a support charity for survivors of sexual violence, and a media representative for StepChange debt relief charity. She is co-author of *Understanding Autistic Relationships across the Lifespan* with Dr Felicity Sedgewick and a contributor to Damian Milton's upcoming "Double Empathy Reader." When she is not sleeping, Sarah is conducting her own MRes research into spiritual abuse and enjoys singing with the Adult Autism Choir, attending rock/metal gigs, theatre, and RockFit classes.

Jessica A. Eccles is Consultant Psychiatrist in the Neurodevelopmental Service at Sussex Partnership NHS Foundation Trust, specialising in adult ADHD, autism, and Tourette syndrome. Within that service, she co-leads the world's first Neurodivergent Brain–Body Clinic. Having trained in medicine at the Universities of Cambridge and Oxford, she completed integrated academic training in psychiatry at Brighton and Sussex Medical School, where she undertook an MRC Clinical Research Training Fellowship. She is now Associate Professor (Reader) in Brain–Body Medicine at the BSMS Department of Clinical Neuroscience where she leads prize-winning research on a broad range of projects that link differences in the body (particularly exemplified by joint hypermobility) to a variety of physical and mental health conditions. She is particularly interested in the emerging link with neurodivergence. She chairs the Neurodevelopmental Psychiatry Special Interest Group of the Royal College of Psychiatrists. She is a passionate educator and committed to public engagement. She hopes to encourage curiosity and challenge stereotypes.

Andrew Eddy (BCom, FCA, FCPA, FAICD) is a senior finance professional passionate about neurodiversity and creating opportunities for neurodivergent individuals. He co-founded Untapped Talent and the Neurodiversity Hub initiative focused on working with employers and higher education institutions to develop a sustainable neurodiverse employment ecosystem to increase opportunities for autistic individuals and those with other neuro-variations, thereby realising their untapped potential. Before this, Andrew had a career in senior finance-related roles with global public companies and was also Deputy Chancellor of La Trobe University in Australia. Andrew has now retired but continues his interest in neurodiversity and advocating for more inclusive workplaces and learning spaces.

Timothy Frawley is Associate Professor in Mental Health Nursing at University College Dublin, with previous roles as Head of Subject and Associate Dean. He teaches on Ireland's only Neurodiversity Professional Certificate and Diploma programme and focuses on inclusive nursing practices in mental health care. His work is dedicated to advancing mental health nursing, neurodiversity awareness and education, aiming to improve support for people within healthcare settings. Dr Frawley's commitment to advancing neurodiversity is also shaped by personal experiences that have provided unique insights into the challenges and strengths of neurodivergent individuals.

Hannah Hayward is a neurodevelopmental specialist in independent practice with over 20 years of experience in the field of autism spectrum and related conditions. In 2003, Hannah started working with the National Autistic Society as Outreach Community Worker before moving into applied research at the University of Oxford. While working at the IoPPN (Institute of Psychiatry, Psychology, and Neuroscience), Hannah worked on multiple studies involving complex, multimodal, in-depth clinical assessments of children, adolescents, and adults. In her current practice, Hannah conducts diagnostic assessments across multiple NHS Trusts, the Criminal Justice System, and private pathways. She also delivers training on gold-standard diagnostic tools and increasing understanding of neurodivergence across public and private sectors, including HMPS.

Eva Loth is Professor of Cognitive Neuroscience at the Institute of Psychiatry, Psychology and Neuroscience, King's College London. Her main interest is in understanding the dynamic interaction between social and biological factors in social, cognitive, and emotional development in autistic and neurodivergent people. She is Deputy Lead of the AIMS-2-TRIALS consortium, which aims to develop precision medicine for autism to better predict a person's developmental outcome and tailor support to individual profiles. She co-lead the biomarker work programme, which comprises a set of large-scale multidisciplinary longitudinal cohorts spanning infants, preschoolers, adolescents, and adults with varying support needs. She is also Principal Investigator of RESPECT4Neurodevelopment, a UKRI Network Plus that brings together bioengineers, physicists, psychologists, psychiatrists, and families with lived experience to develop responsible, reliable, scalable, and personalised neurotechnologies for neurodivergent children. Finally, her emergent interest is in studying the interplay between social–environmental adversities and protective factors in neurodevelopment and mental health in low- and middle income countries. Here, the current focus is on children and young people who experience multiple poverty-related adversities in South Africa.

Liam McGrattan has worked in areas of healthcare since completing his BA in Psychology Studies and Sociology and Politics at the University of Galway. Subsequently he completed a HDipA in Psychology and an MSc in Clinical Neuroscience. He has worked in a multitude of healthcare settings, including social care, mental health, and children's disability; he also had research roles with Royal College of Surgeons Ireland and Trinity College Dublin. His research areas of interest include ADHD, autism, intervention evaluation, and conceptual issues within psychology and healthcare. He currently works with the ParentsPlus charity as Assistant Psychologist and Associate Researcher focused on the evaluation and development of parent-based group interventions.

Jessica Monahan is a neurodivergent researcher, advocate, and educator committed to improving outcomes for disabled folx through meaningful, collaborative research. She has a PhD from the University of Connecticut and a record of published works, book chapters, and nationally invited talks on neurodiversity and mental health. Acutely aware of the systematic barriers in education and employment for the disabled community, Dr Monahan is passionate to shift narratives about disability.

Rachel Mukwezwa-Tapera is a public health specialist, educator, and community advocate passionate about Indigenous and migrant health and health equity. Rachel is keenly interested in Indigenous philosophies and their application to research and practice. She believes in the opportunities for innovation and out-of-the-box theorising provided by embracing diverse ways of knowing and seeing the world. Such opportunities are crucial in decolonising spaces and tackling and eradicating health inequities. Rachel has conceptualised and led critical Indigenist research underpinned by the African philosophy of Ubuntu. The research focused on exploring the social effects of neurodiversity for African migrants in Aotearoa New Zealand. This work has led to the opening up of conversations on how neurodivergent African migrants can be best supported and opportunities for further exploration of this field for other minoritised migrant communities in Aotearoa. Rachel is a passionate champion for change, who, through her neurodiversity work with African communities, is working towards setting up support services to enable equitable access to information and support and raising awareness to dispel the stigma attached to neurodiversity. Rachel is also collaborating on work aimed at bringing together diverse perspectives and understandings of autism by Māori, Pacific, and Indigenous diasporic communities.

Bethany Oakley is Lecturer in Neurodevelopmental Sciences at the Institute of Psychiatry, Psychology, and Neuroscience, King's College London. Bethany holds a BA (Hons) in Psychological and Behavioural Sciences from the University of Cambridge and a PhD in Developmental Psychopathology from King's College London. Bethany's research focuses on the emergence, maintenance, and impact of co-occurring mental health problems (e.g., anxiety, depression), especially as experienced by neurodivergent populations, where rates of mental health problems are elevated. Bethany also researches the development and implementation of novel and adapted support strategies to prevent and manage mental health problems, including through digital technologies and innovations.

Claire O'Neill is an experienced primary teacher, post-primary teacher, and teacher-educator. She has worked previously as a health and well-being advisor with the Professional Development Support Service for Teachers in Ireland. Claire writes regularly about inclusive education, neurodivergence, and neuroaffirmative approaches and her first solo-authored book was published in February 2023. She is research-active in the field of neurodivergence and well-being and contributes to several research advisory panels. Claire is multiply neurodivergent and her lived experience is central to her professional and academic work.

Roderik Plas was born and resides in The Netherlands. He has diagnoses of PDD-NOS and ADHD Type I and has experienced autistic burnout, depression, and sleep problems. These lived experiences have underpinned Roderik's motivation for involvement in (self-) advocacy efforts, and his role in several large-scale European academic research consortia.

Lisa Quadt is an AuDHD cognitive neuroscientist whose interest is in the central and autonomic nervous system, and the interactions between mind, brain, and body are applied to the understanding of neurodivergent individuals. She is a research fellow in the Department of Neuroscience at the Brighton and Sussex Medical School, University of Sussex. She attained her PhD at the Johannes Gutenberg University of Mainz, Germany, taking an interdisciplinary approach towards a theoretical framework for social cognition that integrated philosophy, cognitive psychology, predictive processing, and social neuroscience. Since 2017, at Brighton and Sussex Medical School, she has led the implementation and testing of interoceptive training studies, neuroimaging, behavioural, and self-report studies in clinical and neurodivergent populations.

Sebastian C.K. Shaw ("Seb") is Assistant Professor in Medical Education (Research Methods), Department of Medical Education, Brighton and Sussex Medical School. I'm multiply neurodivergent. I came to my autistic, ADHD, and dyslexic identity as an adult. I am a medical doctor working in the National Health Service in the United Kingdom. At Brighton and Sussex Medical School, I focus my research on the experiences of neurodivergent people in relation to healthcare – looking at neurodivergent people accessing healthcare – and also neurodivergent healthcare staff/students.

Jerneja Terčon is Professor of Educational Sciences, Special Education and Rehabilitation. She works in a Developmental Clinic with the Centre for Early Intervention at the Community Health Centre Domžale, Slovenia. She is Autism Representative in the Aims-2-Trials, being neurodivergent herself and having three neurodivergent children as well. As a researcher, she has spent the last 20 years doing research into Developmental Coordination Disorder, also being a country representative in the ISRA-DCD, as well as a founding member with lived experience. Since her son's autism diagnosis almost a decade ago, she shifted her special interest in research into autism and other coexisting neurodevelopmental conditions. She does a lot of NGO work, being one of the most vocal advocates for neurodivergency shift in clinical practice and policy changes in the EU. Her recent autism, ADHD and DCD diagnosis, and having mental health problems all her life, is testament to how a ND person with lived experiences could be a much-welcomed addition in participatory research. Most recently, her special research interests have extended to autistic burnout, trauma, and PTSD, as well as PDA and selective mutism both in childhood and in adulthood.

Charlotte Valeur is an investment banker and seasoned FTSE Chair, Non-Executive Director, and governance expert with a wealth of board experience across different sectors. She is a professor, author, and public speaker in corporate governance, leadership, equality, and diversity. A lifelong human rights advocate, Charlotte is driven to play her part in creating an inclusive society; she advocates for equality and inclusion for all, working at the intersection of Government, Industry, academia, and the Third Sector. She founded Board Apprentice and the global Institute of Neurodiversity, ION.

Pierre Violland is an autistic Peer Practitioner, living in Switzerland. After a late diagnosis and with a background in engineering, he has started a new full-time professional activity as a peer support to autistic people, their families, the institutions, and the employers. He has a strong interest in participatory research, having collaborated with numerous teams on subjects ranging from ethics to neuroscience, from mental health to policies. He focuses on making links between lived experience of autism and biomedical research, to help improve the latter and make it more usable to increase the quality of life of autistic people.

Blánaid Gavin is Consultant Child and Adolescent Psychiatrist who has worked as a clinician with children who experience mental health difficulties for over 20 years. Dr Gavin's clinical and research interest include service accessibility and outcome optimisation. Dr Gavin is also involved in teaching, training, and research in the field of child and adolescent psychiatry. She works with a variety of voluntary organisations to support collaborative models of awareness and enable co-production in system change. Together with Prof McNicholas, Dr Gavin has co-developed a project to heighten awareness of young people's mental health across a variety of sectors, including health, education, and justice. She led the development of the first interdisciplinary research in Ireland exploring the experiences of young people attending mental health services. As Chair of the university Equity, Diversity and Inclusion subgroup on Neurodiversity, she is co-lead of the research programme on Making UCD a Neurodiversity Friendly Campus.

Introduction

This book is the first in a series of books in the area of neurodiversity that arose from a number of papers presented at an international online conference organised by University College Dublin, Maynooth University, Stanford University, ADHD Ireland, and the Neurodiversity Hub in December 2020. The conference was so successful that a series of master classes was organised whereby the speakers would enter into a dialogue about their areas and provide the audience with a more engaged format to discuss their topics. As a result of the success of the master classes and the conference, it was decided to bring these diverse and important topics into one accessible book format to assist with the development of advancements, and indeed a social paradigm shift, in the area of neurodiversity. A number of speakers were invited to contribute to the book. The framework for the book was one of inclusivity, respectfulness of others' opinions, even where there is disagreement, empowering individuals who are often disempowered by the system, and reflection to allow for contemplation on often complex ideas that push the boundaries of presupposed and long-standing social and biomedical ideas.

The intersection between neurodiversity and mental health is complex and seeps into many areas of individuals' lives, from family to school to work life and, indeed, many other areas. Whilst it is beyond the scope of this book to delve into all of these areas, the book has brought together key areas where this intersection is evidenced. Moreover, this book provides a springboard where other areas of intersectionality can be explored through the other books in this series. Neurodiversity is increasingly recognised as a significant risk factor for mental health challenges and there are competing views as to whether this is as a result of societal triggers and/or other correlating/causal factors. Indeed, this is an area that requires significant attention if services are to meet the specific requirements of neurodivergent persons who experience mental health difficulties. This is particularly important as many mental health services struggle to effectively support neurodivergent individuals due to a lack of specialised knowledge and tailored approaches that can lead to poor services and outcomes. This is often compounded by systemic obstacles, social marginalisation, stigma, and an expectation to adhere to neurotypical norms, which can contribute to stress, lowered self-esteem, and feelings of isolation. A more inclusive society, one that embraces neurodiversity, provides universal

DOI: 10.4324/9781003495949-1

support for individual needs, and promotes understanding, has the potential to significantly alleviate these mental health concerns. When society makes a concerted effort to challenge presuppositions and foster a more inclusive environment, it can lead to opportunities for true acceptance and a sense of belonging. Simple gestures of empathy, accommodation, and support can have a profound positive effect on the well-being of neurodivergent individuals, enabling them to flourish and engage with society meaningfully, without the added strain of unnecessary mental distress. This book aims to bridge this gap by providing evidence-based guidance on supporting neurodivergent individuals with co-occurring mental health conditions. It explores the unique needs of this population, identifies best practices, and advocates for systemic changes to improve mental health care for all.

Moreover, this book dives into tackling difficult areas such as the intersection of mental health and neurodiversity. The neurodivergent community often face significant mental health challenges and the etiology of these challenges is unclear. However, a substantial body of evidence highlights the role of social exclusion. This exclusion manifests across various domains, including social interactions, education, healthcare, employment, and even within families. Understanding how exclusion contributes to mental health difficulties is crucial for developing effective support systems and fostering inclusive environments. Social exclusion refers to the process by which individuals or groups are systematically marginalised from participating fully in societal activities. This marginalisation can occur through discrimination, stigmatisation, and the creation of barriers that prevent equal access to resources and opportunities. For the neurodivergent community, social exclusion often results in limited access to quality education, healthcare services, employment opportunities, and social networks. Exclusion serves as a mechanism to suppress neurological differences by enforcing conformity to societal norms. This suppression invalidates the unique experiences and contributions of neurominorities, pressuring individuals to mask or hide their differences. Such masking is mentally exhausting and can lead to increased stress and mental health issues. The societal expectation to "fit in" disregards the value of diversity and perpetuates a cycle of exclusion and mental distress. A study published in the *British Journal of Psychiatry*[1] highlights the complex relationship between social exclusion and mental health, it outlined that social disadvantage, including mental illness, is both a cause and a consequence of social exclusion. This has led to growing efforts to promote social inclusion for those with mental health problems, who are often among the most excluded in society. The mental health difficulties experienced by the neurodivergent community are deeply intertwined with the pervasive social exclusion they encounter. By recognising and addressing the various forms of exclusion – as mechanisms that suppress neurological differences – society can take meaningful steps towards fostering inclusivity. Such efforts not only alleviate mental health challenges but also enrich communities by embracing the full spectrum of human diversity. This book brings such ideas together to explore new arenas of thought and challenge long-standing narratives that have domination, sometimes with minimal questioning. Social exclusion is one area where shifts in thought are evident.

It highlights where the clinical, structural, social and, importantly, lived experience intersect to provide a new platform of shared knowledge.

A central pillar of this book is it being community-led. This means that, at a very minimum, each chapter has a neuro-mixed team working on the chapter. Authors were provided with a wide scope to write about their experiences of neurodiversity and mental health in the areas of their interest/scholarship. Some authors have written in the identity-first language and discussed their own experiences of academic and mental health. Others have written in a more traditional academic third-person format. As such, both identity-first (e.g., autistic) and person-first language (e.g., with autism) have been used in the books. As this is a global series, different authors have different preferences and there is no unified agreed approach. The editors were not prescriptive in relation to this as the approach taken was to provide a space where authentic scholarship could be developed in a way that suited the author's drafting style. In this sense, the book is pushing the boundaries of typical academic work and providing a safe space where neurodivergent scholars and authors can write in a manner that suits their message dissemination. The flexibility around this is to advance academic scholarship and be inclusive of diverse styles. Whilst this flexible approach was championed in this book, there were clear guidelines around remaining faithful to empirical arguments and theoretical frameworks to guide work. The editors felt this was important as a step to highlight that more flexible and authentic scholarly work can be evidence-based and theoretically framed.

The innovative approach to this book is driven by a wider paradigm shift where the voice and lived experience of researchers and scholars are coming to the fore in an activist and unapologetically authentic manner, whilst remaining faithful to an empirical and theoretical framework. The conference, the master classes, the subsequent conferences, and now the book allow for researchers and scholars to discuss the empirical and theoretical from the perspective of the lived world. Similar to the disability movement, this shift and, indeed, this book aims to bring about change, challenge stigma, and break down presuppositions about neurodiversity. It brings together various voices and perspectives that are not always aligned and, indeed, can sometimes be at odds. This is intentional as it breaks down the echo chamber walls with a view to bringing about authentic critical dialogue and discussion with the objective of advancing this space.

This book is underpinned by the "nothing about us without us" approach whereby no policy, practice, decision-making, or book writing should be undertaken without the central voice of those it is about and will impact. This is an important rights-based approach that upholds inclusivity, empowerment, and the right for people impacted by events and actions to have control over the decisions that affect their lives. Therefore, this book aligns itself with an affirmative approach and is open to dialogue and inclusive advancement of societal change in this space.

Neuroaffirming language is a communication approach that emphasises respect and validation for individuals' neurological differences, particularly in contexts involving neurodiversity. It focuses on recognising and affirming each person's unique experiences and perspectives, avoiding language that is stigmatising or dismissive.

This type of language promotes understanding and acceptance, fostering an inclusive environment where people feel valued and understood.

Key principles include:

1 *Respect for Individual Experiences:* Acknowledging that everyone has their own way of processing and interacting with the world.
2 *Avoiding Pathologising Terms:* Using language that doesn't frame neurominority traits as deficits or disorders.
3 *Empowerment:* Encouraging self-advocacy and valuing diverse ways of thinking and being.

Overall, neuroaffirming language aims to create a supportive atmosphere that recognises and honours neurological diversity.

This book is organised as follows:

Chapter 1 offers a particular overview of neurodiversity, its origins, and its evolving meanings, highlighting both the scientific and social underpinnings of the concept. The chapter begins with an introduction to neurodiversity, defining it as a broad term that encompasses variations in neurological functioning. It explores the brain's complex structure, emphasising its uniqueness and adaptability, which serves as the foundation for understanding neurodiversity. The history of neurodiversity is examined through the lens of past harmful practices, such as pseudoscientific medical treatments and the dominance of psychoanalytic theories, which contributed to the marginalisation of neurodivergent individuals. Key historical events, including the rise of eugenics and the medicalisation of neurodivergence, are discussed in relation to their lasting impacts on societal attitudes and medical practices. The chapter also delves into contemporary debates about the definition of neurodiversity, drawing on contributions from scholars like Nick Walker and Steve Silberman. It emphasises the shift from pathologising differences to recognising them as natural variations, highlighting the importance of social justice movements in advancing neurodiversity. Finally, the chapter contrasts the medical model of disability with the social model, advocating for an affirmative approach and a phenomenological framework to better support neurodivergent individuals. It concludes by raising important questions and challenges that remain in the ongoing development of neurodiversity.

Chapter 2 addresses the prevalence and impact of co-occurring mental health problems in autistic adults, highlighting key factors that contribute to mental health challenges such as anxiety and depression. It begins by emphasising that a significant proportion of autistic individuals experience mental health problems, often emerging in late childhood and continuing throughout life. The chapter details how these mental health issues affect the quality of life, functional outcomes, and increase the risk of self-harm and suicidal ideation. Despite the growing recognition of the need for research and better support, progress remains slow due to a lack of understanding of the mechanisms involved, which may overlap with both neurodivergent and neurotypical groups but be experienced differently. The chapter presents findings from interviews with 19 autistic adults, focusing on their lived experiences and the factors contributing to their mental health challenges. Eight themes are identified, including autistic burnout, stress and trauma, emotion regulation, negative thought patterns, loneliness, societal factors, and the role of resilience. Autistic burnout, a state of chronic exhaustion and loss of function, is highlighted as a major factor affecting mental health. Other contributing factors include heightened sensitivity to stress, trauma, and sensory overload, as well as difficulties in emotional awareness and regulation. The chapter concludes by emphasising the need for research to integrate both risk and protective factors in mental health outcomes for autistic adults. It advocates for neurodiversity-affirmative models, which focus on environmental adaptations and the promotion of positive mental health, and highlights the importance of improving public understanding and access to tailored mental health services.

Chapter 3 critically examines findings from three studies conducted by the authors on the barriers to healthcare access and the challenges faced by autistic individuals. It is written from the perspective of a researcher with lived experience, offering valuable insights into how this positioning informs such research. The chapter addresses key issues such as difficulties in booking appointments, communication challenges, sensory sensitivities, and poorer health outcomes. Furthermore, it highlights the significant implications of these difficulties, including delayed care seeking, increased likelihood of experiencing communication issues when care is sought, and healthcare avoidance, which may result in untreated or delayed treatment for life-threatening conditions. The chapter also introduces the concept of epistemic injustice, wherein the experiences and self-reports of autistic individuals are often dismissed or misunderstood by healthcare professionals. It explores the triple empathy problem, which refers to the layered communication mismatch between autistic patients, non-autistic doctors, and the broader medical system. In response to these challenges, the chapter proposes the Autistic SPACE framework – an acronym for Sensory, Predictability, Acceptance, Communication, and Empathy – as a simple yet effective tool for improving healthcare accessibility for autistic individuals. The framework has been well-received in healthcare settings and seeks to promote more inclusive and empathetic interactions.

Chapter 4 explores the intersection of neurodiversity and mental health, highlighting the importance of understanding and addressing the co-occurrence of neurodivergence and mental health conditions. The author outlines the significance of this understanding, particularly in the context of mental health services, where neurodivergent individuals often experience under-recognition and mischaracterisation of their needs. As such, the chapter reveals the complex relationships between these neurodivergent experiences and mental health illnesses. The author stresses the need for greater awareness of the higher prevalence of mental health issues within neurodivergent populations and advocates for tailored support and services. Additionally, the chapter discusses the structural and institutional challenges within mental health services, including diagnostic overshadowing and the lack of specialised care. It also highlights positive developments in mental health service provision, such as neurodiversity-affirming practices and inclusive service designs. The chapter concludes by emphasising the need for collaborative efforts between healthcare providers, policymakers, and academics to improve mental health care for neurodivergent individuals, suggesting that despite current challenges, there is hope for a more inclusive and supportive future.

Chapter 5 highlights a novel theoretical framework for understanding the co-occurrence of attention-deficit hyperactivity disorder (ADHD) with mood and anxiety disorders in adults, introducing innovative insights into diagnostic and treatment challenges. It critiques traditional concepts of comorbidity, often misleading in psychiatric contexts due to the lack of well-defined pathophysiologies for many mental disorders. The chapter argues for the adoption of the term co-occurrence instead, which avoids the assumptions of causality or distinct pathology, and better reflects the complex interplay between ADHD and other psychiatric conditions. The author highlights a shift from the hierarchical diagnostic approach, traditionally used in psychiatry, to one that recognises ADHD and mood or anxiety disorders as co-occurring traits or states. This model acknowledges the fluctuating nature of symptoms and the possibility of shared neurobiological mechanisms, such as disruptions in prefrontal cortex functioning, which might explain the overlap in symptoms like impulsivity and emotional dysregulation. However, the framework also acknowledges the limitations of current research, especially concerning the genetic and environmental factors driving these co-occurrences. This theoretical shift enhances our understanding of ADHD's co-occurrence with mood and anxiety disorders, challenging traditional diagnostic paradigms and suggesting a more integrative approach to treatment. It calls for further research to substantiate these connections and refine diagnostic criteria to ensure more accurate, nuanced clinical interventions.

Chapter 6 explores the complex interplay between neurodivergence, joint hypermobility, and emotional and physical health challenges. It highlights how individuals with conditions such as ADHD, autism, and Tourette syndrome, along with hypermobility, often experience both mental and physical health issues. Hypermobility, the ability of joints to exceed typical range of motion, can lead to pain, instability, and autonomic dysfunction, while individuals with neurodivergence often encounter heightened anxiety, proprioception issues, and emotional dysregulation. This chapter underscores the importance of recognising the brain-body connection and its implications for health outcomes. It explains the concept of neurodivergence, which includes traits like autism and ADHD, framing these conditions through a strength-based lens rather than the traditional deficit-based approach. The chapter also discusses how neurodivergent individuals are often dismissed in the medical system, which exacerbates mental health challenges. Key findings from research studies illustrate that joint hypermobility is more prevalent in neurodivergent individuals, particularly in those with anxiety, pain, and dysautonomia. It stresses the need for integrated healthcare that addresses both the neurodevelopmental and physical aspects of health, advocating for early screening, better diagnosis, and tailored care strategies to improve outcomes for this population. The chapter concludes by calling for more research into the mechanisms that link neurodivergence with hypermobility, with a focus on improving healthcare practices.

Chapter 7 explores the critical role of schools in supporting the mental health of neurodivergent learners. It begins by highlighting the growing recognition of education as a key space for promoting mental well-being, with an emphasis on the need for tailored mental health strategies for neurodivergent students. Despite the established research on the increased mental health risks faced by neurodivergent individuals, such as higher rates of depression and suicide, there is a notable gap in research on effective school-based supports. The chapter advocates for evidence-based frameworks, like the Continuum of Support, which offer a structured approach to meeting the diverse needs of neurodivergent learners. The chapter outlines three levels of support within the Continuum model: Level 1 (universal support for all students), Level 2 (targeted support for some learners), and Level 3 (individualised, specialised support for those with complex needs). It stresses the importance of creating an inclusive school culture and a supportive environment that fosters positive relationships, autonomy, and equity for neurodivergent students. Additionally, the chapter highlights the potential harm that can arise from poorly understood or misapplied interventions, referred to as iatrogenic harm, and emphasises the need for a deep understanding of the Neurodiversity Paradigm. The chapter concludes by providing future guidelines for educational practices, calling for collaborative, neurodivergent-centred approaches, and the integration of interdisciplinary expertise to enhance the mental health support for neurodivergent students.

Chapter 8 explores the intersection of neurodivergent college students, mental health, and systemic oppression through the lens of the Neurodiversity Paradigm and Critical Disability Theory. The chapter emphasises the need for higher education institutions to become neurodiversity-affirming by critically examining the societal structures that impact neurodivergent students' experiences and mental health. The author discusses how ableism, embedded within both institutional systems and societal norms, can exacerbate mental health challenges for students with disabilities. The author calls for a shift away from the medical model of disability, advocating instead for the Neurodiversity Paradigm, which views neurodivergence as a natural variation rather than a defect. This shift, it is argued, would reduce stigma and promote self-determination in how students engage with their identities and needs. The chapter further outlines the limitations of traditional Student Development Theory and highlights the importance of understanding the diverse experiences of historically marginalised students. The chapter offers practical recommendations at both institutional and individual levels, including the creation of disability cultural centres, reformed accommodation processes, and professional development initiatives aimed at dismantling ableism. Ultimately, it is stressed that true inclusion requires both systemic change and support for neurodivergent students within existing structures. It is argued that by embracing the Neurodiversity Paradigm and Disability Justice Framework, higher education can foster a more equitable environment for all students.

Chapter 9 examines the complexities faced by neurodivergent African migrants in Aotearoa New Zealand, focusing on the intersection of neurodiversity, mental health, and cultural identity. Whilst this study focuses on African migrants in New Zealand, it is likely that the findings apply equally to other migrants in other parts of the world. Drawing from interviews with parents, community leaders, and health professionals, the author explores how African migrants' understandings of neurodiversity differ from the Western medical model. The chapter highlights the challenges African migrant families encounter when seeking support, including cultural misunderstandings, misdiagnosis, and a lack of consideration for diverse worldviews. As such, the stigma surrounding neurodiversity and mental illness is critically discussed, emphasising the compounded effects of racism and migration on African migrants' experiences, leading to further marginalisation. The chapter delves into the overlap between neurodiversity and mental illness, which creates complex social dynamics, especially when cultural differences influence how these conditions are perceived and addressed. The concept of intersectionality is central to understanding the compounded disadvantages faced by these communities, as race, migration status, and neurodivergence intersect to shape their access to services. The author also examines the barriers to healthcare, including systemic racism, cultural insensitivity, and the difficulty of navigating Aotearoa New Zealand's health system, calling for a more inclusive and culturally responsive approach to neurodiversity, advocating for the recognition of diverse perspectives and the involvement of marginalised communities in shaping policies and services. The chapter concludes with recommendations to improve service access, cultural safety, and community awareness.

Chapter 10 brings some of the core arguments from the book together and critically reflects on areas that require urgent attention in this space. It emphasises the evolving nature of neurodiversity, presenting it not merely as an academic concept but as a central element in societal discourse. This chapter discusses how the work in this book highlights the lived experiences of neurodivergent individuals, addressing the challenges they face while recognising their resilience and potential for societal transformation. Moreover, it positions the community-led approach, asserting the principle of "nothing about us without us," which insists on neurodivergent individuals leading conversations about their own needs and experiences. Highlighting that this approach is evident in the book's promotion of neuroaffirming language and practices, which seek to shift societal perceptions of neurodivergence from a deficiency to a natural variation in human cognition. However, tensions emerge in the discussions, particularly regarding the intersection of neurodiversity and mental health. The volume critically engages with challenges such as the co-occurrence of mental health issues and the need for systemic changes in health, public policy, education, immigration, and mental health systems to support neurodivergent individuals. Moreover, the chapter draws from the important work in Chapter 9 that underscores the importance of extending the neurodiversity paradigm globally, incorporating diverse cultural perspectives, and avoiding the imposition of Western-centric models. It calls for interdisciplinary research and a global, inclusive approach to neurodiversity.

Note

1 Morgan C, Burns T, Fitzpatrick R, Pinfold V, Priebe S. Social exclusion and mental health: Conceptual and methodological review. *British Journal of Psychiatry.* 2007;191(6):477–483. https://doi.org/10.1192/bjp.bp.106.034942

Chapter 1

Neurodiversity
Origins, History, Meanings, and Applications

Liam McGrattan

Introduction

Neurodiversity is a complex concept of ever-growing significance in our world. This chapter seeks to provide the reader with a basic introduction to neurodiversity, a definition of neurodiversity, and information on its usage. Beyond this, an emphasis is placed on factors that influenced its growth in popularity, including history and scientific breakthroughs. This chapter finishes by discussing some existing debates and challenges involving neurodiversity. The reader will find a collection of referred-to sources throughout the chapter, which they may wish to explore for further learning.

The Brain: Some Information

The human brain consists of approximately 100 billion neurons. Each neuron is around 4–10 μm in size (equal to one-millionth of a metre). Neurons are in constant communication with one another and do so using chemicals called neurotransmitters at gaps between neurons, commonly called synapses. The synapse act as a venue for neurotransmitters to allow the continuation (excitation) or stopping (inhibition) of electrical impulses along a series of connected neurons. Each neuron is considered to have approximately 7,000 synaptic connections with other neurons, pushing the total synapse count in the brain to around 600 trillion. Long "chains" of connected neurons make up neural pathways that allow different parts of the brain to communicate. These neural pathways are like motorways within the brain, with electrical signals zooming at speeds of up to 120 m/s. With approximately 100 billion neurons, each possessing approximately 7,000 synaptic connections with other neurons, it is no wonder why the brain is described as an electrical circuit of organic origins (Von Bartheld et al. 2016).

In the first few years of life, over 100 million neural connections are created every second. Following this mass expansion of connections, this period is followed by a phase in which certain connections are eliminated. This process is referred to as "pruning" and ultimately allows the working neural networks of the brain to become more efficient. What influences the decline of specific synaptic

DOI: 10.4324/9781003495949-2

connections and neural pathways is thought to be the degree to which they are activated. The Canadian neuropsychologist Donald Hebb famously said, "Neurons that fire together, wire together," highlighting consistent activity between neurons as an influential factor in selecting which neuronal pathways become established (Shatz 1992, p. 64). Throughout life, the brain will alter and adapt the trillions of connections between neurons and is influenced by "living" factors such as lifestyle, genetics, environment, and health.

The brain has a massive number of neural cells, synapses, and neural pathways; its phenomenal ability to alter neural connections throughout life, and its sensitivity to living factors, supports the argument that each human brain in existence is unique and individual. This viewpoint provides a formidable foundation for understanding a concept as expansive as neurodiversity.

Neurodiversity: How History Spurned Direction for Change

This section briefly explores three key examples of areas (pseudoscientific medical practices, overly dominant psychological theories, and political ideologies relevant to the time). These historical "treatments" caused significant harm to the individual, their family, and to society through the commencement and perpetuation of incorrect understandings and practices upheld by dubious scientific efforts. The debates described above are best considered in the historical framework within which they originated. This historical lens continues to evolve providing the opportunity for further learnings which guide against repeating past errors and provide a roadmap to effective action. The 19th and 20th centuries observed numerous developments which saw an overall rise in criticism towards the medical models used in the "treatment of disability." One can begin to understand the growth of criticism by exploring the troubled history of disability treatment and its influences on contemporary debates.

Pseudoscientific Medical Practices

Much of what modern medicine is capable of is due to breakthroughs in scientific research when conducted correctly. Pseudoscience is a "process in which major errors are made in the selection and interpretation of evidence" (Schopler 2001, p. 13). The 20th century observed cases of medicinal practice, for example, surgical procedures and treatments, reliant on improperly interpreted findings actively used in disability treatment. Such cases included the practice of frontal lobotomies or leucotomies, developed by Portuguese neurologist Antonio Egas Moniz. A lobotomy or leucotomy was a form of psychosurgery (brain surgery used to treat mental illness) that involved severing neural connections in the front part of the brain (prefrontal cortex). Moniz viewed this procedure to be a cure for schizophrenia. Without substantial legitimacy, he assumed mental disorders originated from synaptic disorders, stating a "fixation of synapses" caused the expression of "predominant, obsessive ideas'" in individuals with mental illness that "absorbed" other mental activities (Gross & Schäfer 2011, p. 1). Although involved in over 40 lobotomies, Moniz never performed the surgeries himself due to having no experience in neurosurgical training but instructed surgeons to destroy neurons via the injection of alcohol or the use of a retractable wire loop (Tan & Yip 2014). Moniz provided inaccurate descriptions of surgical parameters – depths of insertion and angles – highlighting the inflicted changes to the brain varied from patient to patient. In 1949, he was controversially awarded a Nobel Prize in Medicine amid harsh criticism from other clinicians, one of whom was Siegried Haddenbrock, a German psychiatrist, who had come to disregard forms of psychosurgery and described lobotomy to be a "definitive destruction of the self-confident and free personality of the human being" (Gross & Schäfer 2011, p. 4; Haddenbrock 1949). Haddenbrock's criticisms arose from the fact that severing the neurons of psychiatric patients turned individuals into "living vegetables" (Schopler 2001, p. 13). Following the lobotomy, patients were described by Moniz to be calmer, less paranoid, and well-oriented. Still, in retrospect, the substantial changes in patients' presentations were not that lobotomy "cured," but merely crippled thousands of schizophrenic patients. Lobotomy was regularly used in the United States and posed as a solution to the issue of overcrowding in mental institutions (Faria 2013). Lobotomy was used in cases where patients exhibited erratic behaviours which were deemed overly challenging, including individuals who showed forms of neurodivergence, including autism (Jęczmińska 2017; Morton 2012).

The American psychologist Elliot Valenstein suggested Moniz had been "free" to pursue theories which were "vague and loosely reasoned arguments" (Gross & Schäfer 2011, p. 4) that deviated from correct scientific methods because of his reputation as the former Portuguese minister of foreign affairs and had pioneered a form of brain imaging called cerebral angiography. Because Moniz was older coming into his role in medicine, Valenstein suggested he "sped" up his research because he "had not many years left to achieve a place in history" (Gross & Schäfer 2011, p. 4) and was competing against other scientists who craved a spotlight in medical history.

Examples such as that of lobotomy exemplify the damage pseudoscience can have when put into practice. Psychosurgery has remained a controversial topic impacted by the history of procedures like lobotomy and left a lasting legacy in the inhumanity of its practice culturally embodied in the 1975 film, *One Flew over the Cuckoo's Nest*, starring Jack Nicholson, and the film *Francis* in 1982 about the actress Frances Farmer. Criticism of psychosurgery reached its peak in the final third of the 20th century and was replaced with newly discovered psychotropic medications, psychotherapy, and electroconvulsive therapy (Lichterman et al. 2022).

Overly Dominant Psychological Theories

In the late 19th century, Austrian neurologist Sigmund Freud developed psychoanalytic theory, a different approach to treating psychological issues such as depression and anxiety and by the year 1900, had left his practice of neurology completely (Bogousslavsky 2011). As psychoanalysis developed, it would become a dominant theory in the minds of clinicians, especially in the United States, one of whom was in the process of investigating a collection of symptoms which are now considered features of autism.

The discovery of autism was greatly influenced early on by the works conducted by two psychiatrists, Leo Kanner, based in the United States, and Hans Asperger, in Austria. Kanner and Asperger both were born in the Austrian-Hungarian Empire and trained in Germany and Austria but worked independently for most of their careers. Only once did Kanner acknowledge Asperger's work, having claimed he had no awareness of Asperger's work. Reasons why Kanner did not refer to Asperger's works have involved claims of intellectual theft, the Second World War, and simple ignorance. In Steve Silberman's (2016) book *The Legacy of Autism and the Future of Neurodiversity*, Silberman observes Kanner to be a complex character who "was desperate to make his name in the history of medicine" (Baron-Cohen 2015, p. 1329). This conception of Kanner could quite possibly be applied to a vast number of early clinicians.

Another explanation behind the lack of acknowledgement was that Asperger and Kanner had observed different presentations of autism in the groups of children they were referred to and were thought to be exploring different conditions. Asperger coined the phrase "autistic psychopathy" to describe the symptoms he was observing. Kanner initially used the phrase "autistic disturbance of affective contact" but then introduced "early infantile autism" as a diagnostic term (Harris 2018). Before the creation of these terms, the symptoms of autism were referred to as "childhood schizophrenia."

Both clinicians published studies with small cohorts of children who varied greatly in their strengths and challenges which exemplifies the modern concept of the "autism spectrum." Treatment approaches varied between the two clinicians. Asperger (1944) focused on identifying interventions which focused on the strengths of the individual child rather than on the difficulties. Kanner (1968) initially considered a biological element but, under the heavy influence of psychoanalysis, considered psychosocial factors to be the cause.

With psychosocial factors as the primary focus, Kanner initially blamed parents, especially mothers, for their children's condition and said these parents kept these children "neatly in a refrigerator that did not defrost" (Grinker 2007, p. 72). Kanner was supposed to have regretted saying this when Bruno Bettelheim, another Austrian clinician, developed his "refrigerator mother theory," which suggested a lack of maternal emotional warmth caused autism. Bettelheim suggested autistic children suffered from situations similar to being in the holocaust, and was caused by maternal deprivation. Bettelheim had survived the Holocaust and immigrated to the United States, where he became director of a residential school for children with mental illness at the University of Chicago without any qualification in psychoanalysis. Bettelheim initially gained a following, but following his death from suicide, he was exposed to be greatly fraudulent, and a darker side was revealed.

In his biography of Bettelheim, author Richard Pollack conveyed the director as a tyrant who struck children with belts and verbally humiliated them. A former school student, Ronald Angres, shared that he lived "in abject, animal terror" of Bettelheim (Silberman 2016, p. 207). Children like Ronald Angres had been diagnosed with autism by Bettelheim and, due to the supposed lack of warmth from their parents, were confined to prolonged periods away from their families in the school "for their own good" until their stay had cured them of their autism (Silberman 2016, p. 199). Bettelheim greatly exaggerated such claims of children being cured to the point not one of the first 11 autistic children who attended the school had come close to resembling a "cure" on leaving.

The development and popularity of psychoanalysis as a prominent psychological theory at the time of the preliminary studies of conditions now collectively identified as autism had destructive effects. The consequences of Bettelheim's theory that parents were to blame for their children's symptoms had a lasting legacy (Stace 2010) on how families both cope and see their child's differences. Parents were left with a sense of shame in experiencing the "tragedy of an autism diagnosis" (Stace 2010, p. 68) and followed a life-long process to "becoming experts on autism and . . . pursue various treatments in an attempt to return their child to normality" (Nadesan 2013; Stace 2010, p. 68). Such desires to make an autistic child "normal" coincide with the previously mentioned historical view that forms of neurodiversity were pathological and required a cure.

Such debates of whether autism is normalised or warrants a "cure" have led to violence, exemplified in the United Kingdom in 2007 when actress and advocate Jane Asher was approached with demands for a "cure" during a National Autism Society campaign (Murray 2008). The "cure" approach to understanding autism can be linked to the consequence of the historical cultural and biomedical goal of finding a "cure." Neurodiversity seeks to challenge this approach and acknowledge the compassion, empowerment, and support families need to dismantle decades of shame left in the shadow of inappropriate use of psychoanalytic theories.

Political Ideologies

In the late 19th century, Francis Galton, a scientist and cousin to Charles Darwin, coined the term "eugenics" to describe his idea to improve the human race by getting rid of people deemed "undesirables" and included people living with a disability or mental illness. Eugenics argued disability and mental illness were considered the products of "biologically grounded flaws" (Kevles 1999, p. 319) and associated with poor moral character. Such a theory led people to consider criminality and poverty to result from "bad genes" (Kevles 1999, p. 319).

To comprehend the impact ideology such as eugenics had on the medicinal models for disability, one only needs to look at the growth of national socialism in Germany in the early 1930s. The arrival of Adolf Hitler into power in 1933 brought with it racial ideology heavily influenced by eugenics, which resulted in the legalisation of involuntary euthanasia and the deaths of 275,000–300,000 people with conditions deemed incurable in psychiatric hospitals throughout Germany, Austria, and Czechia, and occupied Poland. This killing campaign was referred to as *Aktion T4*. It included the extermination of 5,000 children, some of whom in modern times would be identified as having forms of neurodivergence such as autism, epilepsy, dyslexia, dyscalculia, and intellectual disability.

The atrocities carried out by Hitler and national socialism were underpinned by the development of ideologies like eugenics (Grodin et al. 2018). Although the focus was placed on Germany, eugenics flourished in countries worldwide. Eugenics initially rose to prominence in the United States. Subsequently, it inspired many European countries, including France, Belgium, Sweden, and the United Kingdom, each of whom practised elements of eugenics to varying degrees (Black 2012).

Beyond the controversy evoked in the history of the medical models influenced by an array of issues and developments, one can see reason in the expansion of concepts such as neurodiversity which counter the idea of a "cure." It is also important to consider how clinicians sought to treat individuals in the absence of modern technology or developed understandings of neurodevelopmental and mental health conditions. As post-war Germany has come to terms with its actions during the war, such moments in history cannot be forgotten, nor hang too much over the minds of the living but warrant deeply humane reflection (MacGregor 2014).

Neurodiversity: A Definition

This section does not claim to deal with all definitions and/or terminology. Rather, it is outlining some key areas of debate in terms of definitions and terminology as a means to contextualise the remainder of the chapter. It is fully accepted that this is a dynamic and fluid space and terminology is still under consideration.

Neurodiversity is a complex concept whereby terminology can be subjective and thus can vary from individual to individual. Moreover, neurodiversity can also be an umbrella term for sub-terminology, which again can be subjective and can vary depending upon on where it is being applied and who the audience is that it is being presented to. The variation in meaning from individual to individual and sub-terminology naturally place it in a position of heavy contention, with the concept becoming prominent in debates about the continuing evolution of human rights, healthcare, education, and much more. The term "neurodiversity" was first used in the 1990s by the journalist Harvey Blume and Australian sociologist Judy Singer. Singer, encouraged variations in "brain styles" to be viewed similarly to how we view variations in organic life – to be understood as examples of biological diversity rather than deficits in biology (Botha et al. 2024) and in this respect, neurodiversity seeks to challenge the "default pathologisation and undue medicalisation" of "natural human variants" (Chapman 2019, p. 371). Neurodiversity, therefore, challenges classifications such as autism, ADHD, and dyslexia as being solely biomedical descriptions of individual presentations that represent cohorts of people who differ in neurocognitive functioning; and seeks to shine an affirmative lens on this space, challenging presuppositions about societal neuro-norms (Chapman

2019). In 2014, Nick Walker, a California-based educator/author, described neuro-diversity by breaking it into three different meanings:

1. The first meaning is "the diversity of human minds, the infinite variation in neurocognitive functioning within our species" (Walker 2023, p. 2). This description refers to the factual reality that all humans are biologically diverse (unique) – biodiversity.
2. The second meaning Walker associates with neurodiversity is what she refers to as the "neurodiversity paradigm" which is a specific stance towards neurodiversity that involves (a) viewing neurodiversity as a natural and valuable form of human diversity, and (b) the idea of one "normal" or "healthy" type of brain or mind, or a "right" style of brain functioning is a fictional product of one's culture which is as invalid as the ideas of one "right" or "acceptable" ethnicity, culture, or gender.
3. The third meaning is that the issues and inequalities that develop in the midst of neurodiversity are similar to those which arise in other aspects of human diversity, such as diversity of ethnicity or culture, which, when embraced, encourage inclusivity.

One can observe a deepening in complexity between these three meanings. The first meaning captures a basic explanation aligned with the factual reality that each human brain carries degrees of neural variation introduced at the beginning of this chapter. Points 2 and 3 of Walker's description of neurodiversity are more elaborate – much of the ideas and terminology associated with neurodiversity only date back to the late 1990s (Dwyer 2022). What Walker refers to as the "neurodiversity paradigm," others refer to as the "neurodiversity framework" (Kapp 2020; Russell 2019) or even the "neurodiversity approach." Although a universal title is still to be agreed upon in academia, points 2 and 3 represent a stance of acceptance in response to the factual evidence supporting point 1. A term often associated with point 3 is the "neurodiversity movement," which represents the social justice movement seeking equal civil rights, equality, inclusion, and respect for all neuro-divergent individuals.

Beyond Walker's in-depth description, other definitions of neurodiversity include that of the American writer Steve Silberman, who, in his exceptionally well-received book *NeuroTribes: The Legacy of Autism and the Future of Neurodiversity*, described neurodiversity as follows:

> The notion that differences like autism, dyslexia, and attention-deficit / hyper-activity disorder (ADHD) should be regarded as naturally occurring cognitive variations with distinctive strengths that have contributed to the evolution of technology and culture rather than mere checklists of deficits and dysfunctions.
> (Silberman 2016, p. 16)

Silberman's monumental work detailing the history of autism and neurodiversity argues that individuals of different neurocognitive functioning have always existed – seeking to wipe the counter clean of misinformation suggesting elements of modern life, for example, vaccinations, have caused an increase in individuals with autism and ADHD. Silberman includes detailed chapters dedicated to some of history's "silent" renaissance men and women who shaped the world we now live in – Henry Cavendish, Paul Dirac, Larry Wall, Hugo Gernsback, Nikola Tesla, and John McCarthy, to name but a few. Idiosyncrasies described by past biographers are now re-examined and recognised as possible characteristics of neurodivergence. The life stories of such people actively break the preconceptions of what it means to have a brain beyond the "norm."

Having briefly covered the complex meaning of neurodiversity, one may or may not be familiar with the term "neurodivergent." Neurodivergent is a describing word for individuals whose brains function in ways that significantly diverge from what society has deemed "normal." Being neurodivergent (or neurodivergence: a state of being neurodivergent) can be (a) genetic, in which one is born with a brain that functions significantly differently to the "norm", or (b) a result of life experiences which alter the way one's brain functions, including brain trauma, and chronic drug usage, and (c) a mixture of both genetic and life experiences.

In applying neurodivergence within the fields of healthcare, conditions and diagnoses of neurodevelopmental and neurological origins such as autism spectrum disorder (past this point referred to as autism), attention-deficit hyperactivity disorder (ADHD), dyslexia, dyscalculia, dyspraxia, epilepsy, Tourette's syndrome, and intellectual disability are viewed as forms of neurodivergence. The collection of diagnoses that belong under the "umbrella" of neurodivergence encompasses any condition associated with brains with "different neurological wiring" (Rothstein 2012, p. 100). In accordance with such a movement away from "pathologising" neurodifference, it is important to highlight existing discussions in search for replacement names for forms of neurodivergence. Words such as "disorder" and "deficit" have been viewed to potentially reinforce the idea of pathology and disease (Hallowell & Ratey 2024). The replacement of deficit-focused terminology requires mutual agreement between advocates and healthcare authorities and coincides with the growing emphasis of Identity-first language, that embodies any form of neurodivergence, for example, autism, with one's personal identity, that is, an Autistic person, instead of saying that person "lives with autism." Such developments are still exemplary of society's tendency towards a style of social categorisation which can instil an "us" and "them" mindset, but aids in the expansion and empowerment of minority groups beyond the "white, western, male, middle-class and heterosexual 'norm' within diagnostic protocols" (Doyle 2024, p. 13). Indeed, recent research suggests that such approaches compound discrimination and feelings of inadequacy whereby neurodivergent individuals do not meet societal expectations of what neurodivergence is and thus perceive themselves as "failing at neurodiversity" (Quigley et al. 2024). These are important considerations because as society progresses to more inclusive societal structures and attitudes, careful critical analysis of such progress needs to be undertaken; otherwise, we run the risk of perpetuating existing discriminatory phenomena under a false veneer of progress.

The number of forms of neurodivergence becomes complicated when one considers mental health conditions such as depression, bipolar disorder, and schizophrenia. There is an active debate amongst scholars and clinicians regarding whether mental illnesses can be considered forms of neurodivergence. Those in favour of the inclusion of mental illnesses as forms of neurodivergence cite discoveries of differences in brain functioning in individuals diagnosed with mental illnesses and modern neurocognitive theories. Beyond the scholarly definitions, neurodivergence can be deeply personal, varying in means from person to person.

In applying neurodivergence beyond the field of healthcare, the term neurodivergent describes individuals with neurodifference that is different to the typical. The term "neurotypical" is often used to describe those who cluster as being the norm with those with neurodifferences being outliers. Nick Walker defines neurotypical individuals as those who have a style of neurocognitive functioning that matches society's standards of "normal"; this standard is socially dominant and leads to certain expectations of neuro-presentation. Those who do not fit within these expectations are often being perceived as different and not fitting within social structures which are by and large designed for the typical presentation.

Understanding the variety and complexity of differences which are considered forms of neurodivergence reveals the potential for a vast number of individuals to identify with neurodivergence. In early 2024, an online study conducted by Red C, a marketing and polling research company, held in conjunction with the Bank of Ireland's launch of their Neuroinclusion Strategy, found that almost one in ten adults living in the Republic of Ireland identify as being neurodivergent and that 26% of adults who engaged in the study reported that they are themselves, or have a family member who is neurodivergent (Bank of Ireland 2024). This information can be compared to the 15–20% of the global population reported as neurodivergent (Doyle 2024; CDC 2024).

The percentage of the global population reported as neurodivergent has seen remarkable growth, quite possibly a response to an increase in the diagnosis of neurodevelopmental conditions exemplified by data collected in the United States; the rate of diagnosis of autism in children rose from one child in 150 in 2000 to 1 in 36 in the year 2020 (Maenner 2023). A similar increase has been observed in ADHD diagnoses – in the year 2000, the prevalence of ADHD amongst individuals aged 4–17 was 6.5%, and by the end of 2020, it had increased to 10% (Li et al. 2023; Xu et al. 2018a, 2018b). The debate continues as to whether the increased numbers described reflect a true increase in prevalence or simply reflect increased diagnosis reflective of increased awareness or in fact reflect a broader interpretation of diagnostic categories influenced in part by sociocultural shifts shaping clinician judgement.

Beyond the observed increase in diagnoses of forms of neurodivergence such as autism and ADHD, neurodiversity's conceptual rise to prominence has been the result of the popularisation of the "neurodiversity paradigm." As per Walker's definition, the neurodiversity paradigm actively disagrees with the idea that there is a "right" style of brain functioning, associating this idea with ideals similar to those that the civil rights movements of the 20th century sought to change, for example, gender and racial inequality.

This highlights a complex picture whereby competing voices disagree as to the reason for the increase in prevalence. On the one hand, it could be argued that the biomedical field has expanded (net widened) to include broader presentations and thus captures more individuals in terms of diagnostic criteria. On the other hand, the gradual destigmatisation of the area, leading to greater emphasis upon an affirmative diagnosis, may be contributing to greater numbers coming forward to have their own space in the neurodiversity landscape. It is beyond this chapter to explore this any further; however, this debate requires further attention and more in-depth exploration.

Neurodiversity: The Medical Model

The neurodiversity paradigm seeks to challenge and exemplify an alternative approach to existing institutional models, such as that of the medical model used in research and clinical care of individuals with disability and mental illness (Singer 2016). The phrase "medical model" has multiple meanings but has "almost always been used pejoratively" (Hogan 2019, p. 16). Historically, both research and clinical care of individuals who presented with atypical development (development beyond what was considered normal) assumed such differences were pathological, meaning they were medical disorders and diseases of mind and body that left individuals with deficits that greatly limited an individual's ability to function. Resulting treatments focused on cure and/or adapting disabled people into typically developing individuals. In other words, they "normalise" the individual (Constantino 2018; Ne'eman 2010).

Attempts to "normalise" individuals with autism have been described as an "explicit goal of autism research" (Dwyer 2022, p. 73). Criticism towards normalisation attempts includes research findings suggesting autistic people attempt to "camouflage" or "mask" their autism to appear "normal" resulting in anxiety, burnout, exhaustion, stress, depression, and suicidality (Raymaker et al. 2020). Further research is required, but it highlights ongoing concerns regarding the traditional goals of the medical models in terms of supporting individuals and understandings of difference (Williams 2021).

Neurodiversity: The Social Model

The traditional medical model outlined above and the oft-used pathway of referral to what are now deemed controversial care practices of those deemed to have had a difference provides a viable backdrop to neurodiversity's expansion and its questioning of the core goals of the traditional and historic medical models. Critics, consisting of disability scholars and people with disabilities, promoted an alternative to the "medical model," referred to as the "social model." The social model resulted from intellectual and political arguments within the Union of Physically

Impaired Against Segregation (UPIAS), founded by Paul Hunt, a British disability advocate, in 1972.

The social model views disability as a product of an "unaccommodating and oppressive society, rather than an individual and medical problem" (Hogan 2019, p. 16). In line with the Limits Model of Disability, Dwyer (2022) writes the social model views disability and/or differences as caused by society's response to an individual's impairment and makes an example of a physically impaired individual unable to access a specific space, that is, an office building, due to the absence of wheelchair ramps because of an inaccessible societal design with exclusion being the societal design rather than bodily impairment. Although developed with a primary focus on the effects of exclusion towards people with physical impairments (Shakespeare 2006), the "neurodiversity movement" (the social justice movement for neurodivergent people) adopted proponents of this model to explain the challenges experienced by individuals with forms of neurodivergence (Dwyer 2022; Barnes & Mercer 2004). Dwyer (2022) provides comprehensive detail on the differences between the medical and social models in relation to neurodiversity, presented in the following section.

Conceptual Differences between the Medical Model, Social Model, and Neurodiversity

Debates between the medical and social models are complex and vary, with sometimes converging but largely diverging voices. Such debates between defenders of the medical models and social model advocates can be observed in an excerpt from Shields and Beversdorf (2020):

> The medical model defender will point to some behaviour or incapacity as exemplifying an intrinsically disabling feature of the condition. Then, the social model proponent will highlight the norm grounding the expectation that humans behave in that way or that humans have the capacity, and they will then argue that this norm is merely rooted in neurotypical or ableist prejudice.
>
> (Shields & Beversdorf 2020, p. 10)

Further development beyond the debates surrounding the appropriate model to practice warrants contributions from clinical, research, and neurodivergent communities to ensure all voices are heard, respected, incorporated, and validated in an ongoing process of communication.

Such a change has proved challenging, with ongoing debates about the degree to which neurodiversity is granted a foothold in clinical practice. For example, the neurodiversity movement's support for ending the view of autism as an illness (Milton 2017) naturally means substantial change for the clinicians involved. Green (2023) argues clinicians now (a) are required to "seriously" consider "autistic lived-experience" (Green 2023, p. 439), enhancing the dependence of clinical understanding in the subjective rather than the objective, (b) understand the importance of reference to social identity and encourage "self-identification" and that autism is no longer solely linked to clinical spheres, and (c) need to understand forms of neurodivergence, such as autism, are concepts now associated with highly developed views of individuality rather than being a pathological category (Green 2023). Such developments highlight the reality that clinicians may require varying degrees of re-education to practice neurodiversity-affirming frameworks and approaches.

Neurodiversity has influenced the replacement of "deficit-focused" with "strengths-based" frameworks. Derivatives of the strengths-based approach were first established in the 1980s at the University of Kansas by social work scholars Bertha Reynolds, Dennis Saleebey, Charles Rapp, and Ann Weick (Healy 2005), who disagreed with the then overemphasis on risks, needs, and weaknesses (Nissen 2006; Laursen 2003). The "strengths model" focuses on "amplifying the well part of the patient" (Rapp & Goscha 2012) and encourages optimism and creativity. The attractiveness of these traits was observed in the expansion of the strengths-based approach in popularity, extending into spheres including child protection, addiction, disciplinary practices, and disability (Healy 2005).

In Western jurisdictions, the strengths-based approach is largely notable in supporting families with autistic children, whereby each child's individual strengths and challenges are identified through child–parent–clinician collaboration within multidisciplinary clinical teams consisting of psychologists, psychiatrists, occupational therapists, social workers, speech and language therapists, and so on. However, whilst it is beyond this chapter to deal with this issue, it must be recognised that this approach and/or indeed understanding of such differences are unlikely to be global and greater collaboration with the lived experience and structural practices in non-Western jurisdictions is much needed (see Chapter 8 for further discussion on this area). Children's healthcare services operating with a strengths-based approach will introduce families to the approach via child and parent interventions can seek to educate and prompt reflection on children's talents. Strengths of autistic children include excellent memory skills, motivation to identify patterns, attention to detail, visual learning, sensory acuity, system-minded, and possess a strong sense of fairness/justice (Cherewick & Matergia 2023). The motion towards strength-based frameworks is still in its infancy. Yet, existing research investigating the effects of strengths-based approaches on individuals with disability identified improvements to self-determination, which subsequently empowers individuals in disability communities, leading to a positive impact on quality of life and life satisfaction (Shogren et al. 2017).

Beyond the adoption of strengths-based approaches, other advances away from deficit-focused frameworks include the practice of phenomenological approaches towards understanding the primary elements of living with a form of neurodivergence. Phenomenology is a flexible philosophical approach that focuses on investigating subjective and objective experiences in full detail (Spiegelberg 1978). Over the 19th and 20th centuries, phenomenology developed in different directions, making an exact definition challenging to define (Moran & Mooney 2002).

Phenomenology's association with psychology is also complex (Brentano 2012) but seeks to unite philosophy and science using the living world, arguing that descriptions of human experience are most important (Davidsen 2013). In focusing on experience, the focus is placed on seeing something as it appears, that is, "the thing itself" (Davidsen 2013, p. 3), "controlling" for pre-existing prejudices so as "to capture as closely as possible the way in which the phenomenon is experienced within the context in which the experience takes place" (Giorgi & Giorgi 2003, p. 27).

Green (2023) describes an explosion in neurodivergent lived experience literature signifying the need to develop the use of phenomenological approaches specific to forms of neurodivergence, for example, autism, dyslexia, ADHD, and so on (Nilsson et al. 2019). The subsequent use of the phenomenological approach in supporting individuals with forms of neurodivergence is still in its relative infancy. Yet, existing research exploring the lived experiences between neurodivergent and neurotypical communities identified similar desires, for example, the need for intimacy, trust, acceptance, and enjoyable social experiences (Murray et al. 2022). Such findings highlight the value of adopting a phenomenological approach and challenging stereotyped conceptions surrounding the behaviours and desires associated with forms of neurodivergence, for example, autism and social avoidance that mark these persons out as being "different." Rather, what the phenomenological research seems to be suggesting is sameness and similarities in desires across neurodivergent and neurotypical communities. Moreover, this research also paints an image of a common set of core values and needs. Using the phenomenological approach, Murray et al. (2022) identified neurodivergent populations that faced prominent challenging experiences involving their sensory processing, being overwhelmed, and being misunderstood by others in their early life; but also highlighted similarities and sameness, areas which are often neglected and ignored.

Developing the "neurodivergence phenomenology" highlights phenomenology's value which is also being explored as a means of enhancing Cognitive Behavioural Therapy (CBT) and Interpersonal Therapies (IPT) for individuals with forms of neurodivergence such as autism to account for features of autism which historically challenged the implementation of CBT and IPT, including sensory challenges during therapy, demanding unachievable cognitive flexibility, and overbearing social interaction (Pantazakos & Vanaken 2023). The aim of these approaches is not to change the individual or make them "more neurotypical" but rather to strengthen and empower through the development of a better understanding of self.

Although there is yet to be a definite set of clinical guidelines for practising neurodiversity, the integration of the strengths-focused and phenomenological approaches are just two examples of how healthcare systems are and could continue to bring about a shift away from deficit-focused practices of the past in favour of healthcare models which affirm the principles embodied within neurodiversity. Such steps towards new therapeutic models depend on ongoing research and debates within psychology, medicine, and philosophy.

Conclusion

This chapter sought to critically engage the reader in the wonderfully expansive, sometimes complicated, concept of neurodiversity. The author sought to focus on neurodiversity's meanings, origins, growth in popularity, and its expression in practice. Readers are encouraged to explore the literature introduced throughout this chapter for further learning.

Neurodiversity is still early in its conceptual development and is not free from criticism. Such criticisms and concerns include the ongoing debate between medical and social models of disability care (Shields & Beversdorf 2020), to what extent mental illnesses and acquired brain injury can be viewed as forms of neurodivergence, the degree to which the neurodiversity paradigm actively benefits individuals with "severe" features of types of neurodivergence, and neurodiversity's role in the midst of the growing hostility between neurodivergent and neurotypical populations as part of "identity politics" (Cameron & Swain 1999). As such, this chapter provides a springboard to think more deeply about some of the questions raised and to advance our understanding in a respectful and dignifying manner. It is hoped, therefore, that this chapter offers food for thought by raising questions for consensus dialogue rather than attempting to answer any.

References

Asperger, H. (1944). Die 'Autistischen Psychopathen' im Kindesalter. *Archiv für Psychiatrie und Nervenkrankheiten*, 117(1), pp. 76–136. doi: https://doi.org/10.1007/bf01837709.

Bank of Ireland Group Website. (2024). *48% of neurodivergent people have not disclosed their condition in work, according to Red C poll – Bank of Ireland group website.* [Online]. Available at: https://www.bankofireland.com/about-bank-of-ireland/press-releases/2024/48-of-neurodivergent-people-have-not-disclosed-their-condition-in-work-according-to-red-c-poll/ [Accessed 4 Sep. 2024].

Barnes, C. and Mercer, G. (2004). *Disability policy and practice: Applying the social model.* Leeds: Disability Press.

Baron-Cohen, S. (2015). Leo Kanner, Hans Asperger, and the discovery of autism. *The Lancet*, 386(10001), pp. 1329–1330. [Online]. doi: https://doi.org/10.1016/s0140–6736(15) 00337–2.

Black, E. (2012). *War against the weak: Eugenics and America's campaign to create a master race.* Washington, DC: Dialog Press.

Bogousslavsky, J. (2011). Sigmund Freud's evolution from neurology to psychiatry: Evidence from his La Salpetriere library. *Neurology*, 77(14), pp. 1391–1394. doi: https://doi.org/10.1212/wnl.0b013e31823152a1.

Botha, M., Chapman, R., Giwa Onaiwu, M., Kapp, S. K., Stannard Ashley, A. and Walker, N. (2024). The neurodiversity concept was developed collectively: An overdue correction on the origins of neurodiversity theory. *Autism,* 28(6), pp. 1591–1594.

Brentano, F. (2012). *Psychology from an empirical standpoint.* Routledge.

Cameron, C. and Swain, J. (1999). *Unless otherwise stated: Discourses of labelling and identity.* Northumbria University Research Portal, pp. 68–78. [Online]. Available at: https://researchportal.northumbria.ac.uk/en/publications/unless-otherwise-stated-discourses-of-labelling-and-identity [Accessed 6 Sep. 2024].

CDC (2024). *Data and statistics on autism spectrum disorder.* Autism Spectrum Disorder (ASD). [Online]. Available at: https://www.cdc.gov/autism/data-research/index.html.

Chapman, R. (2019). Neurodiversity theory and its discontents: Autism, schizophrenia, and the social model of disability. *The Bloomsbury Companion to Philosophy of Psychiatry,* 371.

Cherewick, M. and Matergia, M. (2023). Neurodiversity in practice: A conceptual model of autistic strengths and potential mechanisms of change to support positive mental health and wellbeing in autistic children and adolescents. *Advances in Neurodevelopmental Disorders,* 8. doi: https://doi.org/10.1007/s41252-023-00348-z.

Constantino, C. (2018). What can stutterers learn from the neurodiversity movement? *Seminars in Speech and Language,* 39(04), pp. 382–396. [Online]. doi: https://doi.org/10.1055/s-0038-1667166.

Davidsen, A.S. (2013). Phenomenological approaches in psychology and health sciences. *Qualitative Research in Psychology,* 10(3), pp. 318–339. doi: https://doi.org/10.1080/14780887.2011.608466.

Doyle, N. (2024). *Defining neurodiversity and identifying neurominorities,* pp. 13–38. doi: https://doi.org/10.1007/978-3-031-55072-0_2.

Dwyer, P. (2022). The neurodiversity approach(es): What are they and what do they mean for researchers? *Human Development,* 66(2), 73–92. https://doi.org/10.1159/000523723.

Faria, M.A. (2013). Violence, mental illness, and the brain: A brief history of psychosurgery: Part 1 – from trephination to lobotomy. *Surgical Neurology International,* 4(1), p. 49. [Online]. doi: https://doi.org/10.4103/2152-7806.110146.

Giorgi, A. and Giorgi, B. (2003). *Phenomenology. Qualitative psychology: A practical guide to research methods.* Thousand Oaks, CA, US: Sage Publications Inc., pp. 25–50.

Green, J. (2023). Debate: Neurodiversity, autism and healthcare. *Child and Adolescent Mental Health,* 28(3), pp. 438–442. doi: https://doi.org/10.1111/camh.12663.

Grinker, R. (2007). *Unstrange minds: Remapping the world of autism.* New York: Basic Books.

Grodin, M.A., Miller, E.L. and Kelly, J.I. (2018). The Nazi physicians as leaders in eugenics and 'Euthanasia': Lessons for today. *American Journal of Public Health,* 108(1), pp. 53–57. [Online]. doi: https://doi.org/10.2105/ajph.2017.304120.

Gross, D. and Schäfer, D. (2011). Egas Moniz (1874–1955) and the 'invention' of modern psychosurgery: A historical and ethical reanalysis under special consideration of Portuguese original sources. *Neurosurgical FOCUS,* 30(2), pp. E8–E8. [Online]. doi: https://doi.org/10.3171/2010.10.focus10214.

Haddenbrock, S. (1949). Radikaloperation durch defrontalisation – theoretisches und kritisches zur präfrontalen Leukotomie (Moniz). *Med Klin,* 44(3), pp. 69–74.

Hallowell, E. and Ratey, J. (2024). *ADHD needs a better name. We have one.* ADDitude. Available at: https://www.additudemag.com/attention-deficit-disorder-vast/#:~:text=ADHD%20is%20not%20purely%20a,or%20variable%20attention%20stimulus%20trait [Accessed 15 Nov. 2024].

Harris, J. (2018). Leo Kanner and autism: A 75-year perspective. *International Review of Psychiatry (Abingdon, England),* 30(1), pp. 3–17. [Online]. doi: https://doi.org/10.1080/09540261.2018.1455646.

Healy, K. (2005). *Social work theories in context: Creating frameworks for practice.* 1st ed. New York, NY: Bloomsbury Academic.

Hogan, A.J. (2019). Social and medical models of disability and mental health: Evolution and renewal. *Canadian Medical Association Journal,* 191(1), pp. 16–18. doi: https://doi.org/10.1503/cmaj.181008.

Jęczmińska, K. (2017). History of lobotomy in Poland. *History of Psychiatry,* 29(1), pp. 3–21. doi: https://doi.org/10.1177/0957154x17741231.

Kanner, L. (1968). Autistic disturbances of affective contact. *Acta Paedopsychiatr,* 35(4), pp. 100–136.

Kapp, S. (2020). *Autistic community and the neurodiversity movement*. Singapore: Springer. [Online]. doi: https://doi.org/10.1007/978-981-13-8437-0.

Kevles, D.J. (1999). Eugenics and human rights. *BMJ*, 319(7207), pp. 435–438. [Online]. doi: https://doi.org/10.1136/bmj.319.7207.435.

Laursen, E. (2003). Frontier in strength-based treatment. *Reclaiming Children and Youth*, 12(1), pp. 12–17.

Li, Y., Yan, X., Li, Q., Li, Q., Xu, G., Lu, J. and Yang, W. (2023). Prevalence and trends in diagnosed ADHD among US children and adolescents, 2017–2022. *JAMA Network Open*, 6(10), p. e2336872. [Online]. doi: https://doi.org/10.1001/jamanetworkopen.2023.36872.

Lichterman, B., Schulder, M., Liu, B., Yang, X. and Taira, T. (2022). A comparative history of psychosurgery. *Progress in Brain Research*, pp. 1–31. doi: https://doi.org/10.1016/bs.pbr.2021.12.003.

Macgregor, N. (2014). *Germany: Memories of a nation*. London: Allen Lane.

Maenner, M.J. (2023). Prevalence and characteristics of autism spectrum disorder among children aged 8 years – autism and developmental disabilities monitoring network, 11 sites, United States, 2020. *MMWR. Surveillance Summaries*, 72(2), pp. 1–14. [Online]. doi: https://doi.org/10.15585/mmwr.ss7202a1.

Milton, D. (2017). *A mismatch of salience: Explorations of the nature of autism from theory to practice*. Hove, East Sussex: Pavillion.

Moran, D. and Mooney, T. (2002). *Routledge phenomenology reader*. London: Routledge.

Morton. C. (2012). Not like all the other horses: Neurodiversity and the case of Rose Williams. *The Tennessee Williams Annual Review*, 13, p. 3. doi: https://doi.org/10.2307/45344159.

Murray, D., Milton, D., Green, J. and Bervoets, J. (2022). The human spectrum: A phenomenological enquiry within neurodiversity. *Psychopathology*, pp. 1–11. [Online]. doi: https://doi.org/10.1159/000526213.

Murray, S. (2008). *Representing autism*. doi: https://doi.org/10.2307/j.ctt5vjmwc.

Nadesan, M.H. (2013). *Constructing autism*. Routledge. doi: https://doi.org/10.4324/9780203299500.

Ne'eman, A. (2010). The future (and the past) of Autism advocacy, or why the ASA's magazine, the advocate, wouldn't publish this piece. *Disability Studies Quarterly*, 30(1).

Nilsson, M., Handest, P., Nylander, L., Pedersen, L., Carlsson, J. and Arnfred, S. (2019). Arguments for a phenomenologically informed clinical approach to autism spectrum disorder. *Psychopathology*, 52(3), pp. 153–160. [Online]. doi: https://doi.org/10.1159/000500294.

Nissen, L. (2006). Bringing strength-based philosophy to life in juvenile justice. *Reclaiming Children and Youth: The Journal of Strength-based Interventions*, 15(1), pp. 40–46.

Pantazakos, T. and Vanaken, G.-J. (2023). Addressing the autism mental health crisis: The potential of phenomenology in neurodiversity-affirming clinical practices. *Frontiers in Psychology*, 14, p. 1225152. [Online]. doi: https://doi.org/10.3389/fpsyg.2023.1225152.

Quigley, E., O'Hanlon, M., Brandes, M., Kennedy, R. and Gavin, B. (2024). Neurodiversity and third-level education: A lacuna between the strength-based paradigm shift and the lived experience. *Neurodiversity*, 2, https://doi.org/10.1177/27546330241277427.

Rapp, C.A. and Goscha, R.J. (2012). *The strengths model: A recovery-oriented approach to mental health services*. 3rd ed. New York: Oxford University Press.

Raymaker, D.M., Teo, A.R., Steckler, N.A., Lentz, B., Scharer, M., Santos, A.D., Kapp, S.K., Hunter, M., Joyce, A. and Nicolaidis, C. (2020). Having all of your internal resources exhausted beyond measure and being left with no clean-up crew: Defining autistic burnout. *Autism in Adulthood*, 2(2), pp. 132–143. [Online]. doi: https://doi.org/10.1089/aut.2019.0079.

Rothstein, A. (2012). Mental disorder or neurodiversity? *The New Atlantis*, 36, pp. 99–115. [Online]. Available at: https://www.jstor.org/stable/43152738.

Russell, G. (2019). Critiques of the neurodiversity movement. *Autistic Community and the Neurodiversity Movement*, pp. 287–303. doi: https://doi.org/10.1007/978-981-13-8437-0_21.

Schopler, E. (2001). Treatment for autism. In Schopler, E., Yirmiya, N., Shulman, C. and Marcus, L.M. (eds.) *The research basis for autism intervention*. Boston, MA: Springer US, pp. 9–24.

Shakespeare, T. (2006). The social model of disability. *The Disability Studies Reader*, 2(3), pp. 197–204.

Shatz, C. J. (1992) The developing brain. *Scientific American*, 267(3), pp. 60–67.

Shields, K. and Beversdorf, D. (2020). A dilemma for neurodiversity. *Neuroethics*, 14, pp. 125–141. doi: https://doi.org/10.1007/s12152-020-09431-x.

Shogren, K.A., Wehmeyer, M.L. and Palmer, S.B. (2017). Causal agency theory. *Development of Self-Determination Through the Life-Course*, pp. 55–67. doi: https://doi.org/10.1007/978-94-024-1042-6_5.

Silberman, S. (2016). *NeuroTribes*. Atlantic.

Singer, J. (2016). *Neurodiversity: The birth of an idea*. Lexington, Kentucky: Amazon.

Spiegelberg, H. (1978). *The phenomenological movement: A historical introduction*. Vol. 1. The Hague: Nijhoff.

Stace, H. (2010). Student research report: Mother blaming; or autism, gender and science. *Women's Studies Journal*, 24(2), pp. 66–70.

Tan, S.Y. and Yip, A. (2014). António Egas Moniz (1874–1955): Lobotomy pioneer and Nobel laureate. *Singapore Medical Journal*, 55(4). [Online]. doi: https://doi.org/10.11622/smedj.2014048.

Von Bartheld, C.S., Bahney, J. and Herculano-Houzel, S. (2016). The search for true numbers of neurons and glial cells in the human brain: A review of 150 years of cell counting. *Journal of Comparative Neurology*, 524(18), pp. 3865–3895.

Walker, N. (2023). *Neurodiversity: Some basic terms & definitions*. [Online]. Available at: https://neuroqueer.com/neurodiversity-terms-and-definitions/.

Williams, G.L. (2021). Theory of autistic mind: A renewed relevance theoretic perspective on so-called autistic pragmatic 'impairment'. *Journal of Pragmatics*, 180, pp. 121–130.

Xu, G., Strathearn, L., Liu, B. and Bao, W. (2018a). Prevalence of autism spectrum disorder among US children and adolescents, 2014–2016. *JAMA*, 319(1), p. 81. doi: https://doi.org/10.1001/jama.2017.17812.

Xu, G., Strathearn, L., Liu, B., Yang, B. and Bao, W. (2018b). Twenty-year trends in diagnosed attention-deficit/hyperactivity disorder among US children and adolescents, 1997–2016. *JAMA Network Open*, 1(4), pp. e181471–e181471. [Online]. doi: https://doi.org/10.1001/jamanetworkopen.2018.1471.

Chapter 2

Lived Experiences of Mental Health in Autistic Adults
A Narrative Exploration

Bethany Oakley, Hannah Hayward, Sarah Douglas, Pierre Violland, Jerneja Terčon, Roderik Plas, Charlotte Boatman, Mary Doherty, and Eva Loth

Introduction: Co-Occurring Mental Health Problems in Autistic Adults

Current estimates suggest that at least 20–50% of autistic people will experience one or more co-occurring mental health conditions in their lifetime, such as anxiety and depression (Hollocks et al., 2019; Lai et al., 2019). Mental health problems typically emerge during late childhood into early adolescence (Simonoff et al., 2008) and subsequently persist over time (Gotham et al., 2015; Hollocks et al., 2023). Mental health problems further have a significant impact on the well-being and functional outcomes (e.g., employment; Robertson et al., 2018) of autistic people throughout the lifespan. For instance, mental health problems have been shown to contribute to reduced quality of life in autistic adults, over and above autistic traits like social-communication differences (Oakley et al., 2020; Van Heijst and Geurts, 2015; Mason et al., 2018). Autistic people experiencing mental health problems, like depression, are also at significantly increased risk of self-harm and suicidal ideation and attempts (Richa et al., 2014; Zahid and Upthegrove, 2017; Hedley et al., 2018), which is one of the leading causes of premature mortality in those without co-occurring intellectual disability and epilepsy (Hirvikoski et al., 2016). This emphasises the need for an increasing research focus on the cause(s) of co-occurring mental health problems into and through adulthood.

Indeed, the provision of more effective, accessible, evidence-based support strategies to prevent and manage co-occurring mental health problems has been highlighted as a priority area for research by the autistic community (Pellicano et al., 2014; Autistica, 2017; Roche et al., 2021). However, progress in this area has been slow (Benevides et al., 2020). This is partly due to poor understanding of the candidate social and biological mechanisms underpinning the emergence and maintenance of co-occurring mental health problems in autism that may represent key targets for support, and whether these are the same or different in neurodivergent and neurotypical groups (linked to psychological concepts of equifinality – different mechanisms leading to the same cluster of symptoms; and multifinality – the

DOI: 10.4324/9781003495949-3

same mechanisms leading to different clusters of symptoms; Cicchetti & Rogosch, 1996). Evidence to date suggests that interacting genetic, social–environmental (e.g., stress and trauma), cognitive (e.g., intolerance of uncertainty, emotion regulation difficulties), and physiological and neurobiological (e.g., autonomic function and brain neurotransmitter alterations) factors implicated in mental health problems do appear to largely overlap between neurodivergent and neurotypical groups. However, these factors may be experienced at higher rates and/or qualitatively differently by autistic people (Oakley et al., 2021a).

In this chapter, we (a diverse team of autistic and non-autistic co-authors) present lived experiences of co-occurring mental health problems and the contributing factors for these, as narrated through first-hand accounts by 19 autistic adults (10 females; age range 18–34-years; 2 with mild intellectual disability) who volunteered to be interviewed by authors BO and HH, and the perspectives of co-authors.

Lived experiences are organised into eight key themes that begin to build a conceptual model for better understanding the mechanistic underpinnings of co-occurring mental health problems in autism (Figure 2.1): (1) autistic burnout; (2) stress and trauma; (3) emotion awareness and regulation; (4) negative thought patterns; (5) intolerance of uncertainty; (6) loneliness; (7) societal factors; and (8) the importance of resilience and protective factors, such as positive autistic identity. We close the chapter by summarising contributing factors for mental health problems as experienced by autistic adults and providing recommendations for promoting positive mental health outcomes, including identifying gaps in research that need to be addressed to advance this area.

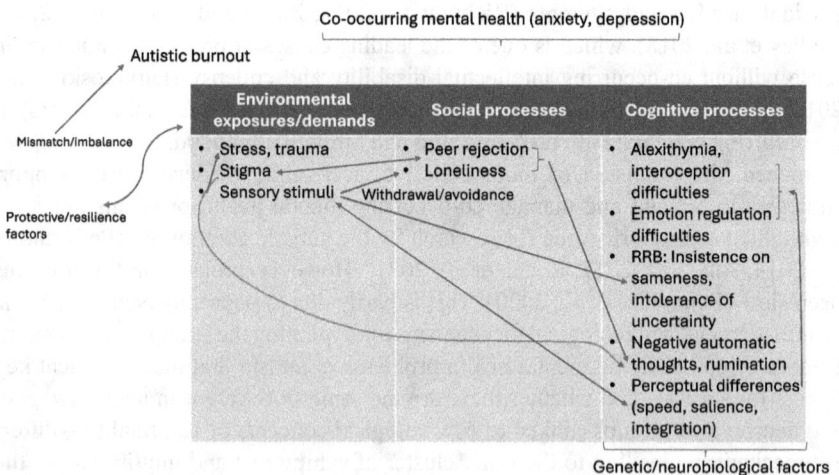

Figure 2.1 Conceptual model of co-occurring mental health problems in autism, based on lived experiences reported by autistic adults.

What Factors Contribute to Mental Health Problems in Autistic Adults?

Autistic Burnout ("I'm Just So Tired All the Time")

Autistic burnout was one of the most frequent issues that autistic adults expressed as having a negative impact on their mental health (and intersecting with physical health):

> I'm just so tired all the time, it's incredible. I don't know what to do about it. I-I'm sure you can have too much sleep. Surely . . . I hate it 'cause it means I can't do stuff, I can't, umm, work towards my goals . . . I'm just so tired that I don't even know what's going on.
>
> (Autistic male, 22-years-old)

Autistic burnout is a relatively new topic in the academic literature, despite being widely represented for some time in the autistic community (e.g., in social media, online blogs; Raymaker et al., 2020; Higgins et al., 2021). Autistic burnout can be defined as a chronic state of exhaustion and distress, which results in a decline in daily living skills (Raymaker et al., 2020; Higgins et al., 2021). This is driven by a high burden of environmental demands unaccommodating to the needs of autistic people and associated pressures to "mask" (conceal) autistic traits during social interactions (Arnold et al., 2023):

> [T]he world's built for and by neurotypical people. So, it's not, it's automatically not helpful, or designed for people with autism. Erm, so they're [the environment], they're always too stimulating or re – in sensory wise [sic], they're really difficult for autistic people.
> if I am masking and camouflaging it's so exhausting that I just can't sustain it
>
> (Autistic female, 22-years-old)

Loss of skills, including speech and executive functions like task-initiation and working memory, are widely reported by autistic people who have experienced, or are experiencing, burnout and some individuals report complete and long-lasting "shutdown":

> I couldn't believe it until I lived it. One of my autistic friends, who was completely functional up until late teen years, had a severe burnout experience due to trauma and PTSD [post-traumatic stress disorder] and collapsed. First literally, then figuratively in terms of a complete shutdown. His functions went from moderate adaptive behavioural issues and "semi-fine" quality of life to a full on catatonic state that lasted for years. He went from a college "almost-graduate" to an individual with massive support needs who can't talk, can't eat by himself, and can't walk from time to time. He now actually has a wheelchair in his worst days to move around and a personal assistant to help him through everyday living.
>
> (Autistic female; 42-years-old)

As such, autistic burnout differs from more widely discussed occupational burnout in its causes (that are not confined to workplace stress, but rather the unique challenges faced by autistic people in a neurotypical world) and manifestation (loss of functional skills) (Raymaker et al., 2020). Discussions in the academic literature are ongoing as to any possible intersections (and neurobiological underpinnings) between autistic burnout and autistic regression (loss of previously required skills, often associated with early developmental milestones, for example, talking, walking), demand avoidance (persistent and marked resistance to everyday demands, for example, following instructions, eating/sleeping), and/or chronic fatigue and pain conditions that impact quality of life (e.g., myalgic encephalomyelitis/ME, fibromyalgia).

Personal coping resources available to manage high environmental demands are also an important factor (Mantzalas et al., 2022):

> [O]n an average day I would say that I'm probably working at about, like, 90% capacity [laughs] of my effort and ability just to do my job description. So, when people start y – y'know, like, y'know, introducing new things . . . that's when it starts going to, like, oh yeah, no, I'm, like, I'm at, like, 100% capacity so, like, I'm – I'm going home after work and having to take like, a nap. Because I'm so tired and so stressed. And . . . I mean, the people in work don't see that side of things . . . And that affects my mental health.
>
> (Autistic male; 31-years-old)

In other words, context and timing may dictate whether similar sensory

> I can get distracted by all kinds of things and that can make me quite anxious
>
> (Autistic female, 29-years-old)

social, and/or cognitive demands constantly . . . thinking about what people are thinking

> (Autistic male, 24-years-old)

are, or are not, manageable, with difficulties particularly experienced during periods of acute stress it varies on how I'm feeling . . . it matters of stress, it matters how tired I am, it matters of everything [sic].

> (Autistic male, 34-years-old)

During episodes of autistic burnout, thresholds for imbalance between environmental demands and coping resources are reduced, as compared to the individual's "baseline" (when not in burnout), and this can lead to negative cyclical effects (i.e., sensory load can reduce personal coping resources, which leads to the burden of the sensory load further increasing).

This is also important when considering possible preventative (via monitoring of early signals of burnout) and protective factors for autistic burnout. The ability to take time out to "decompress" (i.e., remove oneself from the environment/ situation to rebuild personal coping resources) has been reported as a management strategy employed by autistic adults to reduce environmental overload:

I certainly feel more relaxed at home because I'm not having to deal with the social element. . . . I take up the option to work from home at least one day a week. . . . So, I'm like two days, in, one day home and I can recharge.

(Autistic male; 31-years-old)

Nevertheless, societal and cultural systems and infrastructure frequently lack sufficient adaptations and flexibility to enable individuals to be open about, and respond to, their personal needs, with autistic people experiencing being blamed or dismissed when asking for help when life tasks become unmanageable (Raymaker et al., 2020). This is a key issue to be addressed to reduce the impact of autistic burnout and its knock-on effects for mental health problems (and/or vice versa, as directionality of associations between autistic burnout and mental health problems is so far poorly understood).

Stress and Trauma ("It's Not the Autism, It's Just Everything Else")

While factors culminating in autistic burnout remain unclear due to the sparsity of research on this topic to date, chronic stress exposure has been frequently discussed in anecdotal qualitative reports, including discussions with autistic adults involved in the work resulting in this chapter:

[W]here I think this fatigue comes from, part of it is just exhaustion, like, cumulative tiredness from all the years of stress that I've been through but part of it is also a learned association between actually doing things that have to be done hundreds of times a day in order to live, err, and an association between that and just being completely drained afterwards.

(Autistic male, 30-years-old)

It is well documented in the general population literature that exposure to traumatic events (such as domestic or community violence, physical, sexual, and psychological abuse, and ongoing neglect or maltreatment) is associated with mental health problems, including post-traumatic stress disorder (PTSD) (Kessler et al., 2017). PTSD is characterised by repetitive re-experiencing of a traumatic event(s), avoidance of cues associated with the event(s), and behavioural or physiological changes, such as hypervigilance, reactivity, persistent negative thoughts and difficulties with memory recall (American Psychiatric Association, 2013). Rates of probable PTSD in autistic people (~32–45%) are higher than those in the general population (~4–4.5%; Rumball et al., 2020; Rumball et al., 2021; Haruvi-Lamdan et al., 2020). Further, the presentation of PTSD in autism may require particular attention, given that features like working memory difficulties and negative rumination are associated with the autistic phenotype also (developed upon further later in this chapter; Golan et al., 2022; Rumball et al., 2021, Carmassi et al., 2019; Fazel et al., 2020; Kildahl & Jørstad, 2022).

Elevated rates of PTSD in autism are, perhaps, unsurprising, given that autistic people are reported to be at elevated likelihood of experiencing trauma (Kerns et al., 2015; Berg et al., 2016), including significant negative life events (e.g., financial hardship, homelessness, interactions with the criminal justice system; Griffiths et al., 2019), which may contribute to increased rates of mental health problems in the autistic population (and act as a further barrier for accessing mental health support; Taylor and Gotham, 2016; Griffiths et al., 2019). For instance, victimisation experiences, especially bullying and sexual victimisation, are predicted to impact a significant proportion (up to 90% across all forms of victimisation) of autistic people (Douglas and Sedgewick, 2024; Trundle et al., 2022):

I didn't feel particularly safe on a day to day basis, I ended up hiding in the library most days whenever there was a free period or something . . . 'Cause that was the least likely place for those kids to be.

(Autistic male, 28-years-old)

[I] have quite frequent bad dreams about physical, err, err, physical conflicts with my parents. Erm and, and sometimes with, err, with other people. Especially with people from school because that's the period when this was happening.

(Autistic male, 30-years-old)

In addition to having a direct impact on mental health problems, victimisation experiences also have profound consequences for other aspects of emotional well-being that influence mental health outcomes, such as positive self-evaluation and self-esteem (Burrows et al., 2017):

[B]ullying is the most obvious example [of social situations affecting my mental health] . . . that continued right through school, it got a bit better in Sixth Form but even at University there were people who were pretty merciless, erm, and, err, that obviously affected my mental health, err, it affected my self-image, erm, my confidence, err, it made me anxious about social interactions and that's an anxiety that I'm still working to cast off.

(Autistic male, 30-years-old)

Of note, though traumatic experiences are often considered as discrete events, it is increasingly acknowledged that cumulative "microtraumas" (or complex PTSD; cPTSD) may also be experienced at high rates by autistic people. Microtraumas are characterised by multiple exposures to 'smaller' or 'less severe' events, but that remain impactful due to their chronic nature (Seides, 2010). For instance, daily environmental demands (e.g., shopping, travelling on public transport) have been shown to be perceived and experienced as more stressful by autistic, as compared to non-autistic, people (Gillott and Standen, 2007). Autistic people also report a wider range of traumatic experiences than typically reported in the general population and more severe responses to trauma (Rumball et al., 2020; Kerns et al., 2022; Quinton et al., 2024). These include trauma responses to sensory experiences:

> there are days where I'm just too sensitive to be able to leave the house. And that's, you know, being able to leave the house is one of the main things I consider to be part of being independent
>
> (Autistic female, 20-years-old)

transitions and change:

> when I had to move on from college, that was, that made me feel very worried because I didn't know what sort of things was going to happen [sic], things could happen to me once I left college. . . . I'm worried about mee-meeting new people, you know, moving onto something new.
>
> (Autistic male, 25-years-old)

and social misunderstandings, conflicts, and rejection: ("I try being, like, kind to them [people at college] but they, mostly they just, like, ignore me," autistic female, 19-years-old).

Emotion Awareness and Regulation ("I Wasn't Very Good at Communicating When Things Were Going Wrong")

Chronic stressor exposure, in combination with prolonged activation of stress responses due to additive/cumulative load (e.g., cortisol and adrenaline release that typically enable individuals to respond and adapt to stress), can result in disruptions to physiological and neurobiological systems ("allostatic load") that are transdiagnostically implicated in mental health outcomes (McEwen, 2004). Indeed, dysregulation of the hypothalamic pituitary adrenal axis (HPA; responsible for stress hormone production and release) and autonomic nervous system (ANS; fundamental to internal organ/tissue regulation) associated with long-term stress exposure and response activation has been reported in autistic people (Oakley et al., 2021).

On top of elevated stressor exposure, individual differences in perceptions of stressors (i.e., what is stressful, and to what extent) and engagement of regulatory strategies for managing stress are also implicated in allostatic load (McEwen, 2006). This is important in the context of autism, as there is growing evidence to suggest that some autistic people (and other neurodivergent groups, for example, those with attention-deficit hyperactivity disorder – ADHD) may experience differences in awareness, interpretation, and regulation of internal bodily sensations and emotions (and identifying/learning their triggers) linked to arousal and stress:

> I'm not even sure if I'm . . . knowing everything that's bothering me, as such.
>
> (Autistic male, 34-years-old)

For example, greater difficulties with both interoceptive awareness (the ability to interpret internal sensations in the body, such as changes in heart rate) and alexithymia (challenges with identifying and describing emotions) have been reported in autism (DuBois et al., 2016; Kinnaird et al., 2019). Moreover, difficulties with interoceptive awareness and alexithymia have been shown to be related to both concurrent and future mental health symptom severity, particularly in relation to anxiety symptoms (Garfinkel et al., 2016; Milosavljevic et al., 2016; Fietz et al., 2018; Oakley et al., 2020; Brewer et al., 2021; Ozsivadjian et al., 2021; Josyfon et al., 2023).

The lack of longitudinal studies in this area means that it is so far unclear whether difficulties identifying sensations and emotions precedes the onset of co-occurring mental health problems in autism. Nevertheless, emotion regulation processes have been posited as a candidate mechanism linking difficulties identifying sensations and emotions with mental health problems in autism and this is supported by existing evidence from cross-sectional studies (Morie et al., 2019). Awareness and accurate identification of one's own emotions has been argued to be the first stage of adaptive emotion regulation, and this may be disrupted or delayed for some autistic people (Gross, 2015):

> I feel like, I don't know, maybe when things just are, subtly don't go my way [sic], but I don't know what my way is. My mood will pick up on it, but I won't. But I won't really know how to change it.
>
> (Autistic male, 22-years-old)

This is because awareness of and attention to emotion(s) facilitates the subsequent cognitive appraisal of that emotion (how it is interpreted, that is, positively versus negatively, within or outside of one's own control) and subsequent strategies for responding to the emotion according to this interpretation (e.g., asking for help to adjust to a challenging situation, or engaging in mindfulness and relaxation techniques to detract focus and respond to a challenging situation) (Gross and Thompson, 2007).

Engagement of these "voluntary" adaptive emotion regulation strategies is reported to be lower in autistic than non-autistic groups (Cai et al., 2018), though this may in part be explained by a reduced capacity to do so when chronic stress exposure (and thus, the need to engage in voluntary strategies) is so constant. In terms of adaptive emotion regulation strategies like eliciting of social support, this is further impacted by difficulties describing sensations and emotions and asking for help – a facet of alexithymia, as noted above:

> [S]ometimes when there are things going wrong for me, it's very hard for me to be able to articulate them and be able to communicate them to other people. Um, and that can be quite hard for my family to then understand what they need to do to help me.
>
> (Autistic female, 22-years-old)

There is also some suggestion that autistic people may be more likely than their neurotypical peers to engage in "involuntary" maladaptive emotion regulation strategies, such as negative rumination, that are related to negative emotional and mental health outcomes (Mazefsky and White, 2014; Brugginck et al., 2016; Cai et al., 2018).

Negative Thought Patterns ("This Might Be as Good As It Gets")

Negative rumination represents a perseverative and repetitive thought pattern, where the individual focuses attention on negative past and current events and feelings, resulting in emotional distress:

> I was sleeping very lightly a little while ago. And, um, kind of, churning in my mind, like, thoughts and memories and conversations. And going over and over things.
>
> (Autistic female, 28-years-old)

Negative rumination has been found to be prevalent in non-autistic people who have experienced trauma, and has been linked to the development and maintenance of PTSD (Michael et al., 2007). In autism, restricted and repetitive behaviours (RRB), including rigid thought patterns, are a core diagnostic feature (American Psychiatric Association, 2013) and it is plausible that negative rumination may be somewhat linked to RRB.

The pattern of rumination in autistic adults has been reported to predominantly centre around repetitive thoughts about one's lack of motivation,

> I feel bad about my productivity slowing down, so I – then I start feeling negative about myself. Which leads on to, like, you know, feeling depressed
>
> (Autistic male, 31-years-old)

a personal sense of having many problems (and more than others; which is reinforced by actual lived experiences) and difficulties coping with stressors

> Cause there's this strong feeling that we were, sort of, you know, born wrong, and [sighs] designed to fail
>
> (Autistic male, 22-years-old)

and self-critical focus on perceived faults and mistakes (that again are reinforced by pressures to conform to neurotypical expectations) (Williams et al., 2021). Further features of this negative self-schema relate to negative thoughts about the future (Beck, 1979) – that things will never change or get better:

> I just know that, like, it's gonna be the same thing, like, same problems every day.
>
> (Autistic female, 19-years-old)

A similar pattern of rumination has been reported in non-autistic populations and found to be associated with the severity of depression symptoms in particular (Bernstein et al., 2019; Williams et al., 2021). However, in autistic adults, the focus of self-critical thoughts appears to often be linked to self-consciousness in social settings (where social feedback, both positive and negative, is also harder to ascertain and can create uncertainties around social performance that increase rumination), social faux pas, and peer rejection (Gotham et al., 2014; Keenan et al., 2017):

> "then I spent 48 hours just, sort of, torturing myself over that [social encounter]"; "I'm looking at this questionnaire and it was asking about, 'how self-conscious do you feel with i – in social situations?' And that's what I, kind of, worry about, how I'm coming across to people. And that can be due to my physical appearance. And mannerisms and stuff."
>
> (Autistic female, 29-years-old)

These kinds of socially focused negative thoughts may also be linked to difficulties with emotion awareness (described above), since difficulties identifying the emotional and mental states of others – as experienced by some autistic people (Uljarevic and Hamilton, 2013; Chung et al., 2014) – can lead to ambiguity in social interactions. There is evidence to suggest that autistic people are more likely than their non-autistic peers to experience ambiguous social cues and have a greater tendency to interpret these ambiguous social cues negatively (Eack et al., 2014):

> [Y]ou know how some people have a kind of, erm, have a kind of resting neutral face. I get very nervous around people who have that sometimes, 'cause I-I-I-I start worrying if I've, offended them or said something wrong.
>
> (Autistic female, 27-years-old)

Fear of negative social evaluation can be the result of previous negative social experiences, and make future social interactions more difficult, acting as a candidate maintenance factor for socially relevant anxiety (Pickard et al., 2017).

Intolerance of Uncertainty ("Sometimes It's a Complete Lack of Control")

Further to rumination, other forms of cognitive rigidity, such as insistence on sameness and intolerance of uncertainty, are also reported to be related to the autistic phenotype and may be candidate contributing factors for co-occurring mental health problems (South and Rodgers, 2017). Insistence on sameness is conceptualised as a component of RRB in autism and refers to a strong desire for imposing order on the environment through routines and difficulties with change and transitions (including differences in transitions between internal brain states) (Cuccaro et al., 2003; Gotham et al., 2013; Watanabe and Rees, 2017):

> I went downhill really, really fast when I realised I hadn't got control over things. So, I think sometimes it's a complete lack of control [that triggers anxiety and

depression] which is really scary for an autistic person because when you get pushed over the edge and you go into meltdown mode you aren't in control anymore.

(Autistic female, 29-years-old)

Intolerance of uncertainty is a broader concept, having been originally represented in the generalised anxiety literature, and refers to discomfort in ambiguous situations and a desire for predictability (Dugas et al., 1998):

The panic a -attacks. I sort of had a, or, I sort of felt one coming on today when I couldn't find the room I was supposed to be taking a tutorial in . . . Because it was the first time I'd been there.

(Autistic female, 27-years-old)

As evident from these definitions, there is some overlap between insistence on sameness and intolerance of uncertainty, in that the maintenance of routines and rituals can reduce unpredictability in the environment.

"Bayesian brain" models postulate that the brain is a dynamic system – constantly updating beliefs and predictions about the world based on new incoming sensory information, in order to reduce uncertainty and thus enhance predictability and the efficiency of perceptual processing (Friston, 2012). This is particularly important in the context of autism, where predictive coding theories have suggested that the autistic brain may make fewer assumptions about the environment based on prior experiences, leading to increased uncertainty and higher cognitive load for perceptual processing (Van de Cruys et al., 2014). Therefore, predictability and control over the environment, similarly to other RRB like stimming and engaging with strong interests (Kapp et al., 2019), may be a strategy for reducing overwhelming sensory stimuli and cognitive load:

I do expect to be in certain places at certain times. It helps with processing stuff . . . I know I can say, this is this point. I just have to worry about this bit and then I can get on to the next bit. . . . I need to know roughly where I'm going to be at certain times. I need to be able to understand of something [sic], I can – otherwise it builds up a lot of anxiety.

(Autistic male, 34-years-old)

While previously overlooked in the academic literature and in care provision for autistic people, it is increasingly recognised that sensory processing differences are a core feature of autism, given their high prevalence and impact on well-being and functioning (Crane et al., 2009; APA, 2013; McConachie et al., 2018). Higher sensory sensitivities are associated with co-occurring mental health problems, such as anxiety, in autistic people from childhood to adulthood (Tillmann et al., 2020). Furthermore, intolerance of uncertainty has been found to partly mediate this association between sensory sensitivities and anxiety symptom severity, and the association between anxiety symptom severity and insistence on sameness in autistic adults (Hwang et al., 2019).

Loneliness ("Loneliness Is Pretty, Pretty Horrible")

Routine and predictability can act as a coping strategy for avoiding and/or managing sensory overload and feeling autonomous and in control of one's environment:

> [W]hat I tend to do is like, kind of . . . I'll be just very upfront . . . like, 'oh, no, I've got to leave by 10'o'clock', or whatever it is. So, like, then I've got like, a time that I'm going to control myself.
>
> (Autistic male, 31-years-old)

Nevertheless, for some individuals, in the longer term, there may also be unwanted outcomes associated with difficulties with changes in routine and the environment. The experiences of autistic people during the societal restrictions imposed during the COVID-19 pandemic (e.g., staying at home, physical distancing) perhaps encapsulate this best and emphasise that autistic and non-autistic people shared similar social needs and difficulties. While some autistic people reported a sense of relief from social pressures, masking, and sensory overstimulation due to the early COVID-19 restrictions, many also experienced a deep sense of social loss (Pellicano et al., 2022; Scheeren et al., 2022) – highlighting the important distinction between "wanted" alone time and loneliness (unwanted lack of social connectedness – the focus of the rest of this section). Autistic people also reported concerns regarding how they would cope when returning to "normal" life after the pandemic, such as experiencing heightened social anxiety following a period of social withdrawal (Oomen et al., 2021):

> [I]t's one of those sort of things [sic] that when one's with a lot of people one wants to be alone and when one's alone for a long time you want more people.
>
> (Autistic male, 34-years-old)

These contrasting experiences of reduced social demands but increased loneliness are important to emphasise because they challenge a stereotypical view that social connectedness is less important for the quality of life of autistic than non-autistic people (Ayres et al., 2018; McConachie et al., 2018):

> I like to be alone and everything but if I don't really talk to people and feel that there is that support, erm, I do feel, err, I feel like that affects my motivation to do a lot of things.
>
> (Autistic male, 22-years-old)

Indeed, while the number of close social relationships reported by autistic people appears to be fewer than in non-autistic people, on average (and with some differences in the nature of contact, for example, fewer interactions outside of organised settings or increased use of alternative communication styles such as online), many autistic people express a strong desire for social connectedness,

I do like to generally be around people, or feel like I can be around people, 'cause I think that being too isolated sort of, makes me go a bit crazy to be honest,

(Autistic male, 28-years-old)

with high-quality social support being a key contributor to well-being (Howlin et al., 2004; Causton-Theoharis et al., 2009; Mazurek, 2013; Mason et al., 2019):

I don't know what I'd 'ave done, especially in the last couple of years with all the mental illness. If I hadn't had my family there, I don't know what I would've done.

(Autistic female, 22-years-old)

The distinction between objective frequency of social contact and subjective satisfaction with social support is thus relevant here, as the latter is often subjectively prioritised and perhaps most important in relation to loneliness (i.e., being alone does not necessarily equate to feeling lonely and, equally, one can feel lonely in the absence of social isolation) (Mazurek, 2013; Ee et al., 2019).

Loneliness has consistently been found to be elevated in autistic, as compared to non-autistic, people (Grace et al., 2022; Hymas et al., 2024). There is also some emerging evidence that loneliness increases as autistic people transition between developmental stages, contexts, and environments, especially into adulthood, which may be linked to changing social spheres (Schiltz et al., 2023). For instance, during childhood and adolescence, school attendance is mandatory, acting as a regular mechanism for social contact with peers. In contrast, in adulthood, autistic people face barriers accessing social opportunities, such as long-term paid employment (Howlin et al., 2004; Shattuck et al., 2012; National Autistic Society, 2019) and past social contacts may be lost, which adds further challenge to transition periods for autistic people:

I would want to hang around with people, people from my past, my old friends . . . but generally it just doesn't happen . . . if a friend is out of my routine for a while, they quite quickly disappear into the shadows.

(Autistic male, 22-years-old)

Associations between loneliness and mental health problems, such as anxiety and depression, have long been reported in the general population literature (Cacioppo et al., 2006). Similarly, loneliness is associated with anxiety and depression symptoms in autistic adults (Mazurek, 2013; Schiltz et al., 2020; Hymas et al., 2024). In turn, mental health problems have further been shown to exacerbate loneliness. This is possibly due to behavioural changes associated with mental health problems (e.g., depression), where many individuals experience withdrawal and reduced ability to experience pleasure and reward (anhedonia) from activities that can reduce loneliness, such as engagement in group leisure activities (Bishop-Fitzpatrick et al., 2017; Han et al., 2019; Schiltz et al., 2020):

> I think if [you're] depressed and don't wanna go out, then you just, kinda, get trapped inside.
>
> (Autistic female; 28-years-old)

Societal Factors ("Losing the Social Stigma Would Help")

Notably, although autistic experiences of loneliness have often been conceptually linked to social communication difficulties in autism

> It's really hard for me ha-having these communication differences, erm, to properly fit in, maybe?
>
> (Autistic female; 22-years-old)

the role of negative past social experiences and rejection (also see above) and lack of autism awareness and acceptance in society are critical factors (Elmose, 2020):

> ultimately, you know, people would just stop inviting me to things, and then stop being friends with me.
>
> (Autistic male; 31-years-old)

In fact, societal stigma and lack of reasonable adjustments to support autistic people is a theme that has links to all discussion points raised in this chapter so far:

> I feel I can call myself the square peg in a round hole . . . at college I'm, I basic – have basically been a square peg in a round hole.
>
> (Autistic female; 19-years-old)

Several common misconceptions regarding autism are still prevalent in wider society, including the confusion of autism as equivalent to commonly co-occurring intellectual disability (estimated to occur in approximately 55% of autistic people, though this figure varies across studies and countries; Charman et al., 2011), or, conversely, the portrayal of *all* autistic people as being socially withdrawn while having exceptional skills and abilities in particular areas (e.g., mathematical skills, creative arts) (Gillespie-Lynch et al., 2015; Jensen et al., 2015):

> I often seem to get the "oh, but you don't seem autistic 'cause you seem really friendly and you talk to people and you're not, you're not completely withdrawn at all."
>
> (Autistic male, 28-years-old)

These misconceptions regarding autism are problematic because they can lead to assumptions that autistic people who do not present in the ways that are expected (based on stereotypical societal portrayals of autism) or have "hidden difficulties" (i.e., support needs that are not immediately apparent, or only become apparent in certain contexts) do not need access to reasonable adjustments (Social Care Institute for Excellence, 2017):

> It's either one can't do anything, or one can do everything just fine and there's not a – how all the stuff really works [sic]. So, a bit of understanding that one can be capable in one area and still have a lot of needs in another and losing the social stigma would help.
>
> (Autistic male, 34-years-old)

Stereotypes and stigma around both autism and co-occurring mental health problems are particularly concerning, since they have been found to prevent autistic adults from feeling comfortable to disclose their mental health problems to access the support they need, even to healthcare professionals (Crane et al., 2018):

> [my peers would] tell me that mental health was, umm, discriminated against and that you've got to present yourself i – as good as, ahh, just we've all got to present ourselves . . . in the best way possible. . . . Although that's all I had been doing and it wasn't right for me.
>
> (Autistic female, 28-years-old)

Autistic people face a range of barriers in accessing healthcare services, including mental health services, some of which are linked to feeling misunderstood by healthcare providers. This is linked to a substantial lack of neurodevelopmental specialist pathways (National Autistic Society, 2019), which results in long waiting lists and a high threshold (in terms of mental health symptom severity) for referral to services, and underpins a sense that the system cannot offer autistic people the mental health support they require (Mason et al., 2019; Doherty et al., 2022; Shaw et al., 2023):

> If I'm in, say, a psychiatric unit a lot – most of the time the staff don't understand what autism is. That I may be having a meltdown but they're assuming that it's me having a tantrum, or, that I'm being a pain. Intentionally.
>
> (Autistic female, 22-years-old)

Societal barriers are also present in other settings beyond health and social care systems. As noted earlier in relation to autistic burnout, the mismatch between societal norms and expectations and individual profile strengths, difficulties, and preferences present significant challenges:

> I would appreciate it, just a little bit if you [society] could just recognise that maybe some of these expectations you have, don't practically work for me. My brain doesn't operate in the same way that yours does.
>
> (Autistic male, 28-years-old)

These challenges can pertain to feeling underestimated by society and not expected to achieve milestones like educational qualifications, employment, and/or having a partner and family:

> [W]hen you're an autistic person is – the general idea is that, 'oh, just do what you can'. You know, you don't, might not necessarily accomplish what anyone else would but that's alright 'cause you're not living at the same quality of life as other people . . . that you're sub-human, you know?. . . at the end of the day, like, a lot of people on the spectrum, they aren't so different.
>
> (Autistic male, 22-years-old)

Equally, autistic people can experience the opposite pressures – struggling to manage societal demands, but fearful of requesting reasonable adjustments in case of discrimination (e.g., losing employment):

> It bothers me. Makes me feel a bit bad, like, ah, you know it's hard and I feel like I can't do much better.
>
> (Autistic male, 22-years-old)

Discrimination, or "enacted stigma," has both a direct and an indirect impact on the mental health problems of autistic people, with indirect impact acting through internalised self-stigma (Han et al., 2022; Turnock et al., 2022). This is where an individual turns the negative perceptions that they experience from others onto themselves, resulting in decreased self-esteem, reduced expectations for self, increased likelihood of masking, and reduced likelihood that an autistic person will disclose their diagnosis to others (Han et al., 2022). Though diagnostic disclosure is often consequently a major decision, there is some evidence to indicate that disclosure is associated with more positive attitudes towards autistic people by neurotypicals (especially those who already hold higher knowledge and lower stigma towards autism), possibly due to a greater understanding of perceived differences in behaviours and social styles of autistic people when the diagnosis is known (O'Connor et al., 2020; Sasson and Morrison, 2017; Thompson-Hodgetts et al., 2020). In supportive environments, diagnostic disclosure can also reduce pressures to mask (and its knock-on impacts):

> I have to really try and subdue the urge to mask and camouflage otherwise that's like, that friendship kind of breaks down, 'cause I'm not– it takes too much effort to be, in that friendship.
>
> (Autistic female, 22-years-old)

It also enables autistic people to be more open about their needs and preferences and more confident that these will be recognised and accepted:

> [T]he most useful thing to me was actually knowing that there were reasons why I think like this and do these things . . . and actually telling my friends that ahead of time actually saves us a lot of problems.
>
> (Autistic female, 29-years-old)

Autistic Identity as a Resilience Factor ("I Just Want to Be Me, No Matter What")

Similarly, one's own sense of positive autistic identity, which is enhanced by external acceptance and support, has been identified as highly important for promoting positive mental health outcomes (Botha et al., 2022; Cooper et al., 2021; Davies et al., 2024; Gray et al., 2024; Lilley et al., 2022). As such, late diagnosis of autism (the average age of autism diagnosis globally is approximately 60 months, although many autistic people are diagnosed, or have their diagnosis revealed to them, in adolescence or adulthood) (van't Hof et al., 2020) has been shown to be associated with severity of mental health problems (Bargiela et al., 2016; Lupindo et al., 2023). This is likely due to a range of factors that include lack of understanding and responsiveness to individuals' needs by others (e.g., environmental adaptations, such as considering sensory over stimulation) and delayed access to support and services.

Additionally, late diagnosis has been associated with a sense of loss, preventing individuals from embracing their autistic identity earlier in life

> I feel like I've missed my life. And, I could have been myself.
>
> (Autistic female, 28-years-old)

and underpinning a sense of personal blame for experiencing certain challenges in everyday life

> for mood and so on, I don't think I would've beaten myself up about not having friends or not fitting in, or not understanding people. Or any of that. 'Cause it's not my fault.
>
> (Autistic male, 28-years-old) (Leedham et al., 2020; Stagg and Belcher, 2019)

For autistic people who do receive their diagnosis in their teenage years or adulthood, this can act as a "light bulb" moment in explaining earlier differences in cognitions and behaviours and identifying strengths, rather than perceiving these differences as negative attributes:

> [K]nowing I'm "officially different" [laughs] is comforting, because it explains why I felt like this. I never felt like I was, you know, inherently different before my diagnosis it was just, ah yeah, no I-I'm either unfortunate or something like that.
>
> (Autistic male, 31-years-old)

> I think before I had my diagnosis it was more of a problem, because they [my family] didn't really understand me . . . I didn't know why I thought about different things from other people, cared about different things. Um, I didn't know I could do things other people couldn't. Um, it was all a bit . . . f– frustrating.
>
> (Autistic female, 29-years-old)

Diagnosis can also provide a new social support infrastructure and community, with research showing that individuals who feel higher social solidarity with other autistic people report higher psychological well-being (Cooper et al., 2023). Connected to this, there has been increasing interest in the benefits of peer support to improve mental health problems for autistic people (Duerksen et al., 2021), with autistic peers being ideally placed to provide support that authentically nurtures autistic priorities and ways of functioning, learning, developing, and living (Bertilsdotter Rosqvist, 2019; Shea et al., 2024).

Conclusion

In this chapter, we have presented several interconnected contributing factors for co-occurring mental health problems (anxiety, depression, etc.) in autistic adults, narrated by lived experiences. This work begins to build a conceptual model for better understanding high rates of co-occurring mental health problems in autism (see Figure 2.1). Contributing factors for co-occurring mental health problems described here included autistic burnout – a chronic state of exhaustion and loss of function linked to an imbalance between personal coping resources and environmental stressors, such as trauma and victimisation, societal stigma (and the associated lack of adaptations to support autistic people in their daily lives), and overwhelm caused by difficulties processing sensory stimuli. In processing and responding to environmental stressors like sensory stimuli, autistic adults reported difficulties with identifying and describing their emotions and internal bodily sensations, linked to lower engagement of adaptive emotion regulation strategies for managing response to stressors. Other cognitive processes implicated in mental health problems included repetitive and rigid thinking styles, such as negative rumination, as well as insistence on sameness and intolerance of uncertainty – the latter two possibly acting as a buffer against sensory overload (insistence on sameness) and mechanism reinforcing this (intolerance of uncertainty), yet with knock-on impacts for maintaining anxiety, in particular. Negative thought patterns and rumination were reinforced by social processes, such as peer rejection and internalised self-stigma, with autistic adults reporting loneliness (sometimes following withdrawal, linked to sensory overload and/or negative social experiences) that contributed to low mood.

Of importance, autistic adults also highlighted factors that promoted positive mental health – many of these reflected in wider theoretical dimensions of psychological well-being (Ryff, 2013) – such as social support networks, engagement in leisure activities, being empowered to achieve personal goals and to have their contributions to society valued, and positive identity as an autistic person. These experiences emphasise that it is essential to widen research and societal focus beyond risk factors for mental health problems to integrate positive/protective and resilience factors for the psychological well-being of autistic people. In other words, what is important for "autistic flourishing" – to live a (self-defined) good quality of life? (Pellicano and Heyworth, 2023). Increasing focus on positive psychological well-being reflects the shift from medical or "deficit-based" models of autism, where autistic features are viewed as negative outcomes that require treatment to align with neurotypical "norms," to neurodiversity-affirmative models that view neurobiological and functional differences in autism as a natural and valuable component of human variation (Heraty et al., 2023).

Neurodiversity-affirmative models of autism do not negate that autism can cause disability, particularly when the environment is unaccommodating to an autistic person's accessibility needs, as per the social model of disability (Heraty et al., 2023; Leadbitter et al., 2021; Oliver, 1990). Thus, environmental adaptations to social infrastructure (e.g., educational/workplaces, health and social care, public/leisure facilities) that maximise the person–environment fit to minimise barriers to access for autistic people is a priority area for service providers and policymakers (Lai et al., 2020; Turnock et al., 2022). This is in part because they have the potential to reduce the likelihood of the development and/or maintenance of co-occurring mental health problems – for instance, by reducing environmental stressors implicated in autistic burnout. Following the "autistic SPACE" framework (Doherty et al., 2023), environmental adaptations should focus on sensory needs (e.g., dimmable lighting functionality), predictability (e.g., provision of accessible preparatory materials and information ahead of a meeting or medical appointment), acceptance (e.g., not attempting to prevent non-harmful self-stimulating behaviours or "stimming," such as use of a fidget item), communication (e.g., clear, direct, unambiguous language style, providing additional breaks and processing time during interactions), and empathy (e.g., asking autistic people for their interpretations, rather than imposing/assuming neurotypical interpretations). Though these adaptations are essential for addressing access issues for autistic people, they also have promise to improve accessibility to the greatest extent possible by all people, irrespective of neurotype (Milton et al., 2016).

The widespread and effective implementation of the environmental and behavioural adaptations described above is underpinned by improving public awareness and acceptance of autism. Existing recommendations for achieving this include national campaigns and advocacy, guidance, and support for local authorities to promote autism-friendly spaces and initiatives, and further work to understand additional barriers experienced by autistic people from underrepresented groups (e.g., ethnic minorities, those from lower socioeconomic backgrounds) (National Autistic Society, 2019). Improving autism awareness and acceptance can also be enhanced through the provision of high-quality training for professionals who will work with autistic people (e.g., teachers, managers, healthcare professionals), but may not be autism/neurodevelopmental specialists. As an example, the UK Health and Care Act 2022 introduced the requirement for brief, mandatory learning disability and autism training to all health and social care staff. However, how such policies are being implemented in practice and the evaluation of their impact is still yet to be understood (National Institute for Health and Care Research, 2023). Efforts in this area are important, as greater, accurate public understanding of autism is central to reducing stigma and its varied associated impacts on the mental health symptoms of autistic people.

A final priority area for improving mental health outcomes for autistic people is the development and provision of more effective, accessible evidence-based support and therapies to prevent clinically relevant mental health problems from occurring or manage them if/when they do. Cognitive-behavioural and mindfulness-based approaches are currently the only candidates with emerging empirical support for management of mental health problems in autistic adults (Benevides et al., 2020). Existing pharmacological approaches, such as selective serotonin reuptake inhibitors (SSRIs), are useful for some, but robust evidence for their effectiveness in autistic adults is lacking and heightened adverse side effects and sensory aversion to taste and texture of some medications has been reported in autistic populations (Howes et al., 2018; Vasa et al., 2016; Williams et al., 2013). Cognitive-behavioural approaches aim to reduce mental health problems by targeting negative thought patterns (described earlier in this chapter) and encouraging behavioural activation – for instance, gradually reducing avoidance of anxiety provoking situations, while encouraging engagement in pleasurable activities (Beck, 1979; McGillivray and Evert, 2014; Sizoo and Kuiper, 2017). Mindfulness-based approaches target emotion awareness and regulation difficulties and reduce physiological arousal (also described earlier in this chapter) through turning focused attention to thoughts, feelings, and the surrounding environment in the present moment without judgement (Sizoo and Kuiper, 2017; Spek et al., 2013).

Though cognitive-behavioural and mindfulness-based therapeutic approaches targeting co-occurring mental health problems are promising, there is increasing recognition that modifications are required to enhance both effectiveness and accessibility for autistic people (Davidson et al., 2024). Modifications can include psychoeducation on the triggers and presentation of the autistic experience of mental health problems, which may differ in some respects from the non-autistic experience (Kerns et al., 2014; Kerns and Kendall, 2012; Stewart et al., 2006; Wood and Gadow, 2010). Other recommendations are a more concrete and structured approach to sessions in favour of excessive use of metaphor and hypotheticals (particularly around identifying and describing emotions), allowing for more processing time through regular breaks or shorter sessions that take place over a longer period of time, including a support person in sessions where appropriate, and integrating autistic strengths and preferences into the therapy (e.g., specific interests, visual materials) (Chew et al., 2022; Cooper et al., 2018; Spain et al., 2015; Spain and Happé, 2020). Other adjustments are required when working with autistic people with a co-occurring intellectual disability, who may be more likely to present with non-classical mental health symptoms (e.g., externalised presentations of internalising problems, such as irritability/agitation, withdrawal, and loss of skills/behavioural changes) (Stewart et al., 2006) and where excessive use of psychotropic drug prescription has been reported (Sheehan et al., 2015). Furthermore, approaches to mental health support for autistic people must avoid imposing assumptions drawn from evidence in neurotypical populations (where most clinical trials are focused) and be sensitive to potential compensatory mechanisms that may be disrupted by intervention (Dawson and Fletcher-Watson, 2021). For instance, behavioural activation may be harmful rather than beneficial for autistic people in acute burnout (Arnold et al., 2022), where withdrawal from overwhelming environments in the short term is adaptive.

Considering the barriers to accessing healthcare experienced by autistic people (Doherty et al., 2022; Mason et al., 2019; Nicolaidis et al., 2015; Shaw et al., 2023), alternative modes of delivering mental health support to autistic people may also warrant further exploration (Oakley et al., 2021b). There is increasing interest and investment in digital tools and technologies for mental health service delivery, from triage to intervention, with some evidence that they may provide a low-intensity and cost-effective method of providing mental health support for some autistic people (Oakley et al., 2023; Sutherland et al., 2018). Digital (or digitally augmented) mental health assessment and support mechanisms have potential to increase accessibility, particularly for those who experience additional challenges accessing in-person services (e.g., due to cost, mobility), and those living in areas where access to specialist mental health services and professionals is limited. However, research in this area is still in its infancy and more work is needed to ensure that digital healthcare technologies are implemented in a way that promotes equitable access and continuity of care, complements and enhances standard of practice care, and is personalised to the specific needs of the service user (Noel and Ellison, 2020).

In conclusion, autistic people experience a range of interrelated factors that contribute to increased likelihood of co-occurring mental health problems, spanning environmental exposure to stressors (e.g., trauma and victimisation, stigma, sensory stimuli), social factors (e.g., peer rejection, loneliness), and cognitive processes (e.g., difficulties with emotion and sensation awareness and regulation, negative thought patterns and rumination, insistence on sameness and intolerance of uncertainty). Imbalances between environmental stressor exposures and personal coping resources can lead to chronic stress responses and burnout, also elevating vulnerability to co-occurring mental health problems and their maintenance. While autism research has traditionally focused on early development and childhood (given that autism is a neurodevelopmental condition), greater emphasis on autistic experiences of mental health problems in adulthood is imperative, especially since co-occurring mental health problems typically first arise from late childhood and early adolescence and subsequently tend to persist over time. To improve mental health outcomes for autistic adults, key priorities for research and policy/practice include environmental adaptations to social infrastructure to minimise barriers for autistic people, promoting better public understanding and acceptance of autism to reduce stigma, and efforts to develop more effective, evidence-based support strategies that are sensitive to autistic experiences of mental health problems and maximise accessibility. These efforts should not neglect the needs of autistic people with co-occurring intellectual disability. Furthermore, the focus here should not only be on reducing mental health problems, but also on promoting positive well-being and outcomes for all autistic adults for the benefit of both individuals and wider society.

References

American Psychiatric Association, APA. (2013). *Diagnostic and statistical manual of mental disorders* (5th ed.). Washington, DC: American Psychiatric Association Publishing.
Arnold, S. R. C., Higgins, J. M., Weise, J., Desai, A., Pellicano, E., & Trollor, J. N. (2023). Confirming the nature of autistic burnout. *Autism*. https://doi.org/10.1177/13623613221147410
Arnold, S., Higgins, J., Weise, J., Desai, A., Pellicano, L., & Trollor, J. (2022, February). *Investigating autistic burnout (#AutBurnout): Final report*. Brisbane: Autism CRC.
Autistica. (2017). *Research strategy 2017–2021*. 1–15. https://www.autistica.org.uk/downloads/files/Autistica-Research-Strategy-2017-2021.pdf
Ayres, M., Parr, J. R., Rodgers, J., Mason, D., Avery, L., & Flynn, D. (2018). A systematic review of quality of life of adults on the autism spectrum. *Autism, 22*(7). https://doi.org/10.1177/1362361317714988
Bargiela, S., Steward, R., & Mandy, W. (2016). The experiences of late-diagnosed women with autism spectrum conditions: An investigation of the female autism phenotype. *Journal of Autism and Developmental Disorders, 46*(10), 3281–3294. https://doi.org/10.1007/s10803-016-2872-8
Beck, A. T. (1979). *Cognitive therapy of depression*. The GuilfordPress.
Benevides, T. W., Shore, S. M., Andresen, M.-L., Caplan, R., Cook, B., Gassner, D. L., Erves, J. M., Hazlewood, T. M., King, M. C., Morgan, L., Murphy, L. E., Purkis, Y., Rankowski, B., Rutledge, S. M., Welch, S. P., & Wittig, K. (2020). Interventions to address health outcomes among autistic adults: A systematic review. *Autism, 24*(6), 1345–1359. https://doi.org/10.1177/1362361320913664
Berg, K. L., Shiu, C.-S., Acharya, K., Stolbach, B. C., & Msall, M. E. (2016). Disparities in adversity among children with autism spectrum disorder: A population-based study. *Developmental Medicine & Child Neurology, 58*(11), 1124–1131. https://doi.org/https://doi.org/10.1111/dmcn.13161
Bernstein, E. E., Heeren, A., & McNally, R. J. (2019). Reexamining trait rumination as a system of repetitive negative thoughts: A network analysis. *Journal of Behavior Therapy and Experimental Psychiatry, 63*, 21–27. https://doi.org/https://doi.org/10.1016/j.jbtep.2018.12.005
Bertilsdotter Rosqvist, H. (2019). Knowing what to do: Exploring meanings of development and peer support aimed at people with autism. *International Journal of Inclusive Education, 23*(2), 174–187. https://doi.org/10.1080/13603116.2018.1427807
Bishop-Fitzpatrick, L., Smith DaWalt, L., Greenberg, J. S., & Mailick, M. R. (2017). Participation in recreational activities buffers the impact of perceived stress on quality of life in adults with autism spectrum disorder. *Autism Research, 10*(5), 973–982. https://doi.org/https://doi.org/10.1002/aur.1753
Botha, M., Dibb, B., & Frost, D. M. (2022). "Autism is me": An investigation of how autistic individuals make sense of autism and stigma. *Disability & Society, 37*(3), 427–453. https://doi.org/10.1080/09687599.2020.1822782
Brewer, R., Murphy, J., & Bird, G. (2021). Atypical interoception as a common risk factor for psychopathology: A review. *Neuroscience & Biobehavioral Reviews, 130*, 470–508. https://doi.org/https://doi.org/10.1016/j.neubiorev.2021.07.036
Bruggink, A., Huisman, S., Vuijk, R., Kraaij, V., & Garnefski, N. (2016). Cognitive emotion regulation, anxiety and depression in adults with autism spectrum disorder. *Research in Autism Spectrum Disorders, 22*, 34–44. https://doi.org/https://doi.org/10.1016/j.rasd.2015.11.003
Burrows, C. A., Usher, L. V, Mundy, P. C., & Henderson, H. A. (2017). The salience of the self: Self-referential processing and internalizing problems in children and adolescents with autism spectrum disorder. *Autism Research : Official Journal of the International Society for Autism Research, 10*(5), 949–960. https://doi.org/10.1002/aur.1727

Cacioppo, J. T., Hughes, M. E., Waite, L. J., Hawkley, L. C., & Thisted, R. A. (2006). Loneliness as a specific risk factor for depressive symptoms: Cross-sectional and longitudinal analyses. *Psychology and Aging, 21*(1), 140–151. https://doi.org/10.1037/0882-7974.21.1.140

Cacioppo, J. T., Hughes, M. E., Waite, L. J., Hawkley, L. C., & Thisted, R. A. (2006). Loneliness as a specific risk factor for depressive symptoms: Cross-sectional and longitudinal analyses. *Psychology and Aging, 21*(1), 140–151. https://doi.org/10.1037/0882-7974.21.1.140

Cai, R. Y., Richdale, A. L., Uljarević, M., Dissanayake, C., & Samson, A. C. (2018). Emotion regulation in autism spectrum disorder: Where we are and where we need to go. *Autism Research, 11*(7), 962–978. https://doi.org/https://doi.org/10.1002/aur.1968

Carmassi, C., Bertelloni, C. A., Salarpi, G., Diadema, E., Avella, M. T., Dell'Oste, V., & Dell'Osso, L. (2019). Is there a major role for undetected autism spectrum disorder with childhood trauma in a patient with a diagnosis of bipolar disorder, self-injuring, and multiple comorbidities? *Case Reports in Psychiatry, 2019*, 4703795. https://doi.org/10.1155/2019/4703795

Causton-Theoharis, J., Ashby, C., & Cosier, M. (2009). Islands of loneliness: Exploring social interaction through the autobiographies of individuals with autism. *Intellectual and Developmental Disabilities, 47*(2), 84–96. https://doi.org/10.1352/1934-9556-47.2.84

Charman, T., Pickles, A., Simonoff, E., Chandler, S., Loucas, T., & Baird, G. (2011). IQ in children with autism spectrum disorders: Data from the Special Needs and Autism Project (SNAP). *Psychological Medicine, 41*(3), 619–627. https://doi.org/10.1017/S0033291710000991

Chew, X. Y., Ozsivadjian, A., Hollocks, M., & Magiati, I. (2022). Cognitive behavior therapy. In D. Spain, F. Musich, & S. White (Eds.), *Psychological therapies for adults with autism* (online edn). Oxford Academic. https://doi.org/https://doi.org/10.1093/med-psych/9780197548462.001.0001

Chung, Y. S., Barch, D., & Strube, M. (2014). A meta-analysis of mentalizing impairments in adults with schizophrenia and autism spectrum disorder. *Schizophrenia Bulletin, 40*(3), 602–616. https://doi.org/10.1093/schbul/sbt048

Cicchetti, D., & Rogosch, F. A. (1996). Equifinality and multifinality in developmental psychopathology. *Development and Psychopathology, 8*(4), 597–600. https://doi.org/10.1017/S0954579400007318

Cooper, K., Loades, M. E., & Russell, A. (2018). Adapting psychological therapies for autism. *Research in Autism Spectrum Disorders, 45*, 43–50. https://doi.org/https://doi.org/10.1016/j.rasd.2017.11.002

Cooper, K., Russell, A. J., Lei, J., & Smith, L. G. (2023). The impact of a positive autism identity and autistic community solidarity on social anxiety and mental health in autistic young people. *Autism, 27*(3), 848–857. https://doi.org/10.1177/13623613221118351. Epub 2022 Sep 4. PMID: 36062470; PMCID: PMC10074754

Cooper, R., Cooper, K., Russell, A. J., & Smith, L. G. E. (2021). "I'm proud to be a little bit different": The effects of autistic individuals' perceptions of autism and autism social identity on their collective self-esteem. *Journal of Autism and Developmental Disorders, 51*(2), 704–714. https://doi.org/10.1007/s10803-020-04575-4

Crane, L., Adams, F., Harper, G., Welch, J., & Pellicano, E. (2018). 'Something needs to change': Mental health experiences of young autistic adults in England. *Autism, 23*(2), 477–493. https://doi.org/10.1177/1362361318757048

Crane, L. Goddard, L., & Pring, L. (2009). Sensory processing in adults with autism spectrum disorders. *Autism, 13*(3), 215–228. https://doi.org/10.1177/1362361309103794

Cuccaro, M. L., Shao, Y., Grubber, J. *et al.* (2003). Factor analysis of restricted and repetitive behaviors in autism using the autism diagnostic interview-R. *Child Psychiatry & Human Development, 34*, 3–17. https://doi.org/10.1023/A:1025321707947

Davidson, A., Doherty, M., Haydon, & Autism, C. (2024). *Seminars in general adult psychiatry. College seminars series* (D. Kingdon, P. Rowlands, & G. Stein, Eds.). Cambridge: Cambridge University Press, pp. 527–538.

Davies, J., Cooper, K., Killick, E., Sam, E., Healy, M., Thompson, G., Mandy, W., Redmayne, B., & Crane, L. (2024). Autistic identity: A systematic review of quantitative research. *Autism Research*, *17*(5), 874–897. https://doi.org/https://doi.org/10.1002/aur.3105

Dawson, M., & Fletcher-Watson, S. (2021). When autism researchers disregard harms: A commentary. *Autism*, *26*(2), 564–566. https://doi.org/10.1177/13623613211031403

Doherty, M., McCowan, S., & Shaw, S. C. K. (2023). Autistic SPACE: A novel framework for meeting the needs of autistic people in healthcare settings. *British Journal of Hospital Medicine*, *84*(4), 1–9. https://doi.org/10.12968/hmed.2023.0006

Doherty, M., Neilson, S., O'Sullivan, J., Carravallah, L., Johnson, M., Cullen, W., &, Shaw, S. C. K. (2022). Barriers to healthcare and self-reported adverse outcomes for autistic adults: A cross-sectional study. *BMJ Open*, *12*(2), e056904. https://doi.org/10.1136/bmjopen-2021-056904

Douglas, S., & Sedgewick, F. (2024). Experiences of interpersonal victimization and abuse among autistic people. *Autism*, *28*(7), 1732–1745. https://doi.org/10.1177/13623613231205630

DuBois, D., Ameis, S. H., Lai, M.-C., Casanova, M. F., & Desarkar, P. (2016). Interoception in autism spectrum disorder: A review. *International Journal of Developmental Neuroscience*, *52*(1), 104–111. https://doi.org/https://doi.org/10.1016/j.ijdevneu.2016.05.001

Duerksen, K., Besney, R., Ames, M., & McNorris, C. (2021). Supporting autistic adults in postsecondary settings: A systematic review of peer mentorship programs. *Autism in Adulthood*, *3*(1).

Dugas, M. J., Gagnon, F., Ladouceur, R., & Freeston, M. H. (1998). Generalized anxiety disorder: A preliminary test of a conceptual model. *Behaviour Research and Therapy*, *36*(2), 215–226. https://doi.org/10.1016/s0005-7967(97)00070-3

Eack, S. M., Mazefsky, C. A., & Minshew, N. J. (2014). Misinterpretation of facial expressions of emotion in verbal adults with autism spectrum disorder. *Autism*, *19*(3), 308–315. https://doi.org/10.1177/1362361314520755

Ee, D., Hwang, Y. I. (Jane), Reppermund, S., Srasuebkul, P., Trollor, J. N., Foley, K.-R., & Arnold, S. R. C. (2019). Loneliness in adults on the autism spectrum. *Autism in Adulthood*, *1*(3), 182–193. https://doi.org/10.1089/aut.2018.0038

Elmose, M. (2020). Understanding loneliness and social relationships in autism: The reflections of autistic adults. *Nordic Psychology*, *72*(1), 3–22. https://doi.org/10.1080/19012276.2019.1625068

Fazel, M., Stratford, H. J., Rowsell, E., Chan, C., Griffiths, H., & Robjant, K. (2020). Five applications of narrative exposure therapy for children and adolescents presenting with post-traumatic stress disorders. *Frontiers in Psychiatry*, *11*, 19. https://doi.org/10.3389/fpsyt.2020.00019

Fietz, J., Valencia, N., & Silani, G. (2018). Alexithymia and autistic traits as possible predictors for traits related to depression, anxiety, and stress: A multivariate statistical approach. *Journal of Evaluation in Clinical Practice*, *24*(4), 901–908. https://doi.org/10.1111/jep.12961

Friston, K. (2012, August) The history of the future of the Bayesian brain. *Neuroimage*, *15*(2), 1230–1233. https://doi.org/10.1016/j.neuroimage.2011.10.004. Epub 2011 Oct 17. PMID: 22023743; PMCID: PMC3480649

Garfinkel, S. N., Tiley, C., O'Keeffe, S., Harrison, N. A., Seth, A. K., & Critchley, H. D. (2016). Discrepancies between dimensions of interoception in autism: Implications for emotion and anxiety. *Biological Psychology*, *114*, 117–126. https://doi.org/10.1016/j.biopsycho.2015.12.003

Gillespie-Lynch, K., Brooks, P. J., Someki, F., Obeid, R., Shane-Simpson, C., Kapp, S. K., Daou, N., & Smith, D. S. (2015). Changing college students' conceptions of autism: An online training to increase knowledge and decrease stigma. *Journal of Autism and Developmental Disorders*, *45*(8), 2553–2566. https://doi.org/10.1007/s10803-015-2422-9

Gillott, A., & Standen, P. J. (2007). Levels of anxiety and sources of stress in adults with autism. *Journal of Intellectual Disabilities : JOID*, *11*(4), 359–370. https://doi.org/10.1177/1744629507083585

Golan, O., Haruvi-Lamdan, N., Laor, N., & Horesh, D. (2022). The comorbidity between autism spectrum disorder and post-traumatic stress disorder is mediated by brooding rumination. *Autism*, *26*(2), 538–544. https://doi.org/10.1177/13623613211035240

Gotham, K., Bishop, S. L., Hus, V., Huerta, M., Lund, S., Buja, A., Krieger, A., & Lord, C. (2013). Exploring the relationship between anxiety and insistence on sameness in autism spectrum disorders. *Autism Research : Official Journal of the International Society for Autism Research*, *6*(1), 33–41. https://doi.org/10.1002/aur.1263

Gotham, K., Brunwasser, S. M., & Lord, C. (2015). Depressive and anxiety symptom trajectories from school age through young adulthood in samples with autism spectrum disorder and developmental delay. *Journal of the American Academy of Child and Adolescent Psychiatry*, *54*(5), 369–376.e3. doi: 10.1016/j.jaac.2015.02.005

Grace, K., Remington, A., Lloyd-Evans, B., Davies, J., & Crane, L. (2022). Loneliness in autistic adults: A systematic review. *Autism*, *26*(8), 2117–2135. https://doi.org/10.1177/13623613221077721

Gray, S. M., McMorris, C. A., Mudry, T. E., & McCrimmon, A. W. (2024). An exploration of diagnostic identity for autistic individuals: A systematic review of existing literature. *Research in Autism Spectrum Disorders*, *114*. https://doi.org/10.1016/j.rasd.2024.102394

Griffiths, S., Allison, C., Kenny, R., Holt, R., Smith, P., & Baron-Cohen, S. (2019, October). The vulnerability experiences quotient (VEQ): A study of vulnerability, mental health and life satisfaction in autistic adults. *Autism Research*, *12*(10), 1516–1528. https://doi.org/10.1002/aur.2162. Epub 2019 Jul 5. PMID: 31274233; PMCID: PMC6851759

Gross, J. J. (2015). Emotion regulation: Current status and future prospects. *Psychological Inquiry*, *26*(1), 1–26. https://doi.org/10.1080/1047840X.2014.940781

Gross, J. J., & Thompson, R. A. (2007). Emotion regulation: Conceptual foundations. In *Handbook of emotion regulation*. The Guilford Press, pp. 3–24.

Han, E., Scior, K., Avramides, K., & Crane, L. (2022). A systematic review on autistic people's experiences of stigma and coping strategies. *Autism Research*, *15*(1), 12–26. https://doi.org/https://doi.org/10.1002/aur.2652

Han, G. T., Tomarken, A. J., & Gotham, K. O. (2019). Social and nonsocial reward moderate the relation between autism symptoms and loneliness in adults with ASD, depression, and controls. *Autism Research*, *12*(6), 884–896. https://doi.org/10.1002/aur.2088

Haruvi-Lamdan, N., Horesh, D., Zohar, S., Kraus, M., & Golan, O. (2020, May). Autism spectrum disorder and post-traumatic stress disorder: An unexplored co-occurrence of conditions. *Autism*, *24*(4), 884–898. https://doi.org/10.1177/1362361320912143. Epub 2020 Apr 3. PMID: 32245333

Hedley, D., Uljarević, M., Foley, K.-R., Richdale, A., & Trollor, J. (2018). Risk and protective factors underlying depression and suicidal ideation in Autism Spectrum Disorder. *Depression and Anxiety*, *35*(7), 648–657. https://doi.org/10.1002/da.22759

Heraty, S., Lautarescu, A., Belton, D., Boyle, A., Cirrincione, P., Doherty, M., Douglas, S., Plas, J. R. D., Van Den Bosch, K., Violland, P., Tercon, J., Ruigrok, A., Murphy, D. G. M., Bourgeron, T., Chatham, C., Loth, E., Oakley, B., McAlonan, G. M., Charman, T., . . . Jones, E. J. H. (2023). Bridge-building between communities: Imagining the future of biomedical autism research. *Cell*, *186*(18), 3747–3752. https://doi.org/10.1016/j.cell.2023.08.004

Higgins, J. M., Arnold, S. R. C., Weise, J., Pellicano, E., & Trollor, J. N. (2021). Defining autistic burnout through experts by lived experience: Grounded Delphi method investigating #AutisticBurnout. *Autism*, *25*(8), 2356–2369. https://doi.org/10.1177/13623613211019858

Hirvikoski, T., Mittendorfer-Rutz, E., Boman, M., Larsson, H., Lichtenstein, P., & Bölte, S. (2016). Premature mortality in autism spectrum disorder. *British Journal of Psychiatry*, *208*(3), 232–238. https://doi.org/10.1192/bjp.bp.114.160192

Hollocks, M. J., Leno, V. C., Chandler, S. *et al.* (2023). Psychiatric conditions in autistic adolescents: Longitudinal stability from childhood and associated risk factors. *European Child & Adolescent Psychiatry*, *32*, 2197–2208. https://doi.org/10.1007/s00787-022-02065-9

Hollocks, M. J., Lerh, J. W., Magiati, I., Meiser-Stedman, R., & Brugha, T. S. (2019). Anxiety and depression in adults with autism spectrum disorder: A systematic review and meta-analysis. *Psychological Medicine*, *49*(4), 559–572. https://doi.org/10.1017/S0033291718002283

Howes, O. D., Rogdaki, M., Findon, J. L., Wichers, R. H., Charman, T., King, B. H., Loth, E., McAlonan, G. M., McCracken, J. T., Parr, J. R., Povey, C., Santosh, P., Wallace, S., Simonoff, E., & Murphy, D. G. (2018). Autism spectrum disorder: Consensus guidelines on assessment, treatment and research from the British Association for Psychopharmacology. *Journal of Psychopharmacology (Oxford, England)*, *32*(1), 3–29. https://doi.org/10.1177/0269881117741766

Howlin, P., Goode, S., Hutton, J., & Rutter, M. (2004). Adult outcome for children with autism. *Journal of Child Psychology and Psychiatry*, *45*(2), 212–229. https://doi.org/doi:10.1111/j.1469-7610.2004.00215.x

Hwang, Y. I. (Jane), Arnold, S., Srasuebkul, P., & Trollor, J. (2019). Understanding anxiety in adults on the autism spectrum: An investigation of its relationship with intolerance of uncertainty, sensory sensitivities and repetitive behaviours. *Autism*, *24*(2), 411–422. https://doi.org/10.1177/1362361319868907 (Original work published 2020)

Hymas, R., Badcock, J. C., & Milne, E. (2024). Loneliness in autism and its association with anxiety and depression: A systematic review with meta-analyses. *Review Journal of Autism and Developmental Disorders*, *11*(1), 121–156. https://doi.org/10.1007/s40489-022-00330-w

Jensen, C. M., Martens, C. S., Nikolajsen, N. D., Skytt Gregersen, T., Heckmann Marx, N., Goldberg Frederiksen, M., & Hansen, M. S. (2015). What do the general population know, believe and feel about individuals with autism and schizophrenia: Results from a comparative survey in Denmark. *Autism*, *20*(4), 496–508. https://doi.org/10.1177/1362361315593068

Josyfon, E., Spain, D., Blackmore, C., Murphy, D., & Oakley, B. (2023). Alexithymia in adult autism clinic service-users: Relationships with sensory processing differences and mental health. *Healthcare (Basel, Switzerland)*, *11*(24). https://doi.org/10.3390/healthcare11243114

Kapp, S. K., Steward, R., Crane, L., Elliott, D., Elphick, C., Pellicano, E., & Russell, G. (2019). 'People should be allowed to do what they like': Autistic adults' views and experiences of stimming. *Autism*, *23*(7), 1782–1792. https://doi.org/10.1177/1362361319829628

Keenan, E. G., Gotham, K., & Lerner, M. D. (2017). Hooked on a feeling: Repetitive cognition and internalizing symptomatology in relation to autism spectrum symptomatology. *Autism*, *22*(7), 814–824. https://doi.org/10.1177/1362361317709603

Kerns, C. M., & Kendall, P. C. (2012). The presentation and classification of anxiety in autism spectrum disorder. *Clinical Psychology: Science and Practice*, *19*(4), 323–347. https://doi.org/10.1111/cpsp.12009

Kerns, C. M., Kendall, P. C., Berry, L., Souders, M. C., Franklin, M. E., Schultz, R. T., Miller, J., & Herrington, J. (2014). Traditional and atypical presentations of anxiety in youth with autism spectrum disorder. *Journal of Autism and Developmental Disorders*, *44*(11), 2851–2861. https://doi.org/10.1007/s10803-014-2141-7

Kerns, C. M., Lankenau, S., Shattuck, P. T., Robins, D. L., Newschaffer, C. J., & Berkowitz, S. J. (2022). Exploring potential sources of childhood trauma: A qualitative study with autistic adults and caregivers. *Autism, 26*(8), 1987–1998. https://doi.org/10.1177/13623613211070637

Kerns, C. M., Newschaffer, C. J., & Berkowitz, S. J. (2015). Traumatic childhood events and autism spectrum disorder. *Journal of Autism and Developmental Disorders, 45*(11), 3475–3486. https://doi.org/10.1007/s10803-015-2392-y

Kessler, R. C., Aguilar-Gaxiola, S., Alonso, J., Benjet, C., Bromet, E. J., Cardoso, G., Degenhardt, L., de Girolamo, G., Dinolova, R. V, Ferry, F., Florescu, S., Gureje, O., Haro, J. M., Huang, Y., Karam, E. G., Kawakami, N., Lee, S., Lepine, J.-P., Levinson, D., . . . Koenen, K. C. (2017). Trauma and PTSD in the WHO world mental health surveys. *European Journal of Psychotraumatology, 8*. https://doi.org/10.1080/20008198.2017.1353383

Kildahl, A. N., & Jørstad, I. (2022). Post-traumatic stress disorder symptom manifestations in an autistic man with severe intellectual disability following coercion and scalding. *Journal of Intellectual & Developmental Disability, 47*(2), 190–194. https://doi.org/10.3109/13668250.2021.1995930

Kinnaird, E., Stewart, C., & Tchanturia, K. (2019). Investigating alexithymia in autism: A systematic review and meta-analysis. *European Psychiatry, 55*, 80–89. https://doi.org/https://doi.org/10.1016/j.eurpsy.2018.09.004

Lai, M. C., Kassee, C., Besney, R., Bonato, S., Hull, L., Mandy, W., Szatmari, P., & Ameis, S. H. (2019). Prevalence of co-occurring mental health diagnoses in the autism population: A systematic review and meta-analysis. *Lancet Psychiatry, 6*(10), 819–829. https://doi.org/10.1016/S2215-0366(19)30289-5

Lai, M.-C., Anagnostou, E., Wiznitzer, M., Allison, C., & Baron-Cohen, S. (2020). Evidence-based support for autistic people across the lifespan: Maximising potential, minimising barriers, and optimising the person–environment fit. *The Lancet Neurology, 19*(5), 434–451. https://doi.org/10.1016/S1474-4422(20)30034-X

Leadbitter, K., Buckle, K. L., Ellis, C., & Dekker, M. (2021). Autistic self-advocacy and the neurodiversity movement: Implications for autism early intervention research and practice. *Frontiers in Psychology, 12*. https://www.frontiersin.org/journals/psychology/articles/10.3389/fpsyg.2021.635690

Leedham, A., Thompson, A. R., Smith, R., & Freeth, M. (2020). 'I was exhausted trying to figure it out': The experiences of females receiving an autism diagnosis in middle to late adulthood. *Autism, 24*(1), 135–146. https://doi.org/10.1177/1362361319853442

Lilley, R., Lawson, W., Hall, G., Mahony, J., Clapham, H., Heyworth, M., Arnold, S. R. C., Trollor, J. N., Yudell, M., & Pellicano, E. (2022). 'A way to be me': Autobiographical reflections of autistic adults diagnosed in mid-to-late adulthood. *Autism, 26*(6), 1395–1408. https://doi.org/10.1177/13623613211050694

Lupindo, B. M., Maw, A., & Shabalala, N. (2023). Late diagnosis of autism: Exploring experiences of males diagnosed with autism in adulthood. *Current Psychology, 42*(28), 24181–24197. https://doi.org/10.1007/s12144-022-03514-z

Mantzalas, J., Richdale, A. L., & Dissanayake, C. (2022). A conceptual model of risk and protective factors for autistic burnout. *Autism Research, 15*(6), 976–987. https://doi.org/10.1002/aur.2722

Mason, D., Ingham, B., Urbanowicz, A., Michael, C., Birtles, H., Woodbury-Smith, M., Brown, T., James, I., Scarlett, C., Nicolaidis, C., & Parr, J. R. (2019). A systematic review of what barriers and facilitators prevent and enable physical healthcare services access for autistic adults. *Journal of Autism and Developmental Disorders, 49*(8), 3387–3400. https://doi.org/10.1007/s10803-019-04049-2

Mason, D., McConachie, H., Garland, D., Petrou, A., Rodgers, J., & Parr, J. R. (2018). Predictors of quality of life for autistic adults. *Autism Research, 11*, 1138–1147. https://doi.org/10.1002/aur.1965

Mazefsky, C. A., & White, S. W. (2014). Emotion regulation: Concepts & practice in autism spectrum disorder. *Child and Adolescent Psychiatric Clinics of North America, 23*(1), 15–24. https://doi.org/10.1016/j.chc.2013.07.002

Mazurek, M. O. (2013). Loneliness, friendship, and well-being in adults with autism spectrum disorders. *Autism, 18*(3), 223–232. https://doi.org/10.1177/1362361312474121

McConachie, H., Mason, D., Parr, J. R., Garland, D., Wilson, C., & Rodgers, J. (2018). Enhancing the validity of a quality of life measure for autistic people. *Journal of Autism and Developmental Disorders, 48*(5), 1596–1611. https://doi.org/10.1007/s10803-017-3402-z

McEwen, B. S. (2004). Protection and damage from acute and chronic stress: Allostasis and allostatic overload and relevance to the pathophysiology of psychiatric disorders. *Annals of the New York Academy of Sciences, 1032*, 1–7. https://doi.org/10.1196/annals.1314.001

McEwen, B. S. (2006). Protective and damaging effects of stress mediators: Central role of the brain. *Dialogues in Clinical Neuroscience, 8*(4), 367–381. https://doi.org/10.31887/DCNS.2006.8.4/bmcewen

McGillivray, J. A., & Evert, H. T. (2014). Group cognitive behavioural therapy program shows potential in reducing symptoms of depression and stress among young people with ASD. *Journal of Autism and Developmental Disorders, 44*(8), 2041–2051. https://doi.org/10.1007/s10803-014-2087-9

Michael, T., Halligan, S. L., Clark, D. M., & Ehlers, A. (2007). Rumination in posttraumatic stress disorder. *Depression and Anxiety, 24*, 307–317. https://doi.org/10.1002/da.20228

Milosavljevic, B., Carter Leno, V., Simonoff, E., Baird, G., Pickles, A., Jones, C. R. G., Erskine, C., Charman, T., & Happe, F. (2016). Alexithymia in adolescents with autism spectrum disorder: Its relationship to internalising difficulties, sensory modulation and social cognition. *Journal of Autism and Developmental Disorders, 46*(4), 1354–1367. https://doi.org/10.1007/s10803-015-2670-8

Milton, D., Martin, N., & Melham, P. (2016). *Beyond reasonable adjustment: Autistic-friendly spaces and universal design.* Pavilion.

Morie, K. P., Jackson, S., Wei, Z., Marc, Z., & Dritschel, B. (2019). Mood disorders in high – functioning autism: The importance of alexithymia and emotional regulation. *Journal of Autism and Developmental Disorders, 49*(7), 2935–2945. https://doi.org/10.1007/s10803-019-04020-1

National Autistic Society. (2019). *The autism act, 10 years on: A report from the all party parliamentary group on autism on understanding, services and support for autistic people and their families in England.* All Party Parliamentary Group on Autism. https://pearsfoundation.org.uk/wp-content/uploads/2019/09/APPGA-Autism-Act-Inquiry-Report.pdf

National Institute for Health and Care Research. (2023, May 30). *Policy research programme – (36-01-06) an evaluation of the Oliver McGowan mandatory training on learning disability and autism.* NIHR. https://www.nihr.ac.uk/policy-research-programme-36-01-06-evaluation-oliver-mcgowan-mandatory-training-learning-disability-and-autism

Nicolaidis, C., Raymaker, D. M., Ashkenazy, E., McDonald, K. E., Dern, S., Baggs, A. E., Kapp, S. K., Weiner, M., & Boisclair, W. C. (2015). "Respect the way I need to communicate with you": Healthcare experiences of adults on the autism spectrum. *Autism: The International Journal of Research and Practice, 19*(7), 824–831. https://doi.org/10.1177/1362361315576221

Noel, K., & Ellison, B. (2020). Inclusive innovation in telehealth. *NPJ Digit Med, 25*(3).

O'Connor, C., Burke, J., & Rooney, B. (2020). Diagnostic disclosure and social marginalisation of adults with ASD: Is there a relationship and what mediates it? *Journal of Autism and Developmental Disorders, 50*(9), 3367–3379. https://doi.org/10.1007/s10803-019-04239-y

Oakley, B. F., Tillmann, J., Ahmad, J., Crawley, D., San José Cáceres, A., Holt, R., Charman, T., Banaschewski, T., Buitelaar, J., Simonoff, E., Murphy, D., & Loth, E. (2020). How do core autism traits and associated symptoms relate to quality of life? Findings from the Longitudinal European Autism Project. *Autism, 25*(2), 389–404. https://doi.org/10.1177/1362361320959959

Oakley, B., Boatman, C., Doswell, S., Dittner, A., Clarke, A., Ozsivadjian, A., Kent, R., Judd, A., Baldoza, S., Hearn, A., Murphy, D., & Simonoff, E. (2023). Molehill mountain feasibility study: Protocol for a non-randomised pilot trial of a novel app-based anxiety intervention for autistic people. *PLoS One*, *18*(7), e0286792. https://doi.org/10.1371/journal.pone.0286792

Oakley, B., Loth, E., & Murphy, D. G. (2021a). Autism and mood disorders. *International Review of Psychiatry (Abingdon, England)*, 1–35. https://doi.org/10.1080/09540261.2021.1872506

Oakley, B., Tillmann, J., Ruigrok, A., *et al.* (2021b). COVID-19 health and social care access for autistic people: European policy review. *BMJ Open*, 11, e045341. https://doi.org/10.1136/bmjopen-2020-045341

Oliver, M. (1990). *The politics of disablement*. Palgrave. https://doi.org/10.1007/978-1-349-20895-1

Oomen, D., Nijhof, A. D., & Wiersema, J. R. (2021). The psychological impact of the COVID-19 pandemic on adults with autism: A survey study across three countries. *Molecular Autism*, *12*(1), 21. https://doi.org/10.1186/s13229-021-00424-y

Ozsivadjian, A., Hollocks, M. J., Magiati, I., Happé, F., Baird, G., & Absoud, M. (2021). Is cognitive inflexibility a missing link? The role of cognitive inflexibility, alexithymia and intolerance of uncertainty in externalising and internalising behaviours in young people with autism spectrum disorder. *Journal of Child Psychology and Psychiatry*, *62*(6), 715–724. https://doi.org/https://doi.org/10.1111/jcpp.13295

Pellicano, E., & Heyworth, M. (2023). The foundations of autistic flourishing. *Current Psychiatry Reports*, *25*(9), 419–427. https://doi.org/10.1007/s11920-023-01441-9

Pellicano, E., Brett, S., den Houting, J., Heyworth, M., Magiati, I., Steward, R., Urbanowicz, A., & Stears, M. (2022). COVID-19, social isolation and the mental health of autistic people and their families: A qualitative study. *Autism*, *26*(4), 914–927. doi: 10.1177/13623613211035936

Pellicano, E., Dinsmore, A., & Charman, T. (2014). What should autism research focus upon? Community views and priorities from the United Kingdom. *Autism*, *18*(7), 756–770. https://doi.org/10.1177/1362361314529627 (Original work published 2014)

Pickard, H., Rijsdijk, F., Happé, F., & Mandy, W. (2017). Are social and communication difficulties a risk factor for the development of social anxiety? *Journal of the American Academy of Child and Adolescent Psychiatry*, *56*(4), 344–351.e3. https://doi.org/10.1016/j.jaac.2017.01.007

Quinton, A. M. G., Ali, D., Danese, A. *et al.* (2024). The assessment and treatment of post-traumatic stress disorder in autistic people: A systematic review. *Review Journal of Autism and Developmental Disorders*. https://doi.org/10.1007/s40489-024-00430-9

Raymaker, D., Teo, A., Steckler, N., Lentz, B., Scharer, M., Santos, A., Kapp, S., Hunter, M., Joyce, A., & Nicolaidis, C. (2020). Having all of your internal resources exhausted beyond measure and being left with no clean-up crew: Defining autistic burnout. *Autism in Adulthood*, 2. https://doi.org/10.1089/aut.2019.0079

Richa, S., Fahed, M., Khoury, E., & Mishara, B. (2014). Suicide in autism spectrum disorders. *Archives of Suicide Research*, *18*(4), 327–339. https://doi.org/10.1080/13811118.2013.824834

Robertson, A. E., Stanfield, A. C., Watt, J., Barry, F., Day, M., Cormack, M., & Melville, C. (2018). The experience and impact of anxiety in autistic adults: A thematic analysis. *Research in Autism Spectrum Disorders*, *46*, 8–18. https://doi.org/10.1016/j.rasd.2017.11.006

Roche, L., Adams, D., & Clark, M. (2021). Research priorities of the autism community: A systematic review of key stakeholder perspectives. *Autism: the international journal of research and practice*, *25*(2), 336–348. https://doi.org/10.1177/1362361320967790

Rumball, F., Brook, L., Happé, F., & Karl, A. (2021, March). Heightened risk of post-traumatic stress disorder in adults with autism spectrum disorder: The role of cumulative trauma and memory deficits. *Research in Developmental Disabilities*, *110*, 103848. https://doi.org/10.1016/j.ridd.2020.103848. Epub 2021 Jan 15. PMID: 33454451

Rumball, F., Happé, F., & Grey, N. (2020, December). Experience of trauma and PTSD symptoms in autistic adults: Risk of PTSD development following DSM-5 and Non-DSM-5 traumatic life events. *Autism Research, 13*(12), 2122–2132. https://doi.org/10.1002/aur.2306. Epub 2020 Apr 22. PMID: 32319731

Ryff, C. D. (2013). Psychological well-being revisited: Advances in the science and practice of eudaimonia. *Psychotherapy and Psychosomatics, 83*(1), 10–28. https://doi.org/10.1159/000353263

Sasson, N. J., & Morrison, K. E. (2017). First impressions of adults with autism improve with diagnostic disclosure and increased autism knowledge of peers. *Autism, 23*(1), 50–59. https://doi.org/10.1177/1362361317729526

Scheeren, A. M., Howlin, P., Pellicano, L., Magiati, I., & Begeer, S. (2022). Continuity and change in loneliness and stress during the COVID-19 pandemic: A longitudinal study of autistic and non-autistic adults. *Autism Research, 15*(9), 1621–1635. https://doi.org/10.1002/aur.2787

Schiltz, H. K., McVey, A. J., Dolan Wozniak, B., Haendel, A. D., Stanley, R., Arias, A., Gordon, N., & Van Hecke, A. V. (2020). The role of loneliness as a mediator between autism features and mental health among autistic young adults. *Autism, 25*(2), 545–555. https://doi.org/10.1177/1362361320967789

Schiltz, H., Gohari, D., Park, J., & Lord, C. (2023). A longitudinal study of loneliness in autism and other neurodevelopmental disabilities: Coping with loneliness from childhood through adulthood. *Autism, 28*(6), 1471–1486. https://doi.org/10.1177/13623613231217337

Seides, R. (2010). Should the current DSM-IV-TR definition for PTSD be expanded to include serial and multiple microtraumas as aetiologies? *Journal of Psychiatric and Mental Health Nursing, 17*(8), 725–731. https://doi.org/https://doi.org/10.1111/j.1365-2850.2010.01591.x

Shattuck, P. T., Narendorf, S. C., Cooper, B., Sterzing, P. R., Wagner, M., & Taylor, J. L. (2012). Postsecondary education and employment among youth with an autism spectrum disorder. *Pediatrics, 129*(6), 1042–1049. https://doi.org/10.1542/peds.2011-2864

Shaw, S. C. K., Carravallah, L., Johnson, M., O'Sullivan, J., Chown, N., Neilson, S., & Doherty, M. (2023). Barriers to healthcare and a 'triple empathy problem' may lead to adverse outcomes for autistic adults: A qualitative study. *Autism, 28*(7), 1746–1757. https://doi.org/10.1177/13623613231205629

Shea, L. L., Wong, M. Y., & Song, W. *et al.* (2024). Autistic-delivered peer support: A feasibility study. *Journal of Autism and Developmental Disorders, 54*, 409–422. https://doi.org/10.1007/s10803-022-05816-4

Sheehan, R., Hassiotis, A., Walters, K., Osborn, D., Strydom, A., & Horsfall, L. (2015, September). Mental illness, challenging behaviour, and psychotropic drug prescribing in people with intellectual disability: UK population based cohort study. *BMJ, 351*, h4326. https://doi.org/10.1136/bmj.h4326. PMID: 26330451; PMCID: PMC4556752

Simonoff, E., Pickles, A., Charman, T., Chandler, S., Loucas, T., & Baird, G. (2008). Psychiatric disorders in children with autism spectrum disorders: prevalence, comorbidity, and associated factors in a population-derived sample. *Journal of the American Academy of Child and Adolescent Psychiatry, 47*(8), 921–929. https://doi.org/10.1097/CHI.0b013e318179964f

Sizoo, B. B., & Kuiper, E. (2017). Cognitive behavioural therapy and mindfulness based stress reduction may be equally effective in reducing anxiety and depression in adults with autism spectrum disorders. *Research in Developmental Disabilities, 64*, 47–55. https://doi.org/10.1016/j.ridd.2017.03.004

Social Care Institute for Excellence. (2017). *Autism: Improving access to social care for adults*. London: Social Care Institute for Excellence (SCIE).

South, M., & Rodgers, J. (2017). Sensory, emotional and cognitive contributions to anxiety in autism spectrum disorders. *Frontiers in Human Neuroscience, 11*(January), 1–7. https://doi.org/10.3389/fnhum.2017.00020

Spain, D., & Happé, F. (2020). How to optimise cognitive behaviour therapy (CBT) for people with autism spectrum disorders (ASD): A Delphi study. *Journal of Rational-Emotive & Cognitive-Behavior Therapy, 38*(2), 184–208. https://doi.org/10.1007/s10942-019-00335-1

Spain, D., Sin, J., Chalder, T., Murphy, D., & Happé, F. (2015). Cognitive behaviour therapy for adults with autism spectrum disorders and psychiatric co-morbidity: A review. *Research in Autism Spectrum Disorders, 9,* 151–162. https://doi.org/https://doi.org/10.1016/j.rasd.2014.10.019

Spek, A. A., van Ham, N. C., & Nyklicek, I. (2013). Mindfulness-based therapy in adults with an autism spectrum disorder: A randomized controlled trial. *Research in Developmental Disabilities, 34*(1), 246–253. https://doi.org/10.1016/j.ridd.2012.08.009

Stagg, S. D., & Belcher, H. (2019). Living with autism without knowing: Receiving a diagnosis in later life. *Health Psychology and Behavioral Medicine, 7*(1), 348–361. https://doi.org/10.1080/21642850.2019.1684920

Stewart, M. E., Barnard, L., Pearson, J., Hasan, R., & O'Brien, G. (2006). Presentation of depression in autism and Asperger syndrome: A review. *Autism, 10*(1), 103–116. https://doi.org/10.1177/1362361306062013

Sutherland, R., Trembath, D., & Roberts, J. (2018). Telehealth and autism: A systematic search and review of the literature. *International Journal of Speech-Language Pathology, 20*(3), 324–336. https://doi.org/10.1080/17549507.2018.1465123

Taylor, J. L., & Gotham, K. O. (2016). Cumulative life events, traumatic experiences, and psychiatric symptomatology in transition-aged youth with autism spectrum disorder. *Journal of Neurodevelopmental Disorders, 8*(1), 28. https://doi.org/10.1186/s11689-016-9160-y

Thompson-Hodgetts, S., Labonte, C., Mazumder, R., & Phelan, S. (2020). Helpful or harmful? A scoping review of perceptions and outcomes of autism diagnostic disclosure to others. *Research in Autism Spectrum Disorders, 77,* 101598. https://doi.org/10.1016/j.rasd.2020.101598

Tillmann, J., Uljarevic, M., Crawley, D. et al. (2020). Dissecting the phenotypic heterogeneity in sensory features in autism spectrum disorder: A factor mixture modelling approach. *Molecular Autism, 11,* 67. https://doi.org/10.1186/s13229-020-00367-w

Trundle, G., Jones, K. A., Ropar, D., & Egan, V. (2022). Prevalence of victimisation in autistic individuals: A systematic review and meta-analysis. *Trauma, Violence, & Abuse, 24*(4), 2282–2296. https://doi.org/10.1177/15248380221093689

Turnock, A., Langley, K., & Jones, C. R. G. (2022). Understanding stigma in autism: A narrative review and theoretical model. *Autism in Adulthood, 4*(1), 76–91. https://doi.org/10.1089/aut.2021.0005

Uljarevic, M., & Hamilton, A. (2013). Recognition of emotions in autism: A formal meta-analysis. *Journal of Autism and Developmental Disorders, 43*(7), 1517–1526. https://doi.org/10.1007/s10803-012-1695-5

Van de Cruys, S., Evers, K., Van der Hallen, R., Van Eylen, L., Boets, B., de-Wit, L., & Wagemans, J. (2014, October). Precise minds in uncertain worlds: Predictive coding in autism. *Psychological Review, 121*(4), 649–675. https://doi.org/10.1037/a0037665. PMID: 25347312

van Heijst, B. F., Geurts, H. M. (2015). Quality of life in autism across the lifespan: A meta-analysis. *Autism, 19*(2), 158–167. https://doi.org/10.1177/1362361313517053.

van't Hof, M., Tisseur, C., van Berckelear-Onnes, I., van Nieuwenhuyzen, A., Daniels, A. M., Deen, M., Hoek, H. W., & Ester, W. A. (2020). Age at autism spectrum disorder diagnosis: A systematic review and meta-analysis from 2012 to 2019. *Autism, 25*(4), 862–873. https://doi.org/10.1177/1362361320971107

Vasa, R. A., Mazurek, M. O., Mahajan, R., Bennett, A. E., Bernal, M. P., Nozzolillo, A. A., Arnold, L. E., & Coury, D. L. (2016). Assessment and treatment of anxiety in youth with autism spectrum disorders. *Pediatrics, 137*(Supplement 2), S115 LP–S123. https://doi.org/10.1542/peds.2015-2851J

Watanabe, T., & Rees, G. (2017). Brain network dynamics in high-functioning individuals with autism. *Nature Communications, 8*, 16048. https://doi.org/10.1038/ncomms16048

Williams, K., Brignell, A., Randall, M., Silove, N., & Hazell, P. (2013). Selective serotonin reuptake inhibitors (SSRIs) for autism spectrum disorders (ASD). *The Cochrane Database of Systematic Reviews, 8*, CD004677. https://doi.org/10.1002/14651858.CD004677.pub3

Williams, Z. J., McKenney, E. E., & Gotham, K. O. (2021). Investigating the structure of trait rumination in autistic adults: A network analysis. *Autism, 25*(7), 2048–2063. https://doi.org/10.1177/13623613211012855

Wood, J. J., & Gadow, K. D. (2010). Exploring the nature and function of anxiety in youth with autism spectrum disorders. *Clinical Psychology: Science and Practice, 17*(4), 281–292. https://doi.org/10.1111/j.1468–2850.2010.01220.x

Zahid, S., & Upthegrove, R. (2017). Suicidality in autistic spectrum disorders. *Crisis, 38*(4), 237–246. https://doi.org/10.1027/0227-5910/a000458

Chapter 3

The Challenges of Accessing Healthcare When Autistic

Mary Doherty and Sebastian C.K. Shaw

Background (Mary)

In 2018, I was five years into the journey of re-evaluating my life as an autistic woman. I was a single parent of two children, one of whom was autistic with co-occurring ADHD. My career as a doctor and a consultant anaesthetist was on hold due to illness and caring responsibilities, and it felt like I was at a turning point in life. I knew no other autistic doctors. I had heard that there was one in Australia, and I hoped to meet them one day. I knew few other autistic parents, at least not in Ireland. The Irish autistic community at that time was small and fragmented. While accessing services with my child, I repeatedly asked service providers to connect me with other autistic parents, and the usual response was a confused look and a somewhat patronising reply which implied that I was somehow unique; there were no others.

A key moment occurred while attending an information session for parents delivered by my local child psychology service. The information presented was jarring to me as an autistic woman, and I spoke to the presenter afterwards, suggesting they reconsider their language and tone, particularly for the benefit of autistic parents attending the session. I was assured that I need not be concerned as there were no autistic parents to worry about. At this point, I realised I had a newfound purpose because I had an awareness and perspective as both an autistic person and a doctor that needed to be shared. I had noticed several other parents during that session who appeared to me to be autistic, and indeed, several years later, I know that several have been identified as such (permission has been granted to include this).

Five years earlier, my son had been identified as autistic. At that point, I knew nothing about autism beyond the stereotypes as I had received little to no training during my undergraduate medical studies or during my postgraduate medical career. Researching what this new diagnosis meant for my child led me to the realisation that I was also likely to be autistic and my formal autism diagnosis was followed by ADHD two years later.

My older child was at the time experiencing very challenging mental health difficulties. Recognising some familial traits, it seemed to me that a neurodevelopment

DOI: 10.4324/9781003495949-4

assessment might offer some insights into the reasons my firstborn was struggling so much. However, there was little known about neurodivergence at the time, and particularly not how neurodevelopmental issues manifested in girls. Exploration of this avenue was fiercely resisted by mental healthcare providers at the time, and offering new research on the topic (Gould and Ashton-Smith, 2011; Tebartz van Elst et al., 2013) only served to solidify my position as a problem parent to be managed.

I don't remember how the news of my son's diagnosis was delivered, but I will never forget the reaction I received when I shared it with my older child's psychiatrist. I had naively assumed that sharing that information, as well as my own diagnosis would lend weight to my argument that a comprehensive neurodevelopmental assessment was needed for my older child. Instead, I was met with profound sympathy on behalf of my son, and a confident assertion that my own autistic nature was at the root of my older child's difficulties. Luckily, I had the internal resilience to recognise that this was not the case, but the experience was the pivotal moment which altered the trajectory of my academic work and propelled me into advocacy. The quest for an accurate neurodevelopmental assessment lasted several more years, until finally, recognition of being neurodivergent offered a pathway from life-threatening mental illness to good mental health, to peace, joy and a chance to thrive in a way that seemed impossible a decade before.

At that time, I had discovered the autistic community, both online and in person, and I was a regular attendee at "Autscape," an annual residential conference in the UK. However, the early years of the autistic community were shrouded in shame and secrecy. Many Autscape participants used pseudonyms to attend, and while I used my real name, I avoided telling anyone about my professional background. I was either Mary, the doctor, *or* I was Mary, autistic. For several years, there was no part of my life, beyond with immediate family, in which I was both.

Then, in 2018, I was invited to develop and deliver some autism training for healthcare providers as part of an autism-friendly town project in Clonakilty, Co Cork, led by Irish autism charity, AsIAm. I was keen that the training I would develop should reflect the experiences and concerns of the autistic community rather than being based on my own limited experience, and this desire started me on my research journey looking at autistic healthcare and, in particular, the barriers experienced by autistic people when accessing healthcare.

To explore community perspectives on healthcare, I conducted a survey at Autscape 2018, entitled "What do you wish your GP[1] knew about autism?" alongside an information gathering and discussion workshop during the event. I was delighted with the response from participants, receiving 75 responses from a total of about 200 Autscape attendees. When I returned home, I analysed the data to the best of my ability and was shocked to discover that difficulty using the telephone was mentioned by participant after participant. I knew that this was an issue for myself, but I had never considered that it might be an autistic challenge. Instead, I had assumed it was a shameful personal failing. Even being a doctor, I had difficulty accessing healthcare for myself, and I had experienced a significantly delayed diagnosis of a potentially serious health condition simply because an appointment that needed to be rearranged required a phone call that I could not bring myself to make.

I wanted to know more. In a flurry of monotropic (or single-minded) focus, I created an online survey asking about barriers to healthcare and adverse healthcare outcomes. This was the first use of my insider positionality in terms of knowing what to ask and knowing what outcomes would be clinically meaningful. Several autistic adults helped with refining the survey, ensuring it was clear and accessible to autistic people.

As an autistic and, therefore, "insider" researcher, I received a very positive response from the autistic community, and I quickly realised that I had amassed a large amount of potentially important and impactful data, which warranted attention beyond the original purpose which had been to inform a local autism training initiative.

I recruited academic partners to bring skills I did not have, and together, we sought ethical approval to re-run the study. At the time, I was working as a clinician and did not have an academic appointment, although the hospital where I was based was university-affiliated and, therefore, had a Research Ethics Committee. A particular sticking point became whether or not autistic people were, by definition, "vulnerable adults," and approval was repeatedly delayed. This issue was ultimately resolved when I discussed it directly with the Chair of the Ethics Committee, a surgeon with whom I was scheduled to work. When I disclosed that I was autistic myself, about to anaesthetise their patients, and that respondents to the survey were potentially people like me, the issue was instantly resolved. Approval was granted.

Exploring what was known at the time about healthcare experiences and outcomes for autistic people led me down a path of mounting horror and a growing determination to use my medical knowledge to affect change. I discovered that contrary to what I had learned in medical training, most autistic people are adults who do not have an intellectual disability, and most are likely to be undiagnosed (O'Nions et al., 2023).

Healthcare experiences and outcomes are much worse for autistic people when compared to the general population. Lots of health conditions are more common and, most worryingly, it seems that life expectancy is reduced for autistic people, perhaps by decades (Hirvikoski et al., 2016; O'Nions et al., 2024; Ward et al., 2023). In particular, mental health outcomes are particularly poor, with suicide rates significantly higher than for non-autistic people (Cassidy et al., 2020; Lai, 2023). Autistic people are more than twice as likely as non-autistic people to attend emergency departments, three times as likely to require inpatient admission from the emergency department, and then, once admitted to hospital, more likely to die while in hospital than non-autistic patients (Vohra et al., 2016; Akobirshoev et al., 2020). Autistic women have the worst outcomes (Kassee et al., 2020).

The types of barriers autistic people experience have been described by several other research teams, and the findings were consistent. The difficulties centred around communication with healthcare providers, the sensory environment of healthcare settings alongside the challenges of planning, and the practicalities of attending appointments (Mason et al., 2019). Previous negative experiences in healthcare have also been shown to act as a barrier to accessing care again when needed (Vogan et al., 2017).

Doctors tend to underestimate the number of autistic patients in their caseload, and many have limited autism knowledge (Zerbo et al., 2015; Nicolaidis et al., 2021). In one study, almost 40% of general practitioners (GPs) reported not having received any formal training in autism, and they also reported limited confidence in looking after autistic patients (Unigwe et al., 2017). Both GPs and hospital specialists have reported difficulties communicating with autistic patients (Unigwe et al., 2017; Zerbo et al., 2015). This knowledge gap is less where GPs have personal knowledge of autism, either through having a relative or friend on the autism spectrum, or because they themselves are autistic (Unigwe et al., 2017). Another study showed that only one in four primary healthcare providers had a high level of confidence in communicating with autistic adult patients or knowing what accommodations were required and being able to put these necessary accommodations in place so that their autistic patients could access their services (Zerbo et al., 2015).

The Survey

Developing the Survey

We wanted to gather a comprehensive picture of the experiences autistic people had when attempting to access healthcare. Our survey contained a mix of specific questions and free comment boxes. We asked about specific barriers people encountered accessing healthcare, the reasons for delaying or avoiding a visit, and the difficulties people experienced when booking, planning or waiting for a GP visit. We explored the challenges during a consultation, including communication, sensory, and organisation issues, as well as any social supports that were available or needed. We also explored the impact of the access barriers, including, in particular, whether respondents reported negative consequences in terms of health outcomes.

We first ran the study in 2018, which is described in our paper (Doherty et al., 2022) as piloting the survey. Initial analysis of the data showed a recurrent theme of inability to access healthcare at all, which we did not expect. Repeatedly, respondents commented that they didn't have a doctor, could not access healthcare at all, or had given up trying to access healthcare. We realised that we had made a common assumption; as we assumed for non-autistic people, our expectation was that autistic people would somehow be in the healthcare system and would present for care when required. Our initial data showed that this assumption may not be valid. We added some questions to the survey to capture responses from this group of autistic people. The final survey had 52 questions. We recruited autistic people online using a combination of social media platforms and advertising it on the AsIAm website. We wanted to compare autistic experiences with those of non-autistic people accessing healthcare, so we also recruited a group of non-autistic people (who were also not parents of autistic children) to act as a comparison group.

The Respondents to the Survey

We reported the data from the second run of the survey in our first "Barriers to Healthcare" paper, which was published in the *BMJ Open*, an online medical journal that is well known and well regarded amongst medical doctors internationally (Doherty et al., 2022). The survey respondents included 507 autistic and 157 non-autistic people. The average age in both groups was 38. Most were female, which is not unusual for respondents to online surveys, although it contrasts the expected gender breakdown for autistic people. Interestingly, in the autistic group, there were almost as many respondents who identified as non-binary as identified as male. The majority in both groups were located in the United Kingdom or Ireland. In the autistic group, over three-quarters reported a formal autism diagnosis. The average age at diagnosis was 33, although this ranged from 2 years to 67 years of age. Half had been diagnosed by a clinical psychologist, with the others equally split between psychiatrist and a multidisciplinary team. We didn't enquire about intellectual capacity or educational attainment, but respondents had to have been able to access and respond to the online survey.

Results: The "Numbers"

What we found was striking, although perhaps not surprising for us as autistic people. Four out of every five autistic adults who responded to the survey reported that they had difficulty accessing a GP when needed, compared to one in three of the non-autistic group. It is important to note that we asked about going to a GP "when you need to," so it was about having trouble when people already had medical symptoms, or another reason to visit a doctor; we weren't asking about difficulty seeing a doctor in general terms.

We found that most people in both groups visited a doctor for physical illness but that autistic people were much more likely to visit for mental health conditions than the non-autistic group. Both groups reported difficulty deciding whether or not their symptoms were sufficient to need a GP visit, and our data suggested that autistic people were more likely to delay for longer. This suggests a need among autistic people for increased "health literacy," meaning an increased general level of knowledge around health and healthcare. To address this need, we are writing a book specifically on healthcare for autistic people.

As suggested by the initial informal survey conducted at Autscape, the telephone did indeed prove to be one of the biggest barriers to accessing healthcare for the autistic group. Three out of five (3/5) autistic people said the telephone was a barrier, compared to only one in six (1/6) of the non-autistic group. Interestingly, over three-quarters of the autistic group avoided the telephone in general, but the data suggests that some appear able to overcome the barrier to accessing healthcare when needed. This may be possible by particular effort, the urgency of a situation, or by having someone else make a phone call on their behalf.

Mary: "That is one solution I have used at times, and interestingly, I have autistic friends who could make phone calls to make a GP appointment for me when they would experience difficulty doing the same for themselves."

Seb "The phone is something I also really struggle with. Oddly, I seem to find it easier when I am 'the doctor'. However, when I am not at work, I find it nearly impossible to initiate calls without lots of mental preparation. Personally, the solution that I have found revolutionary when accessing healthcare myself has been the introduction of online booking systems and other online ways of accessing my GP's surgery. Being able to type a quick explanation of why I am making contact has not only avoided the need for the phone but has also avoided the need for appointments at times when I have been able to provide enough information on what I am asking for."

The next most common reason for avoiding or delaying a needed GP visit was not feeling understood. Over half of the autistic respondents reported not feeling understood by doctors, compared to one in six of the non-autistic group. As doctors, this is heartbreaking for us to realise, and it is one of the reasons we at Autistic Doctors International are so passionate about improving autism awareness among our colleagues. As documented in the next "Barriers to healthcare" paper (see below), this lack of understanding can potentially have really serious consequences in terms of outcomes for autistic patients. (We shouldn't have to specify this, but just for clarity, when we refer to "autistic patients", we mean autistic people who are sick and need medical care for illness; not that autistic people are "patients" simply because they are autistic.)

Communication with Healthcare Providers

Difficulty with healthcare didn't stop with the problems of accessing care in the first place. Once respondents can access care, the challenges continue, with over half of the autistic respondents reporting difficulty communicating with the doctor during the appointment. In contrast, this was reported by less than one in ten for the non-autistic group. Difficulties communicating with reception staff were almost as frequent, with just under half the autistic group reporting this as a barrier. Again, less than one in ten of the non-autistic group experienced this challenge. Communication difficulties during a medical consultation were reported "all the time" or "frequently" by well over half of the autistic group. Some interesting results show aspects of autistic communication that are not generally appreciated by non-autistic people but are well-recognised features of autistic communication by autistic individuals.

Anxiety makes it harder to communicate. This is common for both autistic and non-autistic people, but it is so much more common for us and can be so much more impactful. Three-quarters of the autistic group reported this, compared to only a quarter of non-autistic respondents. While we didn't explore the precise nature of the anxiety-induced communication difficulty, personal experience and anecdotal evidence suggest this can sometimes amount to situational mutism for autistic people. In other words, a complete loss of access to speech in the context of a medical appointment, and particularly for those who are known to be usually articulate, can lead to unwarranted assumptions about motivation and manipulation.

Sensory issues were also reported to make it harder to communicate by a third of the autistic group. This was not an issue for non-autistic respondents, with only two in the non-autistic group reporting this. It's worth mentioning here that we didn't confirm that those choosing to respond as non-autistic were, in fact, not autistic, so it may be that some actually were autistic but unrecognised. While that is merely speculation, of course, it would be unusual for non-autistic people to be impacted by sensory issues to the same degree.

Some interesting and very recognisable communication features were reported by two-thirds of the autistic group – in particular, difficulty prioritising when describing medical symptoms and the sense of needing to give the whole story and not leave anything out. Also, general difficulty describing pain or symptoms accurately, especially using spoken words. Text is easier, so the increasing use of text-based messaging in healthcare in the United Kingdom is likely to benefit autistic people. Needing extra time to process information was reported by over half the autistic group, which is a specific challenge in the current healthcare climate, with healthcare providers under enormous time pressure and general practice appointments commonly only ten-minutes long.

Just under half of the autistic group said that differences in how they expressed emotion were a difficulty in medical consultations; for example, the possibility of appearing angry when in pain or afraid. Again, as autistic doctors, we can easily see how this can lead to doctor–patient relationship challenges when autistic people are not understood. It is natural for a healthcare provider to respond differently to an apparently aggressive or hostile patient compared to an "easy" patient, and while a professional approach is expected in all cases, it may be more difficult to experience and display empathy for an autistic patient without understanding this aspect of their communication.

Furthermore, the lack of understanding of autistic communication and autistic emotional processing can often lead to inadvertent escalation of difficult situations, as practitioners may not have the autism-specific tools needed to defuse potentially explosive encounters. The simple act of touching an emotionally aroused autistic patient, for example, may have a very different outcome compared to the same action with a non-autistic patient. Tactile defensiveness, which is common for autistic people, is a heightened sensitivity to physical touch and can lead to a reflex response when touched, particularly when already in a state of high arousal.

Other sensory issues impact healthcare access, with half of the autistic group reporting the waiting room environment as a barrier. Sensory challenges described included noise, lighting, music, and smells, as well as the discomfort of a crowded waiting room. Again, while all of these aspects may be experienced as uncomfortable by non-autistic people, the difference is that they are tolerable for most non-autistic people rather than actually preventing them from accessing needed healthcare.

Autistic people described significant anxiety around healthcare, with only 3 out of 100 not feeling anxious about going to the doctor. Autistic people worried about not being taken seriously, being considered a hypochondriac or wasting the doctor's time. They reported difficulty asking for help, difficulty discussing mental health, and concerns that unusual behaviour, for example, stimming, would cause negative reactions from healthcare staff or other patients.

Planning and organising medical care was another challenge for the autistic group. Difficulties making appointments in advance and prioritising health issues, as well as difficulties making lifestyle changes, were reported. Many more autistic than non-autistic respondents had forgotten medical appointments, had turned up on the wrong day, or, indeed, had forgotten what the appointment was for. Difficulties with a lack of predictability were common. Challenges included not knowing how long a wait for a consultation might be, which practitioner would be seen, and what would happen during the appointment.

Autistic people described support needs that were often unmet, and these unmet needs were further barriers to accessing healthcare. Physical mobility needs were more common, as was feeling the need for a support person to accompany respondents to healthcare appointments. Indeed, this also reduced the ability to access hospital-based healthcare, with autistic respondents more likely to not have anyone to take them to appointments or to collect them from the hospital following an emergency attendance or surgical procedure. Imagine having an accident, being taken to hospital by ambulance and not having anyone who could go to your home and collect essential belongings, for example. Also, because as healthcare providers, we tend to assume most people will have family or friends who can meet such needs, it can be difficult for autistic people to admit that, actually, no, there isn't anyone in our lives who can fulfil that role.

Adverse Outcomes

The next part of the project was particularly sobering. We asked respondents to tell us about the health consequences of the barriers they experienced. We wanted to know if having difficulty accessing healthcare led to worse healthcare outcomes. It's worth being clear that the results in this section all related to adverse outcomes that respondents reported themselves. We didn't have any proof of worse medical outcomes, but as we will explain below, when we describe our second "Barriers to Healthcare" paper, these do make sense from a medical perspective. We have no reason to doubt the findings. The adverse outcomes we looked at included untreated conditions, both physical and mental, both of which were reported by two out of three autistic respondents. Delayed treatment was reported, including respondents needing more extensive treatment or surgery than if they had come for care earlier. Other negative consequences included being referred to a specialist but not attending and not attending preventative screening services. Autistic respondents reported more adverse consequences compared to the non-autistic group and far more frequently. Most worryingly, a third of the autistic group reported a "potentially serious or life-threatening condition" for which they did not access healthcare. Next, we looked at just the autistic group and compared the majority group who reported difficulty accessing a GP when needed, compared with the minority who did not. Once again, the differences in terms of adverse outcomes were stark. Those who had difficulty accessing healthcare when needed had more poor outcomes, adverse consequences, and delayed treatment. While it might seem intuitive that this would be the case, this was the first time such research had been done, and so it was the first time an association had been found between healthcare access barriers and poor healthcare outcomes.

It is important to remember that what we found was only an association. We can say that something linked the two things together, but we cannot say with certainty what that is or that one leads to the other. In science, we often repeat, like a mantra, "correlation does not equal causation." This means that while two events are associated with one another, it does not mean that one causes the other. It might mean that an unrelated factor causes both. A different type of research is needed to explore whether healthcare access barriers might actually cause poor outcomes. We will touch on this further when addressing our second "Barrier to Healthcare" paper below. There was a minority group of autistic people who reported no access to primary care at all, or in other words, that they did not have a GP. This was about 1 in 25 of the autistic group. Interestingly, a similar number of non-autistic group reported that they had no GP, but they were only half as likely to report difficulty visiting a doctor when needed or experience adverse outcomes, so the assumption from this might be that this group didn't have a GP but would be able to access one if needed.

We also looked at the autistic group and compared those who had a formal autism diagnosis with those who self-identified, and we found no differences between the two groups in terms of difficulty accessing a GP when needed, the barriers they experienced trying to access care, and the adverse health consequences that were experienced. Given that we know the majority of autistic people, particularly older autistic adults are likely to be unidentified, this suggests there is a large group of autistic adults having difficulty accessing healthcare and experiencing poor healthcare outcomes without any awareness that this may be related to being autistic. The sorts of adjustments that made it easier to access care were being able to make appointments online, being able to indicate in advance what the consultation was for, and being able to wait in a quiet place of even outside the healthcare facility until it was their turn. Booking the first or last appointment of the day was also helpful. Respondents appreciated GP who had a direct communication style, and where they didn't know very much about autism, respondents valued GPs who were honest about this. They also valued GPs who understood that autism isn't a mental illness. Autistic people were much more likely to value their relationship with their GP compared to the non-autistic group, even though only a third reported a good relationship with their GP. Just over half reported that their GP knew they were autistic, and one in five weren't sure.

All of the different access barriers reported were associated with some of the adverse outcomes for the autistic group. Interestingly, communication difficulties with both medical and reception staff were associated with all of the adverse outcomes that we looked at. The inability to see a particular doctor was associated with untreated physical and mental health conditions, as well as with late presentations. Finding waiting too difficult was also associated with untreated conditions and late presentations. Respondents who reported that they didn't experience any healthcare access barriers also didn't report any adverse outcomes.

Results: The "Stories"

There are lots of indications from our research linking healthcare access barriers with poor healthcare outcomes, but these associations are not sufficient for us to be able to clearly state that one leads to the other. It might seem intuitive that they would, but the scientific process requires more – and different – evidence before we can say this. The next part of our project doesn't provide that evidence either, but it does bring us one step closer (Shaw et al., 2024). What was done next was to look at the responses to questions in our survey where respondents could provide free text answers. The questions were open-ended, so people could give as much or as little information as they wanted. For this part of the project, we combined the responses from the pilot survey and subsequent survey, as there were no differences in the questions for which free text answers could be given, and if the same respondent answered the survey twice, that didn't matter as the data was being analysed qualitatively, rather than quantitatively. If the same story was told twice, that wouldn't have a double impact, as it was the themes and patterns in the data we were seeking. Therefore, data were available from 1,248 individual responses from autistic adults, which were then subjected to thematic analysis. Following the analysis, and using our own medical knowledge, we looked for patterns that might explain the links between the barriers respondents were describing and the adverse outcomes.

Improving healthcare access for autistic people requires an understanding of the healthcare access process and the barriers experienced from the perspective of the autistic person, and this was what we were trying to explore and understand. We know from research that autistic people are more likely to use emergency medical services such as out-of-hours doctors or emergency departments. Autistic individuals are more likely to be admitted to hospital when attending the emergency department, and even more shockingly, are more likely to die in hospital compared to non-autistic people after having been admitted from the emergency department.

This suggests that autistic individuals may be presenting later and with more serious illness compared to non-autistic people. We need to understand why this might be the case to make improvements. As we were looking only at the data from the autistic group, and as all of the research team were autistic, this was a rare example of a fully autistic research project. It was an absolute joy to work with a team of autistic researchers who just understood the data, understood each other, and to not have to censor or translate our communication, even though the actual data we were working with was utterly heartbreaking.

The demographics of the respondents was similar to the quantitative sample, except that non-binary respondents outnumbered male respondents slightly. The free text responses amounted to almost 60,000 words of qualitative data. As well as our themes and subthemes, we identified an overarching theme of "epistemic injustice," which came through across all of the themes and acted as a supporting framework for everything else we discovered. We will explain what this means later.

Firstly, before even accessing healthcare, it is necessary to recognise oneself as unwell. Difficulties with recognising internal bodily sensations and changes from one's normal state led to challenges in recognising that healthcare was needed. Differences with pain, in particular, were reported, with participants not recognising that something was wrong until complications had occurred – for example, until an appendix had already ruptured. Once a health condition was recognised, the barriers detailed above were encountered, particularly the need to use the phone to access healthcare. Difficulties travelling to appointments and a lack of predictability then became relevant – followed by the sensory challenges of healthcare facilities, especially waiting rooms. Communication challenges between participants, healthcare providers, and administration staff were the second theme. Respondents described attempting to mask to get the needed healthcare and deliberately trying to emulate non-autistic styles of communication, such as the use of eye contact. There was also an acknowledgement that autistic people were less effective at manipulating the healthcare system to get their needs met compared to non-autistic people. Interestingly, respondents who were healthcare providers themselves reported similar communication challenges in the healthcare system, despite their insider knowledge of medical settings and medical terminology.

Following unsuccessful attempts to access healthcare, respondents reported a sense of self-doubt and even guilt for potentially wasting a doctor's time. This was offset when respondents had a positive relationship with their doctors, but unfortunately, many did not. Such negative relationships led to their credibility being questioned, which was seen as being directly related to being autistic. Not being believed or indeed being infantilised led to frustration and concerns about diagnostic overshadowing, where physical symptoms were wrongly attributed to autism or assumed to be due to anxiety. This fear was a barrier to disclosure for some respondents. The hardest thing to experience after reaching out for help is to find that there is no help available. This was a common occurrence and left autistic people feeling despondent and helpless, which makes it even harder to reach out for help again. Respondents had learned through experience that the healthcare system could not or would not be able to meet their needs. Participants began to fear repercussions if they repeatedly tried to seek help from healthcare providers, with potential risks for child custody if the doctor was to decide a patient was a "bad parent" being mentioned by some autistic respondents. Having experienced negative healthcare encounters, autistic respondents were dissuaded from trying again. For some, this led to a complete inability to access healthcare, even when they knew this was likely to negatively impact their health and even their life. What was most challenging about this part of our project was reading the accounts of what we recognised as medically serious conditions and knowing the potential impact of not getting medical care. Undiagnosed and untreated tumours, heart attacks, ectopic pregnancies, and other conditions are genuinely life-threatening when left untreated. Reading an account by one participant where she described finding a breast lump, but she hadn't seen a doctor, still haunts me. I hope that she found the strength to see a doctor and to do so in time, but sadly, I know that may not have been the case. I think about the multiple studies that show that, as autistic people, we have a reduced life expectancy compared to non-autistic people, and I know that the challenges accessing healthcare play a part in this.

We reluctantly labelled the end result of this process as "healthcare avoidance." That is what happens, autistic people avoid healthcare, but in no way does this imply a voluntary decision to avoid healthcare. It is, for many, a valid response to prior healthcare trauma. But we must label it as it is and acknowledge the result can be serious adverse health consequences.

Epistemic Injustice

This relates to the idea that as autistic people, we are not seen as credible or reliable witnesses to our own experiences, merely because we are autistic.

Respondents reported that healthcare providers simply didn't believe them when they reported their own experiences, and knowing they were likely to not be believed negatively impacted the doctor–patient relationship. Respondents reported experiences of sharing their autism diagnosis and then having their intellectual capacity questioned, even in cases where intellectual capacity was objectively evidenced by educational attainment. One respondent who had achieved a PhD reported being treated "like a stupid child" and the assumption being made that they didn't understand what was being said to them. Others reported that medical issues were attributed to anxiety, despite having explained they were not anxious. Some withheld their autism diagnosis because they anticipated that they would not then be believed about other matters, or fears of being reduced to "a single-dimensional label of autism, and therefore their own thoughts, intelligence and self-awareness were subconsciously considered less valuable or less credible by doctors" (Shaw et al., 2024). Stimming was a particular example of epistemic injustice in practice, where healthcare professionals assumed it was anxiety-driven, instead of believing what an autistic person said about the reasons for stimming. Another was the level of a patient's pain being underestimated because the assessment was based on non-verbal expression of pain, rather than believing what the patient reported verbally, without acknowledging that autistic non-verbal communication is different.

Mary: "The point about stimming being misinterpreted resonated deeply with me. I stim constantly, and although I grew up with the expectation that I should suppress unconventional gestures or body movements, as I embrace my autistic identity, I consciously challenge this tendency and stim openly where it is safe to do so. One of my regular stims is to rub my hands together in a way that resembles the classic gesture of 'wringing one's hands,' which commonly indicates a state of anxiety or anguish. The reality for me is that it simply feels really pleasant and somehow helps me to concentrate. However, I am quite aware that it can be disconcerting to be on the receiving end of such a mixed message – my hands transmit anxiety, while the rest of my demeanour and my words do not. The challenge for the neurotypical observer is to recognise that the meaning for me is different to the meaning they may ascribe to what they are observing and to believe this when told. Failure to do this, to assume that their interpretation is correct despite evidence to the contrary, is an example of epistemic injustice. One aspect of the COVID-19 pandemic which I quite enjoyed was the chance to regularly reach out and use the wall mounted sanitisers as I walked through the hospital and to openly rub my hands together to my heart's content, and have others attribute this to simply practising good hand hygiene."

It was an overarching theme in our research, showing up across all other themes and subthemes. Only by challenging this epistemic injustice on an individual level and systematically will we start to make meaningful changes to healthcare outcomes and access for autistic people.

The Triple Empathy Problem

Another aspect of our research was how we explored the impact of Damian Milton's "Double Empathy Problem" and how it is operationalised in healthcare encounters (2022). The double empathy problem refers to the challenges autistic and non-autistic people can have in communicating with or understanding each other. Crucially, it is a bidirectional phenomenon, in contrast to the more traditional framing of autism, where any communication difficulties are assumed to be a deficit on the part of the autistic person. Research by Catherine Crompton and colleagues has shown that autistic peer-to-peer communication is equally effective as that between non-autistic people, which directly challenges that traditional framing (2020).

As doctors, a large part of our work involves communication with patients, and we receive specific communication skills training during undergraduate and postgraduate medical training. However, that training is generally conducted from a neuronormative standpoint, where the default assumption is that neurotypical communication is the expected standard, and there is little to no appreciation of neurodivergent communication differences. Because neurotypical or non-autistic people are the majority group, there is hardly any incentive or motivation to understand autistic communication, whereas for us, as autistic people, to be able to survive in a largely neurotypical world, we have to at least try to learn to understand non-autistic social interaction and communication. It isn't easy, and it can be compared to trying to learn a foreign language. While we might achieve a high level of competency, even approaching fluency, it is not our native language, and mistakes and misunderstandings are common. I (Mary) often say that "I 'speak neurotypical' fairly well, but I will always have an accent because it is not my mother tongue." When such misunderstandings happen in a medical context, as we have seen above, the consequences can be very serious. In our data, we saw example after example of such miscommunication. And we saw the same pattern even when respondents reported being healthcare providers themselves. Intuitively, you might expect that as medically trained people, we would understand the healthcare system and, therefore, not have the same sort of difficulty accessing care as laypeople. However, that wasn't what our participants reported, and as we analysed the data, both of us recounted our own personal stories of difficulties accessing healthcare.

We could see that the communication challenges between respondents and their doctors seemed to be related to the "double empathy problem." There were repeated examples of bidirectional communication difficulties, perhaps due to the intended meaning of unspoken messages not being inferred by autistic patients as intended by doctors. One example might be where concern on the part of a doctor might be conveyed non-verbally, and this might be missed by autistic patients, leading to the assumption that the doctor is uncaring or worse. However, that did not fully explain what seemed to be happening. The communication mismatch seemed to be more complicated. Then we realised that the same interpersonal dynamics occur between doctors and patients as happens between autistic people and non-autistic people. Because the world of medicine is so specialised, with its own language and culture, which can be quite incomprehensible to outsiders, we see this misunderstanding and lack of a shared perspective between doctors and patients all the time. It is even recognised that such mismatched communication and agendas lead to poor doctor–patient relationships and even worse clinical outcomes for all patients, not just autistic people.

Those of us who work in medicine are used to this culture, and it is easy to forget how alien it can appear to outsiders. We understand that, for example, the primary role of a GP when consulted by a patient with undiagnosed symptoms is to rule out serious causes of symptoms and then to look for and treat common causes. If the first-line treatment works, that confirms the diagnosis, whereas if it doesn't, it is time to move on to the next most likely cause. Even so, it is not uncommon to not find a cause for particular symptoms, and once serious underlying illness is ruled out, as doctors, we are used to accepting that medically unexplained symptoms will sometimes remain. However, from a patient's perspective, medically unexplained symptoms can be very distressing, particularly if the explanation is not clear and the doctor is attempting to provide reassurance non-verbally. This can lead to challenges in the doctor–patient relationship, regardless of whether or not autism is in the mix as well.

The process and impact of these communication challenges between healthcare providers and our respondents seemed to be more complex than could be explained by the "double empathy problem," which explains the mismatch between autistic and non-autistic people. As the same dynamic is at play between healthcare providers and laypeople, when we considered what was happening for our autistic respondents in consultations with non-autistic healthcare providers (who are no doubt the majority of the medical workforce), the dynamic observed seemed to have a three-dimensional quality. On one level, the double empathy problem was operating between autistic and non-autistic people, and simultaneously it was also operating between healthcare professionals and autistic people as laypeople. We call this the "triple empathy problem." Patients can struggle to see their doctor's perspective, and similarly doctors can struggle to see their patient's perspective, in particular bearing in mind the uncertainty that comes from not knowing what we know as doctors. Even when doctors are ill themselves and, therefore, become patients, we do so with our medical knowledge. We cannot "un-know" what we have learned in training. It can be challenging, therefore, to appreciate the perspective of a patient who does not share that medical knowledge, and it takes a conscious effort on the part of the healthcare provider to do so.

We know that autistic people might find it harder to see the perspective of a non-autistic person and vice versa. Therefore, it is even more challenging for autistic people to understand their non-autistic doctor's perspective and, similarly, for non-autistic doctors to understand their autistic patients. The finding that autistic respondents who reported being healthcare professionals themselves experienced similar challenges accessing healthcare supports our extension of the double empathy problem to the triple empathy problem. It is likely that this same dynamic is also at play in other contexts where autistic/non-autistic communication challenges are exacerbated by a professional/layperson divide. Education, social care, and the justice system are examples of where this dynamic may be acting as a cumulative disadvantage for autistic people. The implications for autistic people, and the professionals in those fields, warrant further investigation and this book series goes some way to explore these areas.

Do healthcare barriers lead to adverse health outcomes, including premature mortality for autistic people? We haven't proven this beyond all doubt, but what we have done is create a platform for autistic people to tell their stories about accessing healthcare, and we have analysed those stories in such a way as to paint a picture that shows a plausible pathway from one to the other. More research is undoubtedly needed to definitively prove that one leads to the other, but even more important are solutions. We have countless research papers showing the difficulties autistic people face and the specific access barriers we encounter in the healthcare service. Remember that it is often difficult for autistic people to reach out for help when well, never mind when sick or injured. Urgent changes are needed to ensure that autistic people can avail of health services when needed in the same way that non-autistic people can.

The Solution: Autistic SPACE

We recognise that our medical colleagues have huge demands on their time, both clinical time, where they are seeing patients, and non-clinical time, where they do everything else, from administration to teaching and keeping up with their own professional development. There is pressure to expand the training curriculum to include a vast amount of new medical developments and knowledge, along with multiple single-condition patient lobby groups seeking increased awareness of their particular condition. So, there is a lot of competition for doctors' time and attention. We recognise that our colleagues generally do not have the time to read long and involved research papers or books, even when they may have a particular interest in a condition, so we saw a need for a simple, memorable framework that could be easily applied across a range of healthcare settings.

We had offered a basic version of a framework in our first "Barriers to Health-care" paper, but we recognised that it needed to be significantly upgraded if it was to have the effect we were hoping for. We know that the vast amount of information that must be learned and retained during medical training means that acronyms and mnemonics are very commonly used. Particularly effective are descriptive acronyms, where the main message is contained in the acronym itself. An example of this is the "FAST" campaign for stroke care. FAST stands for Face, Arms, Speech, Time, but the main message is to access care "fast." Similarly, we wanted something that conveyed the most comprehensive description of autistic needs. It was also important that the acronym started with "S" as we believe that sensory differences are at the core of our existence as autistic people, and sensory needs are our primary need.

We felt that the acronym SPACE neatly encompassed our needs, and it stands for Sensory, Predictability, Acceptance, Communication, and Empathy. We described three further domains where the principles apply: physical space, processing space and emotional space. As the framework was developed during the COVID-19 pandemic, it works well from a training perspective that the three domains can be remembered by the acronym "PPE," as that is an acronym all healthcare providers are all too familiar with.

The framework has been well received and found to be helpful in many settings. It is used in healthcare provider training in various contexts, including the Royal College of Psychiatrists' National Autism Training Programme for Psychiatrists. Our goal is to increase knowledge and awareness of the framework in healthcare, so that healthcare providers have a simple, memorable way of remembering how to meet the needs of autistic people when we become patients.

Increasing awareness of any new research or framework can be challenging in healthcare, as there is so much new knowledge constantly being developed and competing for the attention of busy clinicians. It is difficult to find the time to

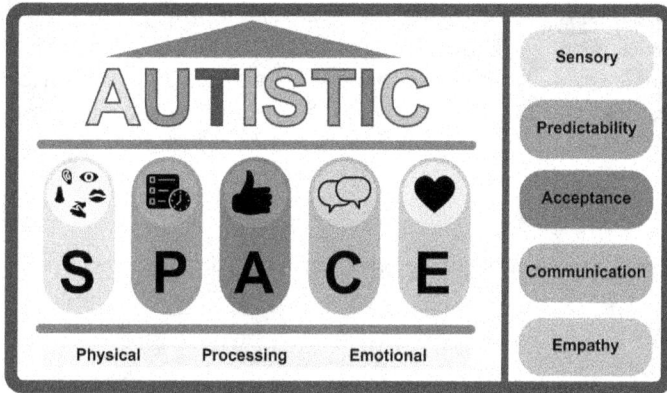

Figure 3.1   Auistic SPACE framework. Reproduced from Doherty, Mary et al. "Autistic SPACE: a novel framework for meeting the needs of autistic people in healthcare settings." British Journal of Hospital Medicine (London, England: 2005), 84, 4 (2023): 1–9. https://doi.org/10.12968/ hmed.2023.0006

read new papers, and that is particularly so when they are difficult to access. It is also important to us that autistic people are empowered to maximise their knowledge about the healthcare issues that impact us and therefore Open Access publishing has been a key goal for us. All of our healthcare papers are freely available open access. Authors must fund Open Access publications, so that readers are not required to pay fees to access the work. Commonly, universities will have funding agreements in place with medical journals, and we were able to make the second of our Barriers to Healthcare papers available under such an agreement. However, we were not able to do this for the first paper, which has an interesting funding source. The AsIAm Autism Friendly Town project was sponsored by SuperValu, an Irish supermarket chain. As the idea for the project originated from the Autism Friendly Town project in Clonakilty, the Scally family, owners of the local SuperValu supermarket in Clonakilty, generously paid the Open Access publication fees. Academic publishing agreements usually only cover original research, so the Autistic SPACE framework wasn't eligible. Instead, the leadership team of Autistic Doctors International clubbed together and contributed the cost of publishing Open Access from our own personal funds.

Conclusion

The Autistic SPACE framework is freely available to be used by anyone in any setting, and we are also working to adapt it to support autistic people in other contexts such as education and employment. We hope you like it, and if you have the opportunity to use it in your life or your work, we would really like to hear about your experiences. If you can conduct a research project where you evaluate it, that would be even better. We know that people who know about it and use it to support autistic people generally find it very helpful, but we need to build an evidence base that proves this, so if you can help with that goal, we believe that autistic people will benefit.

Note

1 GP refers to General Practitioner. This is a term used to describe a primary care doctor in Ireland.

References

Akobirshoev, I., Mitra, M., Dembo, R. and Lauer, E., 2020. In-hospital mortality among adults with autism spectrum disorder in the United States: A retrospective analysis of US hospital discharge data. *Autism*, *24*(1), pp. 177–189.

Cassidy, S.A., Robertson, A., Townsend, E., O'Connor, R.C. and Rodgers, J., 2020. Advancing our understanding of self-harm, suicidal thoughts and behaviours in autism. *Journal of Autism and Developmental Disorders*, *50*, pp. 3445–3449.

Crompton, C.J., Ropar, D., Evans-Williams, C.V., Flynn, E.G. and Fletcher-Watson, S., 2020. Autistic peer-to-peer information transfer is highly effective. *Autism*, *24*(7), pp. 1704–1712.

Doherty, M., McCowan, S. and Shaw, S.C., 2023. Autistic SPACE: A novel framework for meeting the needs of autistic people in healthcare settings. *British Journal of Hospital Medicine*, *84*(4), pp. 1–9.

Doherty, M., Neilson, S., O'Sullivan, J., Carravallah, L., Johnson, M., Cullen, W. and Shaw, S.C., 2022. Barriers to healthcare and self-reported adverse outcomes for autistic adults: A cross-sectional study. *BMJ Open*, *12*(2), p. e056904.

Gould, J. and Ashton-Smith, J., 2011. Missed diagnosis or misdiagnosis? Girls and women on the autism spectrum. *Good Autism Practice (GAP)*, *12*(1), pp. 34–41.

Hirvikoski, T., Mittendorfer-Rutz, E., Boman, M., Larsson, H., Lichtenstein, P. and Bölte, S., 2016. Premature mortality in autism spectrum disorder. *The British Journal of Psychiatry*, *208*(3), pp. 232–238.

Kassee, C., Babinski, S., Tint, A., Lunsky, Y., Brown, H.K., Ameis, S.H., Szatmari, P., Lai, M.C. and Einstein, G., 2020. Physical health of autistic girls and women: A scoping review. *Molecular Autism*, *11*, pp. 1–22.

Lai, M.C., 2023. Mental health challenges faced by autistic people. *Nature Human Behaviour*, *7*(10), pp. 1620–1637.

Mason, D., Ingham, B., Urbanowicz, A., Michael, C., Birtles, H., Woodbury-Smith, M., Brown, T., James, I., Scarlett, C., Nicolaidis, C. and Parr, J.R., 2019. A systematic review of what barriers and facilitators prevent and enable physical healthcare services access for autistic adults. *Journal of Autism and Developmental Disorders*, *49*, pp. 3387–3400.

Milton, D., Gurbuz, E. and López, B., 2022. The 'double empathy problem': Ten years on. *Autism*, *26*(8), pp. 1901–1903.

Nicolaidis, C., Schnider, G., Lee, J., Raymaker, D.M., Kapp, S.K., Croen, L.A., Urbanowicz, A. and Maslak, J., 2021. Development and psychometric testing of the AASPIRE adult autism healthcare provider self-efficacy scale. *Autism*, *25*(3), pp. 767–773.

O'Nions, E., Lewer, D., Petersen, I., Brown, J., Buckman, J.E., Charlton, R., Cooper, C., El Baou, C., Happé, F., Manthorpe, J. and McKechnie, D.G., 2024. Estimating life expectancy and years of life lost for autistic people in the UK: A matched cohort study. *The Lancet Regional Health–Europe*, *36*.

O'Nions, E., Petersen, I., Buckman, J.E., Charlton, R., Cooper, C., Corbett, A., Happé, F., Manthorpe, J., Richards, M., Saunders, R. and Zanker, C., 2023. Autism in England: Assessing underdiagnosis in a population-based cohort study of prospectively collected primary care data. *The Lancet Regional Health–Europe, 29*.

Shaw, S.C., Carravallah, L., Johnson, M., O'Sullivan, J., Chown, N., Neilson, S. and Doherty, M., 2024. Barriers to healthcare and a 'triple empathy problem' may lead to adverse outcomes for autistic adults: A qualitative study. *Autism, 28*(7), pp. 1746–1757.

Tebartz van Elst, L., Pick, M., Biscaldi, M., Fangmeier, T. and Riedel, A., 2013. High-functioning autism spectrum disorder as a basic disorder in adult psychiatry and psychotherapy: Psychopathological presentation, clinical relevance and therapeutic concepts. *European Archives of Psychiatry and Clinical Neuroscience, 263*, pp. 189–196.

Unigwe, S., Buckley, C., Crane, L., Kenny, L., Remington, A. and Pellicano, E., 2017. GPs' confidence in caring for their patients on the autism spectrum: An online self-report study. *British Journal of General Practice, 67*(659), pp. e445-e452.

Vogan, V., Lake, J.K., Tint, A., Weiss, J.A. and Lunsky, Y., 2017. Tracking health care service use and the experiences of adults with autism spectrum disorder without intellectual disability: A longitudinal study of service rates, barriers and satisfaction. *Disability and Health Journal, 10*(2), pp. 264–270.

Vohra, R., Madhavan, S. and Sambamoorthi, U., 2016. Emergency department use among adults with autism spectrum disorders (ASD). *Journal of Autism and Developmental Disorders, 46*, pp. 1441–1454.

Ward, J.H., Weir, E., Allison, C. and Baron-Cohen, S., 2023. Increased rates of chronic physical health conditions across all organ systems in autistic adolescents and adults. *Molecular Autism, 14*(1), p. 35.

Zerbo, O., Massolo, M.L., Qian, Y. and Croen, L.A., 2015. A study of physician knowledge and experience with autism in adults in a large integrated healthcare system. *Journal of Autism and Developmental Disorders, 45*, pp. 4002–4014.

Chapter 4

Neurodiversity and Mental Health Service Provision

Timothy Frawley

Introduction

Neurodiversity and mental health are broad concepts that require unpacking. As an edited book, it is fortunate that other chapters (for example, McGrattan and Oakley and colleagues) helpfully define terms and provide context whilst also outlining interactions between neurodistinct or neurodivergent experience and mental illness. In this chapter, I will set out why understanding neurodiversity in a mental health context is important. I will also outline some information on the co-occurrence of neurodivergence and mental health illness. Lastly, I will explore positive developments within mental health service provision and how more can be done to sustain these.

Please note, in some parts of this chapter, the term 'disorder' is used. This reflects the fact that this is the term used in the referenced research – while I espouse use of neurodiversity-affirming language, I believe it would be incorrect to avoid the term preferred by the original researchers. Moreover, disorder is also the term used in the internationally recognised *Diagnostic and Statistical Manual* (DSM) (American Psychological Association, 2013) which carries some importance in mental health contexts. Furthermore, it is worth noting the difference inherent to the terms 'mental illness' and 'mental health difficulty'. A mental illness is typically clinically diagnosable, usually by a specialist using agreed criteria such as outlined in the DSM. Such clarity and preciseness are important to ensure that, across countries and cultures, there is consistency in the recognition of the phenomenon being explored. Mental health difficulty, on the other hand, is a broader concept incorporating emotional distress, which may not necessarily significantly impair daily functioning. Clinical diagnosis or intervention may not be required and less intensive inputs may lead to an amelioration of the experience.

Perhaps most pertinently, I believe certain arguments around language are reductionist and represent a zero-sum game, potentially leading to an internecine feud. I do not consider this helpful in advancing the cause of improving mental health services for those among us who identify as neurodifferent, neurodistinct, neurospicy, neuroatypical, or neurodivergent. The above highlights my commitment to respectful debate and willingness to learn and adapt, fuelled by a welcoming of differences and of differing perspectives as integral to diversity.

DOI: 10.4324/9781003495949-5

Is Understanding Neurodiversity and Mental Health Service Provision Important?

In Autumn 2023, the BBC carried a stark headline – 'Young autistic people dying despite coroner warnings over care'. They reported that over a 10-year period, UK coroners issued 51 'Prevention of Future Death notices' related to failings in the care of autistic people, with a majority under 30 years old and a third of those being children. The National Institute of Clinical Excellence (NICE, 2021) outline the importance of care coordination where autism co-occurs with mental illness, with social anxiety disorder reported as having a high prevalence. I believe, similar to Hur et al. (2020), that social or generalised anxiety disorder can be a serious mental illness and sometimes its deleterious consequences are under-recognised. Social anxiety commonly co-occurs where there is neurodifference (Jakobsson Støre et al., 2024; Spain et al., 2018). Recognition of coexisting mental illness is important as it facilitates understanding and allows for accommodations. However, despite the recognised higher prevalence of mental illness associated with neurodivergence, it remains under-recognised, mischaracterised, and misunderstood and thus inadequately supported and treated. Such recognition of different experiences is essential to their validation in a mental health context. This, in turn, is imperative to inform an authentic understanding of how to effectively affirm a person's lived experience rather than rely on incomplete formulations seen through a lens of pathology or deficit.

In a recent systematic review, Brown et al. (2024) report that autistic people have an eightfold increased risk of death compared to non-autistic people. Balazs and Kereszteny (2017), in a review of 26 studies, found a positive association between suicide and ADHD with comorbid disorders being mediating factors which heighten risk. A narrative review by Gagliano et al. (2024) also highlights a complex interaction between neurodevelopmental disorders, emotional dysregulation, and adverse childhood experiences. Moreover, in a nationally representative survey (Canadian Community Health Survey), 'specific learning disorders' are associated with an increased risk of suicide attempts (Fuller-Thompson, 2018). It should be noted that some of the studies referenced here only infer an 'association'. It is well understood, that an association is different to attribution of cause. This term describes a statistical link between two factors, indicating that changes in one often accompany changes in the other. However, this does not mean that one directly causes the other. For instance, research might show that neurodivergent individuals have a higher likelihood of facing mental health illness. This suggests a connection, but it does not prove that neurodivergence is the root cause of these challenges. Therefore, I do not purport that being neurodivergent automatically suggests poor mental health or increased suicidality at an individual level. Rather, it is the case that a neurodivergent person *may be or is, from a statistical perspective, compared to the general population, at increased risk* of mental illness.

However, let's go further. Mosner et al. (2019) state that neurodivergent people are at increased risk of mental illness and suicide completion. Lai et al. (2019) report that co-occurring mental illnesses are more prevalent in the autistic population than in the general population, while Mancini et al. (2024) assert a heightened risk of poorer psychosocial outcomes in children experiencing developmental coordination disorder. Therefore, yes, there is a concern, and yes, those of us attending mental health services, working in mental health services, in any of the varied roles, educating professionals or supporting family members should want to do something constructive about it. However, as has been explored by many other authors in this book, how best to do so is largely informed by the paradigm that underpins our sociocultural understanding of the phenomenon at play. As such, whether neurodiversity is deemed a social or pathological phenomenon, an interplay or both, is crucial in determining societal responses. It seems reasonable to assert that those who experience a world that is constructed to function in a neuro-normative way can experience at least some psychological distress. Therefore, to understand the high prevalence of mental health illness associated with neurodivergence, the question of societal responses and impact are important areas to examine.

Milton refers to the double empathy problem (Milton, 2012), which in part relates to a mutual misunderstanding that may occur between autistic and non-autistic people. Perhaps this contributes to the known challenges for neurodivergent people experiencing co-occurring mental health illness attending mental health services. However, this may be putting the cart entirely before the horse. Could it be that we need to simultaneously and with vigour invest in the needs of our workforce alongside the needs of those who avail of health services? Doyle (2020) suggests that 15–20% of the general population may identify as being neurodivergent. Victoria Sweetmore, in the UK, writes of her mixed or difficult experiences of being an autistic woman, nurse, and service user engaging with mental health services (Sweetmore, 2021). Amy Pohlmann, a US-based nurse also refers to her experiences, which are thankfully more positive and fulfilling (Seaberg, 2018), although Shaw et al. (2023), in a small phenomenological study, suggest autistic medical students can feel additionally isolated as compared to their peers. Perhaps paying more attention to the environment within which health or mental health services are delivered is providential.

Should mental health services even provide consultations to neurodivergent people for anything other than a mental health difficulty? Is it right to pathologise a neurotype? Such questions frequently become circular, bearing in mind the difficulty for many, including gatekeepers to service access, in appreciating the nature of co-occurring experiences. Of course, where a co-occurring mental illness is evident, mental health services should provide care. After all, a dyslexic person can experience depression. An autistic person can experience psychosis. Yet is there a schism afoot? The term autistic spectrum disorder (ASD) is anathema to some, but does it have a legitimacy, a currency through which people can access certain aspects of care and treatment. If so, is there merit in maintaining the status quo of this currency or is an entire overhaul in order? I don't have an answer to this question, and in fact, I have no intention whatsoever of trying to answer it here.

I do, however, have an interest in examining whether there are structural, institutional, and practical factors which may constitute barriers to care. There are concerns about diagnostic overshadowing[1] (Hendriksen et al., 2015; Dell' Armo and Tassé, 2024; Frawley et al., 2024) and whether mental health signs and symptoms may be attributed to a neurotype or a neurodifference itself. Sometimes too, the complexity of dual diagnosis is given scant attention (Raines and Netson-Amore, 2024). Specialised diagnostic services may be required, and such specialisation is sometimes beyond the scope of generic mental health/psychiatry teams. This is not a repudiation of the excellent services these teams provide. It is simply a recognition that complexity in mental health care has grown and service fragmentation is a factor of concern (David et al., 2024).

Paradoxically, in an effort to enhance specialisation, mental health and neurodiversity services can be siloed (Brede et al., 2022). There is a myriad of literature, generally, regarding the challenges of inter-disciplinary working. For example, most current designs of clinical environments are not particularly cognisant of, or sympathetic to, sensory sensitivities. Inappropriate sensory environments act as a stressor for many, both those seeking care and the professionals themselves, making effective care and treatment more arduous and draining. Moreover, there is a lack of training and expertise available to mental health professionals (Lipinski et al., 2022). Many mental health practitioners will have studied 'neurodevelopmental disorders', but in some jurisdictions, these may have been seen as other than 'pure' or 'traditional' mental health disorders. In the context of resource constraints, which ultimately is a political and less a clinical matter, eligibility criteria may be tightened to fit a more 'typical' profile. This is not indicative of mental health services or providers seeking to provide a sub-standard service. On the contrary, I contend it represents the effects of chronic under-investment in specific areas of disability or different-ability services. In fact, this underfunding and reactive policy tweaking only creates a 'Street-Level Bureaucratisation' of our mental health services, as theorised by Michael Lipsky (1980), which ill-serves the provider and the 'patient'. Briefly, and for context, in his 1980 work, Lipsky introduced the concept of 'Street-Level Bureaucracy', which explains how public service professionals – such as social workers, educators, police officers, and healthcare practitioners – act as the primary agents of public policy implementation. These 'street-level bureaucrats' possess considerable autonomy in applying policies, especially when operating within environments with limited resources. Mental health services, in particular, often face significant constraints in areas like funding, staffing, and available time. This lack of resources compels these frontline workers to make tough decisions regarding client prioritisation and the distribution of scarce resources.

So, to answer the question first posited in the heading of this section, 'Is Understanding Neurodiversity and Mental Health Service Provision Important? I would say 'yes – yes it is'. The question now arises, what is being done about it? By way of disclosure, I am a mental health nurse. I have worked in mental health services for many years and I believe in them. I believe in the people who work in them and their determination to positively impact people's lives for the better. I also believe in the determination of people attending mental health services, and their families, to recover and to lead meaningful, satisfying lives. Therefore, I am going to unashamedly focus on what is working and where there is an evidence base for good practice. I am not interested in criticising or shining a light on failings. While this has its place, I believe a positive focus can reap richer dividends.

Co-Occurrence of Neurodiversity and Mental Health Illness

Prior to exploring any one specific condition or experience, it may be useful to point out some relevant materials or comments that apply across the neurodiversity spectrum. To understand the prevalence of mental health disorders more generally, with particular reference to children, a paper by Lynch et al. (2023) is rather useful. What can be gleaned from a cursory review of their work is that prevalence varies widely depending on various factors, in particular, the methodology for determining prevalence chosen. In general, many of the neurodistinct experiences discussed in this book are more frequently diagnosed in males rather than females, with autism and ADHD being prominent examples of this (Craddock et al., 2024; Loomes et al., 2017). Below I will focus on four specific experiences/conditions – ADHD, autism, dyslexia, and dyspraxia. I have selected these as a result of the intersection of ADHD, autism, and mental health illness being more prominent in the literature. Meanwhile, dyslexia is a specific learning difference and dyspraxia or developmental coordination disorder relates more so to movement, hence there is some variety in the selected experiences/conditions. I also have some professional interest in these areas.

Autism

Zeidan et al. (2022), taking a global perspective, suggest that 1 in 100 children are diagnosed as being autistic. They suggest there is significant variance internationally, in part due to different methodology to assess prevalence being used, unequal access to awareness, and assessment of autism, as well as variance across time. In Ireland in 2018, the Department of Health suggested a prevalence of 1–1.5% for policy and planning purposes, although there exists concern as to the lack of credible, up-to-date prevalence data relating to mental health and neurodevelopmental conditions in this jurisdiction. However, the work of the United States based Centers for Disease Control and Prevention's (CDC) Autism and Developmental Disabilities Monitoring (ADDM) Network in the United States is notable, wherein it was determined that 1 in 150 children were diagnosed as autistic in 2000, as compared with 1 in 36 in 2020 (Shaw et al., 2025). Therefore, it can be said that prevalence ranges are shifting and depend on a multiplicity of well-established factors, together with unknown factors, and there is evidence to suggest a growing recognition and diagnosis of autism.

Mosner et al. (2019) report that 70–95% of autistic children and adolescents experience at least one co-occurring mental illness. They suggest that similarly high numbers of autistic adults experience a co-occurring illness. It is worth noting the limitations of their work, including small sample size, convenience sampling, and a predominantly male caucasian cohort; however, this should not unduly detract from the fact that co-occurrence rates are generally high. In a systematic review and meta-analysis, Lai et al. (2019, p. 819) reported the following co-occurrence of mental illness with various neurodifferences:

> Pooled prevalence estimates of 28% (95% CI 25–32) for attention-deficit hyperactivity disorder; 20% (17–23) for anxiety disorders; 13% (9–17) for sleep–wake disorders; 12% (10–15) for disruptive, impulse-control, and conduct disorders; 11% (9–13) for depressive disorders; 9% (7–10) for obsessive-compulsive disorder; 5% (3–6) for bipolar disorders; and 4% (3–5) for schizophrenia spectrum disorders.

It is reasonable to assert that the above-mentioned prevalence is in excess of that observed in the general population. This should send a clear message about the possible additional care and support needs that members of the autistic community may require. At a minimum, treatment access, enhanced mental health assessment and treatment for autistic people should be a focus within mental health services. However, as previously outlined, increased awareness of the difference between neurodivergence and mental illness, and their co-occurrence, needs to be more widely recognised and sensitively navigated to ensure pathologisation of neurodifference does not occur. Equally, under-recognition and, by extension, under-treatment of treatable illnesses should not occur secondary to diagnostic overshadowing. Again, based on current levels of competency and service provision, this may be easier to theorise than enact in practice, but that does not mean we should shy away from it.

ADHD

Polanczyk et al. (2014) explore the prevalence of ADHD and make the following observations: the International Classification of Diseases (ICD) reports a prevalence of 1–2%, while the Diagnostic and Statistical Manual (DSM) suggests rates of 3–5%. It is suggested that 30–50% of children referred to child psychiatry clinics have ADHD and it is diagnosed three to four times more often in boys than in girls. It can persist into adolescence and adulthood, although the symptom profile may change.

At the intersection with mental health, Bussing et al. (2010) outline that children with ADHD are more likely to experience anxiety or depression and functional impairment in adolescence. Barkley (2015) noted the occurrence of difficulties in emotional self-regulation in the context of ADHD. Emotional regulation is an important concept in mental health, and where dysregulation occurs, distress may arise. More broadly, individuals diagnosed with ADHD and their parents report greater degrees of family stress, overt and unresolved conflict between parents and between parent and child, poorer communication, and greater anger intensity and aggression (Grilli et al., 2024; Wymbs et al., 2008). Therefore, increased exposure to childhood verbal abuse may occur (Dube et al., 2023; Swedo et al., 2023) which may have damaging impacts on a child's development. In seminal earlier research, specifically the National Survey Replication study (Kessler et al., 2006), anxiety co-occurred in almost half of those diagnosed with ADHD, with mood disorders following at 38% and 15% experiencing substance use disorders. Comorbid anxiety disorders are associated with a higher number of ADHD symptoms in childhood, higher scores on adult ADHD rating scales, and a presentation with more emotional dysregulation (Reimherr et al., 2017).

Taking the foregoing into consideration, mental health services should have a keen focus on supporting the needs of people with ADHD. In fact, whether proactive screening should be implemented is a matter of debate (de la Viuda Suárez et al., 2021; Adamis et al., 2018; Corbisiero et al., 2017). At a minimum, the relatively recent policy in Ireland to create a national clinical programme (Health Service Executive, 2020) for the treatment of ADHD in adults seems prudent.

Dyslexia

Dyslexia is a specific learning difference that predominantly affects reading and writing. As a specific learning difference, anecdotally in my practice as a mental health nurse, I have not observed much discussion around connections, links, or associations with mental illness. In fact, this is not surprising as the evidence of a link between these experiences is mixed (Georgiou et al., 2024). However, Kargiotidis and Manolitsis (2024) do report an association between dyslexia and anxiety with social withdrawal symptoms being more prominent. Vieira et al. (2024) highlight the possible deleterious effects of social withdrawal (leading to isolation, impact on physical health, and loss of self-esteem) in dyslexia which may be experienced by some people. Co-occurrence of other neurodifferences adds a complication wherein McArthur et al. (2024) demonstrate that the association with anxiety was more common in children with both dyslexia *and* ADHD as opposed to dyslexia alone.

Dyslexia may, for some, have a profound impact on myriad interconnecting aspects of psychological and social development which undoubtedly confers risks relating to mental health. Wilmot et al. (2023) discuss impacts on self-esteem, identity, and engagement with peers as being affected at the primary school level. Other studies refer to the emotional impact of living with dyslexia (Xiao et al., 2023) and impact on school connectedness (Wilmott et al., 2024), while Deighton et al. (2020) refer to low self-esteem, bullying, and stigma as concerns. Therefore, at a minimum, for those interacting with children, such as parents, teachers, and health service providers, recognition of these experiences and possible implications for mental health is important. I will add that the concept of school connectedness piques my interest. Perhaps a lack of or absence of connectedness to one's school may have wider effects on academic or career trajectory, which may interact negatively with a person's overall well-being. The increasing access to advanced assistive technology, as discussed by Almgren Bäck et al. (2023), is likely to enhance well-being, particularly in post-second-level contexts. Furthermore, Murphy (2023) and Hamilton-Clarke (2024) provide useful insights regarding identity and disclosure in higher education contexts, suggesting that navigating education (or employment) for members of the dyslexic community acts as a dynamic stressor throughout development.This brings us back to our initial discussion on where mental health sits with neurodivergent people and suggests a lack of societal adaptation, historically, for dyslexic people, thus causing increased stress and anxiety. Moreover, this heightened stress may be compounded by the different ways dyslexic people experience the world, a world which has evolved to function in a manner where certain practices are valued if performed in a particular way (neurotypical) but devalued if performed in a different way (neurodivergent), this would suggest a strong correlation between such stress and anxiety and societal organisation.

Dyspraxia

Dyspraxia or developmental coordination disorder is said to impact 2–7% of children (Caçola, 2016), although prevalence differs, as previously noted in respect of other neurodistinct experiences. In a systematic review and meta-analysis, Omer et al. (2018) demonstrate that there is mixed evidence of an association between dyspraxia and mental illness, with no firm consensus apparent. However, they conclude that there is evidence of an association between dyspraxia and internalising problems. Internalising problems are those that reflect inwardly, rather than externally through overt behaviours and may include sadness, loneliness, and anxiety. While sadness, loneliness, and anxiety are part of the human condition, and I do not wish to conflate these experiences with mental illness, it is worth acknowledging that such feelings are typically amplified in scenarios involving mental health challenges. Given Purcell (2024) suggests that dyspraxia can affect or influence a person's leisure and vocational pursuits alongside academic performance, it is possible to infer that such experience can negatively impact an individual's well-being. A systematic review and meta-ethnography by O'Dea et al. (2021, p. 1) offers useful qualitative data outlining a 'mismatch between their [people with dyspraxia] abilities and performance norms for daily activities that led to a cascade of negative consequences including negative self-appraisal, bullying and exclusion'. Helpfully, the paper also synthesises strategies for successful adjustment and inclusion.

Zaragas et al. (2023) examine the effects of physical activity in children and adolescents with dyspraxia and perhaps unsurprisingly find a positive association with improved daily functionality. This may have important implications for mental health, when we consider the work of Nash (2014, 2022, 2024) who explores the nexus of physical and mental health within mental health services. Taking all of the foregoing into account, it is reasonable to suggest that those with a stake in the care and support of people with dyspraxia should be at least aware of the possibility of psychosocial distress and discomfiture in this population. In fact, in considering the work of Mancini et al. (2024) and O'Dea et al. (2021), the broader incorporation of a more psychosocially focused and mental health aware model of care for people with dyspraxia is a welcome proposition.

Enhancing Mental Health Service Provision: Opportunities and Best Practices

The purpose of this section is to offer some examples of worthy practices within mental health services which support the needs of the neurodistinct community. I believe there are many examples, several of which will not be explored here due to space constraints.

I regularly receive calls from clinical colleagues asking how their environment can be made more neurodiversity-friendly. The question is: How can we ensure best practice is more widespread and universally accessible? In a 2018 paper (Frawley et al., 2018), with colleagues, I explore challenges and opportunities regarding policy implementation, the existence of a post-code lottery, and uneven access to services in a mental health service context. I posit there is no easy answer to the question posed, however, in the context of neurodiversity, there is evidence that clinical practice guidelines, national clinical programmes and pathways, as well as inclusive design practices can at least help (Castle, 2024; NHS England, 2023).

Starting with the built environment, and taking a transdisciplinary perspective, there is much to glean from the world of architecture and spaces. For example, Totaforti (2018) applies learning from biophilic theory to hospital design; sound and acoustics (Reavey and Harding, 2018); neuro-adaptive architecture, and embracing technology as discussed by Makanadar (2024) and *Design for the Mind – Neurodiversity and the Built Environment – Guide* (PAS 6463:2021), published by the British Standards Institution (2021), all offer specific guidance on how clinical environments can incorporate architectural and interior design learnings. Bond et al. (2024), from a clinical perspective, offer guidance on ways to reduce sensory overstimulation in hospital settings. These include designated quiet waiting rooms, provision of noise cancelling headphones, weighted blankets and fidgets, and increased functionality to control lighting, among other items.

A second item of note, previously alluded to, is how we support the segments of our workforce who are potentially neurodistinct themselves. Johnson and Aluwalia (2024) and Moore et al. (2020) explore staff challenges and opportunities from a physician's perspective. Cleary et al. (2023, p. 799) explore how certain traits, for example, making eye contact, may be perceived as a 'poor cultural fit' for certain caregiving roles. This may ignore the presence of other desirable characteristics, and lead to masking or camouflaging of one's neurodifference. Clearly, this may stop members of the neurodistinct community from even considering a career in healthcare, let alone continuing in their chosen profession. I wager this is unhelpful to employees' mental health, and also, due to inadequate awareness and acceptance, potentially entrenching a culture of neuroexclusion for those attending mental health services.

However, the present and the future is far from bleak. Currow et al. (2024) in the UK offer a helpful guide exploring topics, including disclosure, creating a neuro-affirming work environment, adaptations to recruitment, and normalising reasonable adjustments designed to support autistic healthcare professionals. Duong and Vogel (2022) provide an uplifting account of disclosure from a medical practitioner's perspective. Similarly, in nursing, Hedlund (2023, p. 210) argues the need for space for 'theoretically and empathetically inclined nurses'.

Examples of good practices with respect to being neurodiversity-affirming are plentiful. Take the Strengths Based Model of Neurodiversity (SBMN) developed by Fung and colleagues (Fung, 2021). While a number of neurodistinct people, and indeed their families, may not see their experience as being a strength, and indeed there is evidence to suggest that this characterisation is not universally accepted (Bury et al., 2020), the concept of a strengths-based, as opposed to deficit only, approach, as explicated by Rapp and Goscha (2011), has much to offer in mental health contexts. Similarly, in Scotland, Rutherford et al. (2023) argue that, while they occupy key leadership roles, community mental health teams (CMHTs) alone cannot meet the needs of the neurodistinct population. They recommend a Stepped Care Adult Neurodevelopment Pathway in each locality. A view was taken that single-condition pathways wasted time and resources due to high levels of co-occurrence. As a tiered approach, primary care level neurodevelopmental teams, with prescribing and differential diagnosis capability as well as direct access interventions and supports (Rutherford et al., 2023, p. 10) would be needed alongside adequately resourced 'secondary care, neurodevelopmentally-informed teams'. Clearly, sufficient resourcing, recruitment, and empowerment of services is essential. In the absence of same, I contend that such developments, while well intended, can exacerbate public frustration and seriously undermine the clinicians tasked with delivering innovative services.

Examples of good practice within mental health services are apparent and I anticipate will grow. Quinn et al. (2023) propose working relationally and providing bespoke housing, in particular where concurrent intellectual disability is evident. Equally, while I have shared my views on language at the outset of this chapter, that is not to suggest it does not matter. Neurodiversity-affirming practice and language is important (Fitzpatrick et al., 2024; Cobbaert et al., 2024). Therefore, for the neurodivergent person to have their life experience characterised as a symptom may be insulting at best and significantly damaging at worst. In this context, the SPACE model as advanced by Doherty et al. (2023) may have relevance – as explored in Chapter 3.

Conclusion

Are we there yet? I believe so. In this chapter, I have sought to affirm why neurodiversity is important within mental health service provision. I have also outlined certain details of the prevalence of the co-occurrence of neurodivergence and mental health illness. In focusing on ADHD, autism, dyslexia, and dyspraxia, I hope

I have impressed the urgent need for awareness, acceptance, and enhanced mental health service provision for these populations. Strategically, I have called attention to areas of positive focus and opportunity within mental health services. I have done so as a mental health nurse, having worked clinically in services. I have only the highest regard for those who work diligently in the provision of mental health-care and support. Generally, a constructive approach is more helpful, too. Based on the recency of certain references utilised in constructing this chapter and observing societal trends towards inclusion, I believe the future is bright. However, realising this vision requires strong leadership, sustained government funding, and robust collaboration among policymakers, practitioners, service and technology providers, advocates, academics, and, of course, neurodivergent individuals themselves.

Note

1 Overshadowing refers to a situation where one condition, illness, or factor becomes more prominent or noticeable, thereby overshadowing or masking other conditions or needs.

References

Adamis, D., Graffeo, I., Kumar, R., Meagher, D., O'Neill, D., Mulligan, O., Murthy, S, O'Mahony, E., McCarthy, G., Gavin, B. & McNicholas, F., 2018. Screening for attention deficit-hyperactivity disorder (ADHD) symptomatology in adult mental health clinics. *Irish Journal of Psychological Medicine,* 35(3), pp. 193–201. https://doi.org/10.1017/ipm.2017.49

Almgren Bäck, G., Lindeblad, E., Elmqvist, C. & Svensson, I., 2023. Dyslexic students' experiences in using assistive technology to support written language skills: A five-year follow-up. *Disability and Rehabilitation: Assistive Technology,* 19(4), pp. 1217–1227. https://doi.org/10.1080/17483107.2022.2161647

American Psychiatric Association, 2013. *Diagnostic and statistical manual of mental disorders* (5th ed.). Arlington, VA: American Psychiatric Publishing.

Balazs, J. & Kereszteny, A., 2017. Attention-deficit/hyperactivity disorder and suicide: A systematic review. *World J Psychiatry,* 22(7), pp. 44–59. https://doi.org/10.5498/wjp.v7.i1.44. PMID: 28401048

Barkley, R. A., 2015. Emotional dysregulation is a core component of ADHD. In R. A. Barkley (Ed.), *Attention-deficit hyperactivity disorder: A handbook for diagnosis and treatment* (4th ed., pp. 81–115). London: The Guilford Press.

Bond, L., Frawley, T., Moore, K., Gavin, B. & McNicholas, F., 2024. Challenges for neurodiverse children in acute medical hospitals and opportunities for the new National Childrens Hospital to be neurodiversity friendly. *Irish Journal of Medical Science,* 193(1), pp. 253–261. https://doi.org/10.1007/s11845-024-03850-y

Brede, J., Cage, E., Trott, J., Palmer, L., Smith, A., Serpell, L., Mandy, W. & Russell, A., 2022. "We have to try to find a way, a clinical bridge" - autistic adults' experience of accessing and receiving support for mental health difficulties: A systematic review and thematic meta-synthesis. *Clinical Psychology Review,* 93, p. 102131.

British Standards Institution, 2021. *PAS 6463:2021 – design for the mind: Neurodiversity and the built environment: Guide.* London: BSI.

Brown, C. M., Newell, V., Sahin, E. et al., 2024. Updated systematic review of suicide in autism: 2018–2024. *Current Development Disorders Reports,* 11, pp. 225–256.

Bury, S. M., Hedley, D., Uljarević, M. & Gal, E., 2020, October. The autism advantage at work: A critical and systematic review of current evidence. *Research in Developmental Disabilities*, 105, p. 103750. https://doi.org/10.1016/j.ridd.2020.103750

Bussing, R., Mason, D. M., Bell, L., Porter, P. & Garvan, C., 2010. Adolescent outcomes of childhood attention-deficit/hyperactivity disorder in a diverse community sample. *Journal of the American Academy of Child and Adolescent Psychiatry*, 49(6), pp. 595–605. https://doi.org/10.1016/j.jaac.2010.03.006

Caçola, P., 2016. Effects of two distinct group motor skill interventions in psychological and motor skills of children with developmental coordination disorder: A pilot study. *Disability and Health Journal*, 9(1), pp. 172–178. https://doi.org/10.1016/j.dhjo.2015.07.007

Castle, H. (2024). Why do architects need to understand neurodiversity? *RIBA Journal*. Online. Available at: https://www.ribaj.com/intelligence/why-do-architects-need-to-understand-neurodiversity

Cleary, M., West, S., Kornhaber, R. & Hungerford, C., 2023. Autism, discrimination and masking: Disrupting a recipe for trauma. *Issues in Mental Health Nursing*, 44(9), pp. 799–808. https://doi.org/10.1080/01612840.2023.2239916

Cobbaert, L., Millichamp, A. R., Elwyn, R. et al., 2024. Neurodivergence, intersectionality, and eating disorders: A lived experience-led narrative review. *Journal of Eating Disorders*, 12, p. 187.

Corbisiero, S., Hartmann-Schorro, R. M., Riecher-Rössler, A. & Stieglitz, R. D., 2017. Screening for adult attention-deficit/hyperactivity disorder in a psychiatric outpatient population with specific focus on sex differences. *Frontiers in Psychiatry*, 8, p. 115. https://doi.org/10.3389/fpsyt.2017.00115

Craddock, E., 2024. Being a woman is 100% significant to my experiences of attention deficit hyperactivity disorder and autism: Exploring the gendered implications of an adulthood combined autism and attention deficit hyperactivity disorder diagnosis. *Qualitative Health Research*, 34(14), pp. 1442–1455.

Curnow, E., Rutherford, M., Maciver, D., Johnston, L., Utley, I., Murray, M., Johnstone Cooke, V., Muggleton, J., Jenkins, N. & Gray, A., 2024. *Beyond accommodations: Supporting autistic health professionals*. Edinburgh: National Autism Implementation Team (NAIT).

David, N., Rahlff, P., König, H., Dückert, S., Gewohn, P., Erik, F., Vogeley, K., Schöttle, D., Konnopka, A., Schulz, H. & Peth, J., 2024. Barriers to healthcare predict reduced health-related quality of life in autistic adults without intellectual disability. *Autism*, 29(2), pp. 476–489. https://doi.org/10.1177/13623613241275406

de la Viuda Suárez, M. E., Alonso Lorenzo, J. C., Ruiz Jiménez, F. J. & Luciano Soriano, M. C., 2021. Assessing ADHD symptoms in clinical public practice: Is a reliable final diagnosis possible? *Atención Primaria*, 53(3), p. 101945. https://doi.org/10.1016/j.aprim.2020.10.004

Deighton, J., Gilleard, A., Cortina, M. & Woodman, J., 2020. *Dyslexia and allied reading difficulties and their relationship with mental health problems: A rapid review of evidence*. NIHR Children & Families Policy Research Unit, UCL and University College London.

Dell'Armo, K. & Tassé, M. J., 2024. Diagnostic overshadowing of psychological disorders in people with intellectual disability: A systematic review. *American Journal on Intellectual and Developmental Disabilities*, 129(2), pp. 116–134. https://doi.org/10.1352/1944-7558-129.2.116

Department of Health, 2018. *Estimating prevalence of autism spectrum disorders (ASD) in the Irish population: A review of and epidemiological data studies sources*. Dublin: Government of Ireland.

Doherty, M., McCowan, S., & Shaw, S. C., 2023. Autistic SPACE: A novel framework for meeting the needs of autistic people in healthcare settings. *British Journal of Hospital Medicine*, 84(4), pp. 1–9. https://doi.org/10.12968/hmed.2023.0006

Doyle, N., 2020. Neurodiversity at work: A biopsychosocial model and the impact on working adults. *British Medical Bulletin*, 135(1), pp. 108–125. https://doi.org/10.1093/bmb/ldaa021

Dube, S. R., Li, E. T., Fiorini, G., Lin, C., Singh, N., Khamisa, K., McGowan, J. & Fonagy, P., 2023. Childhood verbal abuse as a child maltreatment subtype: A systematic review of the current evidence. *Child Abuse and Neglect*, 144, p. 106394. https://doi.org/10.1016/j.chiabu.2023.106394

Duong, D. & Vogel, L., 2022. Untapped potential: Embracing neurodiversity in medicine. *Canadian Medical Association Journal (CMAJ)*, 194(27), pp. E951–E952. https://doi.org/10.1503/cmaj.1096006

Fitzpatrick, A., Wicks, R., Trembath, D. & Sulek, R., 2024, 18 March. New *guidelines for neurodiversity-affirming practice*. MJA InSight+.

Frawley, T., Gavin, B., Valeur, C. & Morin, K., 2023. Enhancing the nursing profession's awareness of neurodiversity. *Journal of Clinical Nursing*, 33(2), pp. 419–421.

Frawley, T., Meehan, A. & De Brún, A., 2018. Impact of organisational change for leaders in mental health. *Journal of Health Organization and Management*, 32(8), pp. 980–1001. https://doi.org/10.1108/JHOM0820180220

Fuller-Thomson, E., Carroll, S. Z. & Yang, W., 2018. Suicide attempts among individuals with specific learning disorders: An underrecognized issue. *Journal of Learning Disabilities*, 51(3), pp. 283–292. https://doi.org/10.1177/0022219417714776

Fung, L. K., 2021. *Neurodiversity: From phenomenology to neurobiology and enhancing technologies*. Arlington, VA: American Psychiatric Association Publishing.

Gagliano, A., Costanza, C., Di Modica, I., Carucci, S., Donno, F., Germanò, E., Abbate, C. S., Roccella, M. & Vetri, L., 2024. Neurodevelopmental disorders and suicide: A narrative review. *Journal of Clinical Medicine*, 13(6), p. 1627. https://doi.org/10.3390/jcm13061627

Georgiou, G. K., Parrila, R. & McArthur, G., 2024. Dyslexia and mental health problems: introduction to the special issue. *Annals of Dyslexia*, 74, pp. 1–3. https://doi.org/10.1007/s11881-024-00300-3

Grilli, S., D'Urso, G., Buonomo, I. et al., 2024. The mediating role of parent stress in the relationship between children's emotion dysregulation and ADHD risk: A pilot study. *Current Psychology*, 43, pp. 26144–26153.

Hamilton Clark, C. H., 2024. Dyslexia concealment in higher education: Exploring students' disclosure decisions in the face of UK universities' approach to dyslexia. *Journal of Research in Special Educational Needs*, 24(4), pp. 932–935. https://doi.org/10.1111/14713802.12683

Health Service Executive, 2020. *National working group, & college of psychiatrists of Ireland. Clinical advisory group. ADHD in adults: Attention deficit hyperactivity disorder: Model care for Ireland*. Dublin: Health Service Executive.

Hedlund, Å., 2023. Autistic nurses: Do they exist? *British Journal of Nursing*, 32(4), pp. 210–214. https://doi.org/10.12968/bjon.2023.32.4.210

Hendriksen, J. G., Peijnenborgh, J. C., Aldenkamp, A. P. & Vles, J. S., 2015. Diagnostic overshadowing in a population of children with neurological disabilities: A cross-sectional descriptive study on acquired ADHD. *European Journal of Paediatric Neurology*, 19(5), pp. 521–524. https://doi.org/10.1016/j.ejpn.2015.04.004

Hur, J., DeYoung, K. A., Islam, S., Anderson, A. S., Barstead, M. G. & Shackman, A. J., 2020. Social context and the real-world consequences of social anxiety. *Psychological Medicine*, 50(12), pp. 1989–2000. https://doi.org/10.1017/S0033291719002022

Jakobsson Støre, S., Van Zalk, N., Granander Schwartz, W., Nilsson, V. & Tillfors, M., 2024. The relationship between social anxiety disorder and ADHD in adolescents and adults: A systematic review. *Journal of Attention Disorders*, 28(9), pp. 1299–1319. https://doi.org/10.1177/10870547241247448

Johnson, J.-A. & Ahluwalia, S., 2025. Neurodiversity in the healthcare profession. *Postgraduate Medical Journal*, 101(1192), pp. 167–171.

Kargiotidis, A., Manolitsis, G., 2024. Are children with early literacy difficulties at risk for anxiety disorders in late childhood? *Annals of Dyslexia*, 74, pp. 82–96. https://doi.org/10.1007/s11881-023-00291-7

Kessler, R. C., Adler, L., Barkley, R., Biederman, J., Conners, C. K., Demler, O., Faraone, S. V., Greenhill, L. L., Howes, M. J., Secnik, K., Spencer, T., Ustun, T. B., Walters, E. E. & Zaslavsky, A. M., 2006. The prevalence and correlates of adult ADHD in the United States: Results from the national comorbidity survey replication. *American Journal of Psychiatry*, 163(4), pp. 716–23. https://doi.org/10.1176/ajp.2006.163.4.716

Lai, M. C., Kassee, C., Besney, R., Bonato, S., Hull, L., Mandy, W., Szatmari, P. & Ameis, S. H., 2019. Prevalence of co-occurring mental health diagnoses in the autism population: A systematic review and meta-analysis. *The Lancet Psychiatry*, 6(10), pp. 819–829. https://doi.org/10.1016/S2215-0366(19)30289-5

Lipinski, S., Boegl, K., Blanke, E. S., Suenkel, U. & Dziobek, I., 2022. A blind spot in mental healthcare? Psychotherapists lack education and expertise for the support of adults on the autism spectrum. *Autism*, 26(6), pp. 1509–1521. https://doi.org/10.1177/13623613211057973

Lipsky, M., 1980. *Street level bureaucracy: Dilemmas of the individual in public services.* Russell Sage Foundation.

Loomes, R., Hull, L. & Mandy, W., 2017. What is the male-to-female ratio in autism spectrum disorder? A systematic review and meta-analysis. *Journal of the American Academy of Child and Adolescent Psychiatry*, 56(6), pp. 466–474. https://doi.org/10.1016/j.jaac.2017.03.013

Lynch, S., McDonnell, T., Leahy, D., Gavin, B. & McNicholas, F., 2023. Prevalence of mental health disorders in children and adolescents in the Republic of Ireland: A systematic review. *Irish Journal of Psychological Medicine*, 40(1), pp. 51–62. https://doi.org/10.1017/ipm.2022.46

Makanadar, A., 2024. Neuro-adaptive architecture: Buildings and city design that respond to human emotions, cognitive states. *Research in Globalization*, 8, Article 100222.

Mancini, V. O., Licari, M. K., Alvares, G. A., McQueen, M. C., McIntyre, S., Reynolds, J. E., Reid, S. L., Spittle, A. J. & Williams, J., 2024. Psychosocial wellbeing, parental concerns, and familial impact of children with developmental coordination disorder. *Research in Developmental Disabilities*, 144, p. 104659. https://doi.org/10.1016/j.ridd.2023.104659

McArthur, G. M., Doust, A., Banales, E., Robidoux, S. & Kohnen, S., 2024. Are comorbidities of poor reading related to elevated anxiety in children? *Annals of Dyslexia*, 74(5), pp. 47–65. https://doi.org/10.1007/s11881-023-00292-6

Milton, D., 2012. On the ontological status of autism: The "double empathy problem". *Disability and Society*, 27(6), pp. 883–887. https://doi.org/10.1080/09687599.2012.710008

Moore, S., Kinnear, M. & Freeman, L. 2020. Autistic doctors: Overlooked assets to medicine. *The Lancet Psychiatry*, 7(4), pp. 306–307. https://doi.org/10.1016/S2215-0366(20)30087-0

Mosner, M. G., Kinard, J. L., Shah, J. S., McWeeny, S., Greene, R. K., Lowery, S. C., Mazefsky, C. A. & Dichter, G. S., 2019. Rates of co-occurring psychiatric disorders in autism spectrum disorder using the mini-international neuropsychiatric interview. *Journal of Autism and Developmental Disorders*, 49(9), pp. 3819–3832. https://doi.org/10.1007/s10803-019-04090-1

Murphy, K., 2023. The [DIS] advantage of studying higher education (HE) with Dyslexia. *Journal of Franco-Irish Studies*, 7(1), Article 7. https://doi.org/10.21427/EMP6KZ6

Nash, M., 2014. Mental health service users experiences of diabetes care by mental health nurses: An exploratory study. *Journal of Psychiatric and Mental Health Nursing*, 21(6), pp. 479–485. https://doi.org/10.1111/jpm.12104

Nash, M., 2022. Examining the preventive health-screening activities of mental health nurses. *Mental Health Practice,* 25(5), pp. 18–26. https://doi.org/10.7748/mhp.2022.e1576

Nash, M., D'Astoli, P. & Molloy, R., 2024. Preventing diagnostic overshadowing to improve the physical health of people with severe mental illness. *Mental Health Practice,* 27(6), pp. 33–41. https://doi.org/10.7748/mhp.2024.e1707

National Institute for Healthcare and Excellence, 2021. *Autism spectrum disorder in adults: diagnosis and management.* Online. Guidance | NICE.

NHS England, 2023. *A national framework to deliver improved outcomes in allage autism assessment pathways: Guidance for integrated care boards.* NHS England.

O'Dea, Á., Stanley, M., Coote, S. & Robinson, K., 2021. Children and young people's experiences of living with developmental coordination disorder/dyspraxia: A systematic review and metaethnography of qualitative research. *PLoS ONE,* 16(3), p. e0245738. https://doi.org/10.1371/journal.pone.0245738

Omer, S., Jijon, A.-M. & Leonard, H. C., 2019. Internalising symptoms in developmental coordination disorder: A systematic review and meta-analysis. *Journal of Child Psychology and Psychiatry,* 60(6), pp. 606–621. https://doi.org/10.1111/jcpp.13001

Polanczyk, G. V., Willcutt, E. G., Salum, G. A., Kieling, C. & Rohde, L. A., 2014. ADHD prevalence estimates across three decades: An updated systematic review and meta-regression analysis. *International Journal of Epidemiology,* 43(2), pp. 434–442. https://doi.org/10.1093/ije/dyt261

Purcell, C., Dahl, A., Gentle, J. et al., 2024. Harnessing real-life experiences: The development of guidelines to communicate research findings on developmental coordination disorder/dyspraxia. *Research Involvement and Engagement,* 10(1), Article 84. https://doi.org/10.1186/s40900-024-00611-0

Quinn, A., Wood, A., Lodge, K.-M. & Hollins, S., 2023. Listening to the experts: Person-centred approaches to supporting autistic people and people with an intellectual disability in the mental health system. *BJPsych Advances,* 29(5), pp. 308–317. https://doi.org/10.1192/bja.2023.31

Raines, J. & Netson-Amore, K., 2024. A - 61 lifelong intellectual developmental disorder and autism spectrum disorder diagnosed in early adulthood: Implications for a patient residing in frontier America. *Archives of Clinical Neuropsychology,* 39(7), p. 999.

Rapp, C. A. & Goscha, R. J., 2011. *The strengths model: A recovery-oriented approach to mental health services* (3rd ed.). New York: Oxford University Press.

Reavey, P. & Harding, K., 2018. *Design with people in mind: The sound issue. Design in mental health network.* Online. The-Sound-Issue.pdf

Reimherr, F. W., Marchant, B. K., Gift, T. E. & Steans, T. A., 2017. ADHD and anxiety: Clinical significance and treatment implications. *Current Psychiatry Reports,* 19(12), p. 109. https://doi.org/10.1007/s11920-017-0859-6. PMID: 29152677

Rutherford, M., Boilson, M., Johnston, L., MacIver, D., Curnow, E. & Utley, I., 2023. *Adult neurodevelopmental pathways: Report on actions, outcomes and recommendations from pathfinder sites in Scotland. National autism implementation team.* Edinburgh: Government of Scotland.

Seaberg, M., 2018. Meet the nurse who's superpower is feeling your pain – literally. *Glamour.* Online. Available at: How mirror-touch synesthesia makes this nurse a superhero. *Glamour.*

Shaw, K. A., Williams, S., Patrick, M. E. et al., 2022. Prevalence and early identification of autism spectrum disorder among children aged 4 and 8 years — autism and developmental disabilities monitoring network. *MMWR Surveillance Summaries,* 74(SS-2), pp. 1–22. https://doi.org/http://dx.doi.org/10.15585/mmwr.ss7402a1

Shaw, S. C. K., Doherty, M. & Anderson, J. L., 2023. The experiences of autistic medical students: A phenomenological study. *Medical Education,* 57(10), pp. 971–979. https://doi.org/10.1111/medu.15119

Spain, D., Sin, J., Linder, K. B., McMahon, J. & Happé, F., 2018. Social anxiety in autism spectrum disorder: A systematic review. *Research in Autism Spectrum Disorders*, 52, pp. 51–68. https://doi.org/10.1016/j.rasd.2018.04.007

Swedo, E. A., D'Angelo, D. V., Fasula, A. M., Clayton, H. B. & Ports, K. A., 2023. Associations of adverse childhood experiences with pregnancy and infant health. *American Journal of Preventative Medicine*, 64(4), pp. 512–524. https://doi.org/10.1016/j.amepre.2022.10.017

Sweetmore, V., 2021. Mental health nursing and autism: I am a mental health nurse so why did it take me so long to realize I'm autistic? *Journal of Psychiatric and Mental Health Nursing*, 29(6), pp. 770–773. https://doi.org/10.1111/jpm.12762

Totaforti, S., 2018. Applying the benefits of biophilic theory to hospital design. *City, Territory and Architecture*, 5(1), pp. 1–9. https://doi.org/10.1186/s40410-018-0077

Vieira, A. P. A., Peng, P., Antoniuk, A., DeVries, J., Rothou, K., Parrila, R. & Georgiou, G., 2024. Internalizing problems in individuals with reading, mathematics and unspecified learning difficulties: A systematic review and meta-analysis. *Annals of Dyslexia*, 74(1), pp. 4–26. https://doi.org/10.1007/s11881-023-00294-4

Wilmot, A., Hasking, P., Leitão, S., Hill, E. & Boyes, M., 2023. Understanding mental health in developmental dyslexia: A scoping review. *International Journal of Environmental Research and Public Health*, 20(2), p. 1653. https://doi.org/10.3390/ijerph20021653

Wilmot, A., Hasking, P., Leitao, S., Hill, E. & Boyes, M., 2024. Understanding mental health in developmental dyslexia through a neurodiversity lens: The mediating effect of school connectedness on anxiety, depression and conduct problems. *Dyslexia: An International Journal of Research and Practice*, 30(3), p. e1775. https://doi.org/10.1002/dys.1775

Wymbs, B. T., Pelham, W. E. Jr., Molina, B. S., Gnagy, E. M., Wilson, T. K. & Greenhouse, J. B., 2008. Rate and predictors of divorce among parents of youths with ADHD. *Journal of Consulting and Clinical Psychology*, 76(5), pp. 735–744. https://doi.org/10.1037/a0012719

Xiao, P., Zhu, K., Feng, Y., Jiang, Q., Xiang, Z., Zhang, Q., Wu, X., Fan, Y., Zou, L., Xiao, H. & Song, R., 2023. Associations between dyslexia and children's mental health: Findings from a follow-up study in China. *Psychiatry Research*, 324, p. 115188. https://doi.org/10.1016/j.psychres.2023.115188

Zaragas, H., Fragkomichelaki, O., Geitona, M. et al., 2023. The effects of physical activity in children and adolescents with developmental coordination disorder. *Neurology International*, 15(3), pp. 804–820.

Zeidan, J., Fombonne, E., Scorah, J., Ibrahim, A., Durkin, M. S., Saxena, S., Yusuf, A., Shih, A. & Elsabbagh, M., 2022. Global prevalence of autism: A systematic review update. *Autism Research*, 15(5), pp. 778–790. https://doi.org/10.1002/aur.2696

Chapter 5

Adult Attention-Deficit Hyperactivity Disorder (ADHD) and Co-Occurring Mood and Anxiety Disorders

Dimitrios Adamis

Introduction

Attention-deficit hyperactivity disorder (ADHD) is a childhood-onset disorder with a prevalence of around 5–7% in childhood (Polanczyk et al., 2014), reducing to 2–5% among adults (Kooij et al., 2010). In adults, ADHD is often co-occurring with other psychiatric disorders, more often mood and anxiety disorders (Bitter et al., 2019; Adamis et al., 2023). It is important to understand the co-occurrence of adult ADHD with other psychiatric disorders because this can increase diagnostic accuracy and avoid misdiagnoses (as there is an overlap of symptoms), optimise treatment strategies, improve patient engagement, and have better outcomes. In the first part of this chapter, some definitions of the terms of comorbidity and co-occurrence/coexistence will be given, as well as some basic epidemiological definitions, which will help the reader to clarify and better understand the second part of the chapter in which the co-occurrence of ADHD with mood and anxiety disorders will be examined. The second part of this chapter focuses only on those two specific disorders mainly because they co-occur more often with ADHD in adults. For each, updated reviews of research in epidemiological studies, possible explanations or theories for the co-occurrences, and possible clinical strategies for prevention/treatment (if and when applicable), will be provided. Other chapters in this book have addressed the non-clinical aspects of these areas, and therefore, this chapter will not rehash these discussions. This chapter is not attempting to counter or detract from these discussions. Quite the opposite, it is written to complement these shifts in ideas and aims to provide a clinical voice as a means to stitch our knowledge together. The terms disorder and, indeed, other clinical language may be used, but this is primarily in response to long-standing terms that are now being questioned. As such, all efforts have been made to adopt an affirmative approach to understandings and practices that are within the clinical space.

DOI: 10.4324/9781003495949-6

On Definitions and Biases: Theories and Definitions about Comorbidity and Co-Occurrence

Comorbidity

Comorbidity is a relatively new concept introduced by Feinstein in 1970 under general medicine to define the co-occurrence of two medical diseases, which can synergistically alter the time of detection of the disease, the prognosis, the treatment, and the outcome of a patient (Feinstein, 1970). In psychiatry, it was first introduced during the 1980s, and at the outset, it was defined as the coexistence of one medical disease with a psychiatric disorder, but later, the definition included the coexistence of more than one psychiatric disorder (Plana-Ripoll et al., 2019; Nordgaard et al., 2023). According to Feinstein, comorbidity implies a distinct new clinical disease on top of the existing (index) disease or medical condition, which has to fulfil two diagnostic principles: "toponymy" (anatomical area) and "chronometric reasoning" (the new disorder needs to be connected chronically, either prior to or concurrently with, the index disease, and to impact the natural course of the index disease). In addition, to qualify a new disease as comorbid, this new medical condition must have either known aetiology and/or defined pathology (Feinstein, 1970). With the last postulation, the problems of the term comorbidity in psychiatry begin. To qualify as distinct additional clinical entities (according to Feinstein), mental disorders must have either known aetiology or circumscribed pathology. However, for most mental disorders, if not for all, known aetiology does not exist (thus the reason that they are called disorders and not diseases or illnesses). Further, mental disorders do not have restricted psychopathology, and there is overlap of symptoms among different disorders. Indeed, the Diagnostic and Statistical Manual of Mental Disorders (DSM-5-TR) states:

> Despite the categorical framework, it is important to recognise that in DSM-5 there is no assumption that each category of mental disorder is a completely discrete entity with absolute boundaries dividing it from other mental disorders or from no mental disorder.
> (American Psychiatric Association, 2022, p. 16)

Therefore, at the theoretical level (at least) as opposed to general medicine, comorbidity of mental disorders cannot exist (See Valderas et al., 2009; Nordgaard et al., 2023; Ghaemi, 2019, pp. 209–230). To overcome this problem, other theoretical frameworks have been proposed, like the one from First (2005). First (2005) accepted that there are co-occurrences among psychiatric disorders, but the lack of a clear definition reflects the inability of psychiatry to provide a single diagnosis to account for all symptoms. Therefore, he proposed a distinction between three types of psychiatric comorbidity: (a) *true comorbidity* that fulfils Feinstein's requirement of distinct additional clinical entities, for example, delirium due to urine infection co-occurring with Alzheimer's disease, is a true comorbidity; (b) *artefactual comorbidity* which is the consequence of the classification systems which split diagnostic entities into many specific narrowly defined disorders, for example, substance dependence (each substance receive a separate diagnosis instead of one multi-substance dependency); and (c) *spurious comorbidity* when two disorders share symptoms in common. Thus, First argues that comorbidity in psychiatry does not imply the presence of multiple diseases or dysfunctions but is merely of the form of artefactual comorbidity.

Although a theoretical framework is lacking, the situation becomes more complicated when it comes to diagnosis and treatment, especially pharmacologically. Traditionally, since the Kraepelinian era, psychiatry has followed a hierarchical diagnostic framework; however, with the last two editions of DSM, this tends to be abandoned, leaving more room for *spurious comorbidity*. In the DSM system, all diagnoses are created equal, and clinicians are encouraged to diagnose as many disorders as possible. In practice, multiple drugs are given for multiple disorders; thus "comorbidities" lead to polypharmacy despite the fact that the second disorder may be a different label for many of the same symptoms (Ghaemi, 2019). In addition, the lack of a hierarchical diagnostic approach can also lead to false genetic heritability. For instance, in ADHD, a very high heritability of around 80% is reported (Faraone and Larsson, 2019), similar to bipolar disorder (Barnett and Smoller, 2009) and schizophrenia (Trifu et al., 2020), which are the only two other major psychiatric illnesses with such a high heritability. However, adults with ADHD who participated in those studies can also be diagnosed with bipolar disorder and still be included in the genetic studies of ADHD, or vice versa. In other words, the "comorbidity" of bipolar disorder (which shares many symptoms of ADHD) is not an exclusion criterion for diagnosing adult ADHD and including such "ADHD patients" in genetic studies can increase the heritability. If an empirically based diagnostic hierarchy was used, then the apparently high genetic heritability of adult ADHD could simply reflect the underlying primary disease of bipolar disorder (Ghaemi, 2019). Indeed, recent studies estimate the proportion of heritability in ADHD based on single-nucleotide polymorphism variants (SNPs) at 22% (Grimm et al., 2020).

Furthermore, especially for ADHD, the DSM-5-TR, using the criterion E, allows the exclusion of ADHD during psychotic disorder or schizophrenia or if the symptoms can be better explained by another mental disorder; so in this case, it is using the hierarchical diagnostic model. However, as is evident from a few lines after that, it allows the comorbidity of ADHD with other organic syndromes with a known cause, (e.g., fragile X or 22q11 deletion syndrome), which in fact violates the diagnostic hierarchy principle (organic first). Therefore, in the space of few lines, the DSM-5-TR accepts and at the same time rejects the use of diagnostic hierarchy by accepting the second level of hierarchy (e.g., schizophrenia) as a reason for the exclusion of ADHD diagnosis.

In addition, a recent theoretical framework that is more relevant to the present work is the one suggested by Nordgaard et al. (2023). Nordgaard and colleagues suggest that Feinstein's concept of comorbidity and his differential diagnostic principles need to be abandoned in psychiatry, given that known aetiology and bounded pathology cannot adequately qualify mental disorders as distinct additional clinical entities. Thus, they suggested that a distinction between *trait* and *state* conditions can be used in determining whether a patient's symptomatology amounts to a distinct clinical entity in addition to the index disorder. As *trait* conditions, they define the mental disorders that are long-lasting even where their symptoms fluctuate; for instance, ADHD, schizophrenia, personality disorders, and so on. As *state* conditions, they define the mental disorders that are presented in one or more restricted episodes, for example, major depression. Thus, comorbidity can be defined as a *trait* and *state* condition that co-occur. However, this model still has difficulties if two *state* conditions co-occur, for example, ADHD and personality disorder. Can they be defined as comorbidity according to this model?

Co-Occurrence

Co-occurrence is another term that is used alternatively to describe disorders that frequently occur together and that may or may not be comorbid. This term is used more often to avoid the term "morbid", as some conditions in psychiatry are not necessarily morbid under the biopsychosocial model, for example, addiction and homelessness. Co-occurrence means that two disorders are present together, but we do not know, or we are uncertain if they act together or are independent (Valderas et al., 2009; Tyrer, 2017; Nordgaard et al., 2023). The term avoids the complications of the term comorbidity, but at the same time, because it has the potential to list every possible disorder or condition, assuming that they are independent and without using a hierarchical diagnostic model, it can increase the co-occurrence of disorders with false positive results (Lilienfeld, 2003; Hartman et al., 2023; Nordgaard et al., 2023). However, especially for developmental differences like ADHD, the term co-occurrence is preferable because it implies temporality and may reflect an underlying causality or even completed unrelated aetiologies (Kaplan et al., 2006).

Coexisting

Coexisting is also an alternative term to co-occurring, which is more regularly used in the recovery approach of psychiatry.

From the above, it seems that the term comorbidity, although helpful in general medicine, has no relevance and is misleading in psychiatry because (a) psychiatric disorders do not have distinct and well-known pathophysiologies and aetiologies, (b) the diagnostic criteria often change from edition to edition of DSM and ICD, and (c) when using the biopsychosocial model certain conditions in psychiatry are not "morbid" or necessarily disease or disorders but could also be social problems. Given that the term co-occurrence is neutral and does not imply either causality or independence of one condition to another (despite its problems with diagnostic accuracy), perhaps it is a preferable term for the time being. For this reason, it will be used also in this chapter. Further, some epidemiological issues about the co-occurrence of mental disorders will be briefly discussed below.

Epidemiological Issues

Screening Scales versus Diagnostic Scales

Accurate estimates of the prevalence of co-occurrence of adult ADHD with other psychiatric disorders are crucial for service planning and resource allocation, including the development of special ADHD clinics. However, the accuracy depends on many factors. For instance, the scales used for ADHD or other differences. Screening scales are faster and cheaper, but their accuracy is not always good and usually they report an increased prevalence, while diagnostic scales followed by detailed clinical examination are more accurate but are lengthy, expensive, and time-consuming (Adamis et al., 2022). Similarly, some scales are dichotomous (depression-no depression) while others allow a dimensional approach that measures, what is often called "severity", for example, the Hamilton Depression Rating Scale. Those severity scales can also be used as categorical if a cut-off point is applied. Therefore, depending on the cut-off point, the prevalence can change. In short, symptom overlap (as discussed above), classification, measurement errors, and scales used can affect the prevalence of the coexistence of adult ADHD with one or more other disorders (Klein and Riso, 1993; Lilienfeld, 2003; Hartman et al., 2023; Nordgaard et al., 2023).

Impact of the Setting

Setting can affect the prevalence of co-occurrence of two disorders. Generally, in population settings, the prevalence of adult ADHD is smaller, at around 2.5% (Simon et al., 2009), compared to clinical settings in which the prevalence of ADHD increases, for example, in outpatient psychiatric clinics, the prevalence of ADHD is up to 19.3% (Leung and Chan, 2017). Therefore, it is expected that the co-occurrence of other psychiatric disorders will increase in clinical psychiatric settings as well. Similarly, this percentage increases when examining selective populations. For instance, in a meta-analysis of 29 studies of adolescents and adults with various substance use disorders, the prevalence of ADHD was estimated at 23% (van Emmerik-van Oortmerssen et al., 2012), while a meta-analysis of outpatient psychiatric clinics showed a prevalence of 14.6% (Adamis et al., 2022). Thus, not only the prevalence is influenced by the setting, but also the nature of co-occurrence (e.g., in addiction services, it is more likely that a high percentage of addiction disorders will be found rather than depression or anxiety only). Furthermore, it has been shown that apart from the settings, registries that are often used to estimate the prevalence of co-occurrence may differ among themselves in registry characteristics, for example, focus on specific disorder(s), number of disorders registered (all or one to two being more important), the diagnostic method used, and the origin of the data (e.g., population or setting). This may also influence the prevalence and the type of co-occurrence (Schram et al., 2008). This highlights a complicated picture, with many moving parts and dependent variables, which, if altered, can change the entire perspective.

Biases in Epidemiological Samples Examining Co-Occurrence of Disorders

Perhaps the most important and most often unrecognised problem in epidemiological studies looking for co-occurrences is the selection biases (Lilienfeld, 2003). Given that most of the studies are conducted in clinical populations, two types of biases have been encountered. The first refers to the fact that individuals with multiple diagnoses are usually more functionally impaired and clinically present with more severe psychopathology. Thus, they are more likely to look for treatment and, therefore, present at clinics. In contrast, people with mild symptoms of one disorder may or may not seek treatment and are thus less likely to present at clinics. So, clinical samples are not representative and introduce biases towards the increased prevalence of co-occurring disorders. The second bias often introduced by the clinical samples is the *Berkson's bias* (Berkson, 1946). Berkson's bias refers to a type of *collider bias* (*or collider-stratification bias*) that occurs when there is a systematic difference between the characteristics of individuals included in a study and those who are excluded. This bias typically arises in case-control studies, particularly when the cases and controls are drawn from a hospital or clinical population, leading to distorted associations between variables (Westreich, 2012). The bias occurs because the sample in the study may not represent the general population. For instance, a study examines the relationship between alcohol use and mental disorders in an inpatient psychiatric population. Because alcohol abuse and mental health disorders often coexist in individuals hospitalised for psychiatric conditions, the study might find an artificially strong link between alcohol use and psychiatric disorders, even though the relationship might not be as pronounced in the general population.

To overcome those shortcomings and eliminate the biases, researchers need to choose participants from the general population rather than exclusively from hospital or clinical settings to ensure a more representative sample, to use in-depth clinical assessments rather than screening scales, and, in case-control studies, to match cases and controls based on key characteristics to control for underlying differences rather than simply demographic characteristics. Finally, it is important to use statistical techniques to adjust for any confounding variables that may arise from the selective nature of hospital-based sampling.

Co-Occurrence of Adult ADHD with Mood and Anxiety Disorders

Mood Disorders: Bipolar Type I and II, Major Depression, Persistent Depression, Cyclothymic Disorder, Premenstrual Dysphoric Disorder

Adult ADHD often co-occurs with mood disorders, including various types of bipolar (BP) and depressive conditions. This co-occurrence can make diagnosis and treatment more complex, as symptoms may overlap or mimic each other. Below is an overview of the co-occurrence of adult ADHD with specific mood disorders.

Bipolar (BP) Type I and II

The co-occurrence of adult ADHD with BP type I and II is relatively common, and both conditions share overlapping symptoms, such as impulsivity, mood swings, and irritability, which can make it challenging to differentiate them. BP is seen in about 5.1–47.1% of individuals with ADHD, and 9.5–21% of individuals with BP may have co-occurring ADHD, particularly those with a more severe course of the disorder, for example, earlier onset or more frequent episodes. The co-occurrence is more frequently observed in individuals with BP type II, which involves hypomanic episodes rather than full manic episodes (Katzman et al., 2017). In a recent meta-analysis of 71 studies, a rate of 7.95% (CI 5.31–11.06) of those diagnosed with ADHD were also diagnosed with BP and 17.11% (CI 13.05–21.59 %) of those diagnosed with BP also presented as ADHD (Schiweck et al., 2021). Furthermore, it was reported that the co-occurrence of ADHD did not differ between patients with BP type I or type II (Schiweck et al., 2021). Longitudinal studies of children with ADHD also highlighted a connection between ADHD and BP developed later in life, with a likelihood 7.9 times higher when compared to a control group of boys and 10 times higher for girls (Biederman et al., 2006, 2010). The likelihood of changes in BP in adolescents with major depression with or without ADHD was also investigated. Biederman and colleagues (2009) followed 168 adolescents with a history of major depression for seven years. In those with ADHD and depression, a manic episode occurred in 28% of cases, versus only 6% in those without ADHD (Biederman et al., 2009). A second study from a registry in Taiwan (Chen et al., 2015), based on ten years of follow-up, reported that 19% of patients with baseline ADHD during the period were also diagnosed with BP, versus 11% for the control group, with a 50% higher risk of developing BP after adjusting for several confounding factors among all psychiatric co-occurrence (Chen et al., 2015). Furthermore, family-based studies suggest a relative risk of about 2% for the coexisted phenotype in first-degree relatives (Faraone et al., 2012). Genetic studies also showed a genetic overlap between ADHD and BP (van Hulzen et al., 2017; Consortium, 2019). Symptoms that are similar to both disorders are impulsivity, restlessness, distractibility, fidgeting, hyperactivity, and mood instability. There are also important differences as ADHD traits tend to be more chronic, persistent, and stable over time and ADHD involves difficulties with attention, organisation, and focus, as well as impulsivity and hyperactivity. These presentations are generally consistent and not episodic, while mood episodes in BP are typically more episodic, with distinct periods of manic, hypomanic, or depressive episodes, which may last for days to weeks or longer. These episodes are more severe and typically involve significant changes in behaviour, energy, and functioning. In addition, age of onset differs between BP and ADHD. With ADHD, onset is usually during childhood (symptoms occurring before the age of 12), while the age of onset of BP peaks in late adolescence or early adulthood. Regarding the treatment of BP depression, the use of stimulants remains unclear, and concerns exist about the use of stimulants, which can increase the risk of mania/hypomania. In the case of a manic or hypomanic episode, it is typical to first treat BP with mood stabilisers and then to look at ADHD (Katzman et al., 2017). Therefore, generally, it is advised to first treat the BP and then move on to ADHD by adding specific ADHD medications such as methylphenidate, atomoxetine, or amphetamine salts, which have proven effective and well-tolerated in adults with ADHD. However, only a few studies have examined the efficacy and tolerability of these psychopharmacologic interventions in individuals with ADHD and co-occurring BP (Salvi et al., 2021).

In summary, adult ADHD and BP share common symptomatology and at times it is difficult to make differential diagnoses. However, there are population, clinical, genetic, and longitudinal studies that show that these two disorders can co-occur with resulting lower functionality, worse quality of life, and a higher number of mood episodes. There is not strong evidence of the best pharmacological treatment, but mood stabilisation should be the first goal of treatment and then the treatment of ADHD with stimulants or non-stimulant medications. However, a treatment-induced manic or hypomanic episode should always be a possibility.

Major Depressive Disorder (MDD)

MDD is characterised by a persistent feeling of sadness and low mood, loss of interest or pleasure in activities, along with other symptoms like changes in sleep, appetite, cognition, and concentration. Studies on the prevalence of ADHD in adults with MDD have reported rates ranging from 5% to 22%, and the prevalence of individuals with ADHD who receive a diagnosis of depression during their lifetime has been reported to be approximately 30–50% (Di Lorenzo et al., 2021). A recent meta-analysis indicates lower percentages, whereby the prevalence of ADHD and MDD in adulthood was reported to be 7% (CI 4–11) (Sandstrom et al., 2021). Regarding gender, there are conflicting results in the literature, but it seems that MDD and ADHD co-occurrence in adulthood did not differ between the two genders or perhaps is a little higher in females (Hartman et al., 2023). Both ADHD and MDD can feature concentration difficulties, lack of motivation, and feelings of restlessness or irritability. However, depression typically involves more pervasive feelings of hopelessness, while ADHD symptoms are more related to attention and executive function. In addition, both can contribute to low self-esteem, though for different reasons. ADHD-related difficulties may lead to chronic feelings of inadequacy in work and social settings, while depression can lead to a more pervasive sense of worthlessness. MDD co-occurring with ADHD can be more severe, more dysfunctional, resistant to treatment, and result in higher rates of suicidality (Di Lorenzo et al., 2021). Also, the co-occurrence of ADHD and MDD can severely affect an individual's overall quality of life more than either alone. Individuals who experience a co-occurrence are at greater risk of chronic stress, low life satisfaction, and poor mental health outcomes (McIntyre et al., 2010). Furthermore, several possible reasons have been suggested for the co-occurrence of ADHD and MDD. Family and twin studies have found that there are overlapping genetic risk factors for both, which may predispose individuals to experience both (Faraone and Larsson, 2019). Moreover, environmental risk factors, like childhood trauma and maltreatment, have been suggested as a link for the co-occurrence of ADHD and MDD (Dvir et al., 2014). Psychological factors have also been suggested as an explanation for the co-occurrence of ADHD and MDD, such as low self-esteem, poor social skills, and academic and occupational failure as a consequence of ADHD, which may, in later life, lead to depression (Henriksen et al., 2017).

Treating adults with both ADHD and MDD requires an integrated approach that addresses both simultaneously, including pharmacological interventions, psychotherapy, and lifestyle modifications. In terms of medication use, an antidepressant alongside an ADHD medication with careful management of side effects can ameliorate the symptoms/presentations. Serotonergic agents alone are not expected to improve ADHD symptoms, which typically respond to norepinephrine-reuptake inhibitors or stimulants. Therefore, a good choice is to use atomoxetine, which also has antidepressant effects, to avoid polypharmacy. Antidepressants such as venlafaxine, vortioxetine, duloxetine, viloxazine, and bupropion have also been evaluated as treatment options for ADHD, but there is not strong enough evidence about their efficacy for ADHD symptomatology in contrast to their efficacy as antidepressants (Nageye and Cortese, 2019; Ilipilla and Arnold, 2024). Alternate pharmacological strategies are a Selective Serotonin Reuptake Inhibitor (SSRI) or Serotonin-Norepinephrine Reuptake Inhibitor (SNRI) together with stimulant medications, which have been shown to be effective for the treatment of co-occurrence ADHD and MMD or anxiety (Katzman et al., 2017).

In conclusion, the co-occurrence of MDD and ADHD in adults is common and requires careful clinical attention. With an integrated approach to treatment, including pharmacological interventions, psychotherapy, and lifestyle modifications, individuals can manage the presentation and symptoms of both and improve overall their quality of life.

Persistent Depressive Disorder (PDD)/Dysthymia

Persistent depressive disorder (a merging of previous definitions of chronic major depressive disorder and dysthymic disorder in the current DSM-5-TR) is a chronic form of depression lasting for at least two years, with symptoms that are less severe but more enduring than major depression. There is an overlap of presentation/ symptoms of PDD with ADHD, which includes the chronicity of both, and can contribute to persistent feelings of low mood, fatigue, and difficulties with concentration and motivation. Difficulties with planning, organising, and completing tasks are also evident in both, but these difficulties may stem from different underlying processes (e.g., motivation issues with PDD versus attention issues with ADHD). The distinction between them is that PDD typically involves a more enduring, subtle depressive state, while in ADHD, depressive symptoms do not have that enduring aspect, and ADHD also manifests mainly with presentations of inattention and hyperactivity and impulsivity rather than depression. Another distinction is the age of onset. Typically, ADHD presents in childhood, whereas PDD presents in adolescence or later in life. The prevalence of co-occurrence varies from study to study, and rates from 17.4% to 22.6% of PDD are reported in adults with ADHD, while a rate of 12.8% of ADHD was reported in those diagnosed with dysthymia/PDD. (Goodman, 2009; Ómarsdóttir et al., 2021). The presence of PDD in individuals with ADHD may lead to a more persistent and complicated clinical course and greater impairment in daily functioning, including difficulties in work, school, relationships, and overall well-being. As for MDD, several possible reasons have been suggested to explain the co-occurrence of ADHD and PDD – genetic, environmental, and psychological – however, the evidence has been weak in terms of aetiological factors for co-occurrence until now. Regarding treatment, several strategies have been suggested. For instance, Goodman (2009) refers to the Texas Algorithm, stating that in adults, the most severe disorder should be treated first and the ADHD last, but in children it is recommended the ADHD be addressed first. The reason given for this is that the clinician should avoid any exacerbation of a manic episode by using ADHD medication in a case of underlying, untreated BP in adults. However, this could happen with any antidepressant, so in any case, close monitoring is needed even if stimulants or atomoxetine are used in treating ADHD and PDD. Nonetheless, the pharmacological treatment of PDD alone is difficult and a combination of different medications may be needed. Therefore, it was suggested the opposite strategy be employed; treat the ADHD presentation first and then administer antidepressants (Regnart et al., 2017).

In summary, the co-occurrence of PDD and ADHD is not uncommon, and it can significantly impact an individual's emotional, cognitive, and social functioning. Accurate diagnosis and careful, tailored treatment plans are essential for addressing both effectively.

Cyclothymic Disorder (CD)

CD is characterised by periods of hypomanic symptoms and depressive symptoms lasting for at least two years, but these symptoms do not meet the full criteria for a manic episode or major depression. There is limited data on CD's co-occurrence with ADHD in adulthood, but one study reports a prevalence rate of 23.8% (Brancati et al., 2021). Both ADHD and CD involve mood swings and impulsivity, though cyclothymia has more defined episodic mood fluctuations compared to the chronic pattern of ADHD. In addition, diagnosis is often more difficult as CD may be identified as emotional dysregulation and/or as cyclothymic temperament, which can both coexist with adult ADHD (Eich et al., 2014; Unal, 2024). Therefore, careful diagnosis is important because this has implications for treatment. The management of ADHD and CD in tandem requires a careful balance of medication to avoid worsening either. For instance, stimulants or non-stimulants (such as atomoxetine) are often used in ADHD management, but caution is necessary for individuals with CD, as these medications may potentially exacerbate mood swings or lead to hypomanic symptoms. A study (Mauer et al., 2023) reported that in amphetamine-treated cases, mood/anxiety symptoms worsened notably in 27% of the sample, whereas 24% had moderate improvement in cognition. This indicates that the treatment needs to be personalised, and no standard pharmacological treatment has been established or approved for CD yet (Bielecki and Gupta, 2023). Mood stabilisers (e.g., lithium or valproate) or atypical antipsychotics may be used to treat the mood instability in cyclothymia. Separately ADHD stimulants or non-stimulants can also be prescribed. Cognitive Behavioural Therapy (CBT) can be helpful for both ADHD and CD, especially in terms of managing emotional dysregulation, improving attention and organisation, and addressing mood fluctuations. Psychoeducation and perhaps InterPersonal and Social Rhythm Therapy (IPSRT), which are used in BP, have also been shown to be beneficial. ·

The co-occurrence of CD and ADHD can present significant diagnostic and treatment challenges due to overlapping symptoms such as mood instability, impulsivity, and attention difficulties. This combination can lead to more severe functional impairment, requiring careful and individualised treatment strategies that address both mood regulation and attention difficulties. Accurate diagnosis and a holistic treatment approach, including a combination of medication, therapy, and lifestyle interventions, are key to effectively manage both ADHD and CD when they co-occur.

Premenstrual Dysphoric Disorder (PMDD)

PMDD is a severe form of Premenstrual Syndrome (PMS), with mood swings, irritability, fatigue, and depression occurring during the luteal phase of the menstrual cycle. The DSM-5-TR requires at least one of the following core emotional symptoms: (i) affective lability, (ii) irritability or anger, (iii) depressed mood, or (iv) anxiety. Supporting symptoms include poor concentration, lethargy, overeating, hypersomnia, and physical symptoms such as breast tenderness, swelling, and joint pain (American Psychiatric Association, 2022). ADHD and PMDD can co-occur, but available data is limited. A study reported co-occurrence of PMDD and ADHD at the rate of 45.5% (Dorani et al., 2021), while another small study (Lin et al., 2024) has shown that women with co-occurrence of ADHD and PMDD had greater everyday memory problems and difficulties maintaining focused attention compared to those with only PMDD. Both disorders ADHD and PMMD can involve irritability, mood swings, and concentration difficulties, but PMDD is specifically tied to the menstrual cycle, while ADHD is lifelong. Although the mechanisms behind the co-occurrence are not clear, sex hormones and central neurotransmitters are most likely involved. Camara et al. (2022) attempted a meta-analysis to find a relationship between sex hormones and ADHD, but there was an inadequate number of studies, and those that were found were contradictory and thus inconclusive. A number of studies have shown a change in ADHD presentation during the menstrual cycle (e.g., Roberts et al., 2018), and hormones like oestradiol and progesterone in higher levels have generally been linked to enhanced executive function and attention (e.g., Hatta and Nagaya, 2009). Therefore, it is expected, although not fully investigated, that further research will point to a change in ADHD presentation during the menstrual cycle. In addition, because levels of oestrogen and progesterone fluctuate during the menstrual cycle and differently influence the effect of stimulant drugs at different points of the month in adolescent and adult females (Kok et al., 2020), higher levels of medication may be needed. In a case study of nine women with ADHD and co-occurring mood disorders, including PMDD, an elevated dose of stimulants was given during the premenstrual period, showing improvements and good tolerability (de Jong et al., 2023). However, more work is needed to establish rates of co-occurrence, more precise diagnosis, and differential diagnosis before attempting any treatment.

The above highlights that the co-occurrence of adult ADHD with mood disorders is very common, and managing these conditions requires careful diagnosis and an integrated treatment approach. Recognising the overlap in symptoms is essential for effective treatment planning, as addressing one condition may improve the symptoms of the other.

Anxiety Disorders: Generalised Anxiety Disorder, Social Anxiety Disorder

The co-occurrence of ADHD and anxiety disorders (ADs) is a common phenomenon. Research suggests that individuals with ADHD are at a higher risk of developing an anxiety disorder, but at the same time people diagnosed with anxiety disorder may have underlying ADHD, and often the anxiety is the primary reason for referral (Katzman et al., 2017). The prevalence of ADs in ADHD patients is estimated at about 25–50% (Koyuncu et al., 2022) and the prevalence of adult ADHD in patients with ADs is around 28% (Van Ameringen et al., 2011). People with co-occurrence of ADHD and ADs tend to present with more severe anxiety symptoms, more severe ADHD presentation, an earlier age of onset, and a higher co-occurrence of other mental health disorders (Koyuncu et al., 2022). Adults with both ADHD and ADs are often characterised by poor occupational outcomes, with higher unemployment, higher rates of sick leave, being recipients of disability benefits or social welfare, and having higher rates of prison experience (Halmøy et al., 2009). ADs and ADHD share symptoms/presentations such as restlessness, attentional problems, and emotional dysregulation. Both ADHD and ADs can result in a feeling of restlessness and difficulty concentrating. For example, a person with anxiety might have racing thoughts, which makes it difficult to focus, while a person with ADHD may have difficulty sustaining attention and staying organised. Also, both can lead to difficulty managing emotions. ADs often involve intense emotional responses to perceived threats, while ADHD can cause impulsivity and difficulty managing frustration or anger. It is possible that such overlapping features can lead the clinician to not recognise the presence of ADHD in an individual suffering from ADs. An interesting study that addressed the overlap between ADHD and generalised anxiety disorder (GAD) in adults found that 75% of individuals continued to meet ADHD criteria and 76% continued to meet GAD criteria after the removal of common symptomatology (Milberger et al., 1995). It has been suggested that in people suffering from ADs, ADHD is recognised later because of the inhibitory effect of anxiety over impulsivity (Schatz and Rostain, 2006).

Generalised Anxiety Disorder (GAD)

GAD is characterised by excessive, uncontrollable worry about a variety of topics, such as work, health, social interactions, and daily tasks. Individuals with GAD often experience physical symptoms like restlessness, muscle tension, fatigue, and difficulty concentrating. Also, individuals with GAD present with emotional dysregulation, due to persistent worry and fear, and can experience difficulty relaxing, which can lead to irritability. Like ADHD, GAD has a significant impact on quality of life and social functioning, especially when GAD co-occurs with mood disorders and other anxiety disorders (Fuller-Thomson et al., 2022). The co-occurrence of ADHD and GAD is estimated at 8–15.1% in community samples (Kessler et al., 2006; Hesson and Fowler, 2018), while in selected samples, for example, in hospital psychiatric patients, this rate increases up to 47.4% (Woon and Zakaria, 2019). Explanations about this high co-occurrence have not been established yet. One hypothesis suggests that both ADHD and GAD are distinct, and that the co-occurrence is simply by chance or by referral bias (Milberger et al., 1995). However, the rate of co-occurrence is too high to only be explained by chance or referral bias alone (Weiss et al., 2011). Another hypothesis suggests that the overlap between ADHD and GAD can result from common neurobiological underpinnings, particularly at the level of the prefrontal cortex. The impairment of prefrontal cortex activity determines inattention, distraction, impulsivity, hyperactivity, and dysfunctional emotional control. Although the amygdala is considered the main structure for anxiety disorders, recently, the dorsal medial prefrontal cortex–amygdala circuit has been recognised as a central node of a broader anxiety circuit involved in both social and generalised anxiety (Robinson et al., 2014). In the same biological line, it was proposed that this co-occurrence may be partially explained by genetic factors. The genetic components of ADHD and anxiety may share some commonalities. Therefore, they may coexist, but transmission of the genetic elements occurs independently (Weiss et al., 2011). The third hypothesis is that one leads to the development of the other. In other words, anxiety may occur as a result of persistent negative experiences caused by the lived experience of ADHD, like efforts with organisation, time management, and consistent performance in various areas of life. Fear of failure, negative evaluation from others, and increased stress related to unmet goals can contribute to the onset of GAD in individuals with ADHD. On the other hand, individuals with GAD may develop symptoms that resemble or heighten those of ADHD, such as difficulty focusing, restlessness, and impulsivity, particularly when their anxiety levels are high. Anxiety-driven cognitive overload can make it challenging to stay on task, leading to symptoms that appear similar to ADHD (Reimherr et al., 2017; Koyuncu et al., 2022). Given the close association of ADHD with anxiety, it has been suggested that ADHD combined with anxiety might be regarded as a distinct ADHD subtype (Jensen et al., 2001; Reimherr et al., 2017). Regarding pharmacological approaches when GAD or anxiety co-occur with ADHD, the most impairing disorder should be treated first. Milder anxiety disorders may respond to the treatment of ADHD and, therefore, can be treated at the same time as ADHD (Kooij et al., 2019). It is supported that stimulants for ADHD can increase the levels of anxiety, but there is some data supporting a reduction of anxiety with ADHD management (Bloch et al., 2017; Koyuncu et al., 2022). If stimulants are not tolerated, switching to atomoxetine is a solution. Atomoxetine has been associated with improvements in both ADHD and GAD or anxiety (Kooij et al., 2019; Koyuncu et al., 2022). Several studies have reported the efficacy on functional outcomes, of co-administration of an SSRI, such as sertraline or escitalopram, which are commonly prescribed for GAD, with a stimulant prescribed for ADHD co-occurring with GAD or anxiety or depressive symptoms (Katzman et al., 2017). In addition, it has been suggested that early detection and optimal support of those with ADHD through stimulants could reduce the risk of later development of anxiety and depressive disorders in adulthood (Biederman et al., 2009; Katzman et al., 2017). Apart from medication, psychotherapeutic interventions are also needed, with CBT or mindfulness having been shown to reduce symptoms of GAD, as well as occupational therapy for improving an individual's daily functioning. Indeed, medication alone cannot build skills such as planning, organisation, control of frustration, and study skills (Kooij et al., 2019) and, therefore, medication is but one step towards good outcomes for those with co-occurring GAD and ADHD.

The co-occurrence of ADHD and GAD is common, and the overlap of symptoms can complicate diagnosis and treatment. Both can exacerbate each other, creating emotional dysregulation, difficulty focusing, and increased stress. Proper diagnosis is crucial to ensure both are addressed effectively with a multidisciplinary treatment approach.

Social Anxiety Disorder (SAD)

SAD, or social phobia, is characterised by persistent fear or anxiety about social situations in which a person might be scrutinised or judged by others. This fear can be so intense that it leads to avoidance of social situations or extreme distress when interacting with others, although the affected person knows that the fear is exaggerated compared to the actual danger of the social situation. Physical symptoms can also be present, including sweating, trembling, rapid heart rate, blushing, or dry mouth when faced with social situations, which in turn increase avoidance (APA, 2022). However, a specific subgroup of people with social anxiety display impulsive actions, which can present as assertiveness, aggressiveness, or a willingness to take risks and has been described as a type of social anxiety characterised by anxiety-driven impulsivity (Tillfors et al., 2013).

The prevalence of ADHD in adults and adolescents with a diagnosis of SAD ranged from 1.1% to 72.3%, while the prevalence of SAD in adolescents and adults with ADHD ranged from 0.4% to 46.7% across the studies (Jakobsson Støre et al.,2024), and the predominantly inattentive type of ADHD was most often associated with SAD (Koyuncu et al., 2022). Thus, SAD and ADHD are often co-occurrent, but the potential links between the two disorders remain unknown (Koyuncu et al., 2019). The same authors (Koyuncu et al., 2019) proposed a causal relationship between SAD and ADHD, but also suggest that mediators like societal and environmental factors may be adding to social difficulties and the negative events caused by ADHD, which can lead to secondary development of SAD. However, they do not offer an explanation for the high rates of ADHD in populations diagnosed with SAD. Are they undiagnosed ADHD cases where the same link applies? According to another model, the "motivational model", children with ADHD do not have typical responses to cues for the consequences of their reward-seeking behaviour, which leads to impulsive and socially inappropriate behaviour and, as adolescents, may have an elevated risk of social rejection. This, in turn, might increase their vulnerability to develop SAD over time (Jakobsson Støre et al., 2024). Nevertheless, a recent systematic review showed that the co-occurrence of ADHD and SAD in adults exacerbates ADHD symptoms, leading to lower educational attainment, lower functioning, and greater and higher severity of symptoms of both ADHD and SAD, which in turn results in greater social difficulties (Jakobsson Støre et al., 2024).

Medications and psychotherapeutic interventions have been proposed as treatment approaches for the co-occurrence of ADHD and SAD. Stimulants (e.g., methylphenidate or amphetamines) are commonly prescribed for ADHD, but they can sometimes exacerbate anxiety as discussed above. Non-stimulant medications like atomoxetine or guanfacine may be used if anxiety is a significant issue. Also, SSRIs, such as sertraline or escitalopram, are often prescribed to treat SAD to reduce anxiety symptoms in combination with stimulants. CBT is effective for both ADHD and SAD and social skills training is an effective behaviour therapy for SAD. Mindfulness-based interventions have been shown to help both ADHD and SAD by fostering emotional regulation and reducing impulsivity in ADHD, while helping individuals manage anxiety and fear in social situations.

As with the GAD, SAD often co-occurs with ADHD. Impulsivity, distractibility, and poor social skills, associated with ADHD, can increase the likelihood of developing SAD, while social anxiety can exacerbate the social challenges of ADHD. As with other disorders, proper diagnosis and multidisciplinary management are essential for the reduction of symptoms and treatment for such co-occurrence.

From the above, it seems that the co-occurrence of ADHD and anxiety disorders is prevalent. However, caution is needed with the mood disorders discussed because the interpretation of the rates of co-occurrence can be misleading, especially in studies that investigate clinical populations. The potential for bias is a real risk that could lead to problematic research findings. The relationship between ADHD and anxiety is often bidirectional – ADHD can contribute to anxiety, and anxiety can exacerbate ADHD-like presentation. The underlying pathophysiological link(s) are still unknown. Effective treatment typically involves a multidisciplinary approach, including medication, psychotherapy, and occupational therapy.

Conclusions

In the first part of this chapter the difficulties to find a term suitable in psychiatry for the co-occurrence of two disorders has been discussed. The current co-occurrence term is preferable as it does not imply any relationship between the two. However, in the second part of the chapter, the potential underlying links between ADHD, mood, and anxiety disorders that may exist were discussed, but these have not been adequately proven as yet. Therefore, co-occurrence is not the perfect term but can be used for the time being as no better term is available. Similarly, in the first part of this chapter, the risk of potential bias in epidemiological studies, especially when clinical samples were investigated, was highlighted. This was obvious in the high rates of co-occurrence between ADHD and mood and anxiety disorders, outlined in the second part of the chapter. However, despite the high rates reported, little is really known about the co-occurrence identified. This has clinical implications for a more holistic diagnostic and therapeutic approach for individuals with ADHD.

References

Adamis, D., Flynn, C., Wrigley, M., Gavin, B. & McNicholas, F., 2022. ADHD in adults: A systematic review and meta-analysis of prevalence studies in outpatient psychiatric Clinics. *J Atten Disord*, 26, 1523–1534.

Adamis, D., Fox, N., de Camargo, M., Saleem, F., Gavin, B. & McNicholas, F., 2023. Prevalence of attention deficit hyperactivity disorder in an adult mental health service in the Republic of Ireland. *Int J Psychiatry Med*, 58, 130–144.

American Psychiatric Association, 2022. *Diagnostic and statistical manual of mental disorders (DSM-5-TR)*, Arlington, VA, US: American Psychiatric Publishing, Inc.

Barnett, H. & Smoller, W., 2009. The genetics of bipolar disorder. *Neuroscience*, 164, 331–343.

Berkson, J. 1946. Limitations of the application of fourfold table analysis to hospital data. *Biometrics*, 2, 47–53.

Biederman, J., Monuteaux, C., Mick, E., et al., 2006. Young adult outcome of attention deficit hyperactivity disorder: A controlled 10-year follow-up study. *Psychol Med*, 36, 167–179.

Biederman, J., Petty, R., Byrne, D., Wong, P., Wozniak, J. & Faraone, V., 2009. Risk for switch from unipolar to bipolar disorder in youth with ADHD: A long term prospective controlled study. *J Affect Disord*, 119, 16–21.

Biederman, J., Petty, R., Monuteaux, C., et al., 2010. Adult psychiatric outcomes of girls with attention deficit hyperactivity disorder: 11-year follow-up in a longitudinal case-control study. *Am J Psychiatry*, 167, 409–17.

Bielecki, E. & Gupta, V. 2023. *Cyclothymic disorder*. StatPearls [Internet]. https://www.ncbi.nlm.nih.gov/books/NBK557877/.

Bitter, I., Mohr, P., Balogh, L., et al., 2019. ADHD: A hidden comorbidity in adult psychiatric patients. *Atten Defic Hyperact Disord*, 11, 83–89.

Bloch, Y., Aviram, S., Segev, A., et al., 2017. Methylphenidate reduces state anxiety during a continuous performance test that distinguishes adult ADHD patients from controls. *J Atten Disord,* 21, 46–51.

Brancati, E., Barbuti, M., Schiavi, E., et al., 2021. Comparison of emotional dysregulation features in cyclothymia and adult ADHD. *Medicina (Kaunas),* 57.

Camara, B., Padoin, C. & Bolea, B., 2022. Relationship between sex hormones, reproductive stages and ADHD: A systematic review. *Archiv Women's Mental Health,* 25, 1–8.

Chen, H., Chen, S., Hsu, W., et al., 2015. Comorbidity of ADHD and subsequent bipolar disorder among adolescents and young adults with major depression: A nationwide longitudinal study. *Bipolar Disord,* 17, 315–22.

Consortium, 2019. Genomic relationships, novel loci, and pleiotropic mechanisms across eight psychiatric disorders. *Cell,* 179, 1469–1482.e11.

De Jong, M., Wynchank, D., van Andel, E., Beekman, F. & Kooij, S. 2023. Female-specific pharmacotherapy in ADHD: Premenstrual adjustment of psychostimulant dosage. *Front Psychiatry,* 14, 1306194.

Di Lorenzo, R., Balducci, J., Poppi, C., et al., 2021. Children and adolescents with ADHD followed up to adulthood: A systematic review of long-term outcomes. *Acta Neuropsychiatr,* 33, 283–298.

Dorani, F., Bijlenga, D., Beekman, F., van Someren, W, Kooij, J. S., 2021. Prevalence of hormone-related mood disorder symptoms in women with ADHD. *J Psychiatr Res,* 133, 10–15.

Dvir, Y., Ford, D., Hill, M. & Frazier, A., 2014. Childhood maltreatment, emotional dysregulation, and psychiatric comorbidities. *Harv Rev Psychiatry,* 22, 149–61.

Eich, D., Gamma, A., Malti, T., Vogtwehrli, M., Liebrenz, M., Seifritz, E. & Modestin, J., 2014. Temperamental differences between bipolar disorder, borderline personality disorder, and attention deficit/hyperactivity disorder: Some implications for their diagnostic validity. *J Affect Disord,* 169, 101–104.

Faraone, V., Biederman, J. & Wozniak, J., 2012. Examining the comorbidity between attention deficit hyperactivity disorder and bipolar I disorder: A meta-analysis of family genetic studies. *Am J Psychiatry,* 169, 1256–66.

Faraone, V. & Larsson, H., 2019. Genetics of attention deficit hyperactivity disorder. *Mol Psychiatry,* 24, 562–575.

Feinstein, R., 1970. The pre-therapeutic classification of co-morbidity in chronic disease. *J Chronic Dis,* 23, 455–468.

First, B., 2005. Mutually exclusive versus co-occurring diagnostic categories: The challenge of diagnostic comorbidity. *Psychopathology,* 38, 206–210.

Fuller-Thomson, E., Carrique, L. & Macneil, A., 2022. Generalized anxiety disorder among adults with attention deficit hyperactivity disorder. *J Affect Disorders,* 299, 707–714.

Ghaemi, S. N., 2019. *Clinical psychopharmacology: Principles and practice.* New York, NY: Oxford University Press.

Goodman, D., 2009. Adult ADHD and comorbid depressive disorders: Diagnostic challenges and treatment options. *CNS Spectr,* 14, 5–7; discussion 13–4.

Grimm, O., Kranz, M. & Reif, A., 2020. Genetics of ADHD: What should the clinician know? *Curr Psychiatry Rep,* 22, 18.

Halmøy, A., Fasmer, B., Gillberg, C. & Haavik, J., 2009. Occupational outcome in adult ADHD: Impact of symptom profile, comorbid psychiatric problems, and treatment: A cross-sectional study of 414 clinically diagnosed adult ADHD patients. *J Atten Disord,* 13, 175–87.

Hartman, A., Larsson, H., Vos, M., et al., 2023. Anxiety, mood, and substance use disorders in adult men and women with and without attention-deficit/hyperactivity disorder: A substantive and methodological overview. *Neurosci Biobehav Rev,* 151, 105209.

Hatta, T. & Nagaya, K., 2009. Menstrual cycle phase effects on memory and Stroop task performance. *Archiv Sex Behav*, 38, 821–827.

Henriksen, O., Ranøyen, I., Indredavik, S. & Stenseng, F., 2017. The role of self-esteem in the development of psychiatric problems: A three-year prospective study in a clinical sample of adolescents. *Child Adolesc Psychiatry Ment Health*, 11, 68.

Hesson, J. & Fowler, K., 2018. Prevalence and correlates of self-reported ADD/ADHD in a large national sample of canadian adults. *J Atten Disord*, 22, 191–200.

Ilipilla, G. & Arnold, E., 2024. The role of adrenergic neurotransmitter reuptake inhibitors in the ADHD armamentarium. *Expert Opin Pharmacother*, 25, 945–956.

Jakobsson Støre, S., Van Zalk, N., Granander-Schwartz, W., Nilsson, V. & Tillfors, M., 2024. The relationship between social anxiety disorder and ADHD in adolescents and adults: A systematic review. *J Atten Disord*, 28, 1299–1319.

Jensen, S., Hinshaw, P., Kraemer, C., et al., 2001. ADHD comorbidity findings from the MTA study: Comparing comorbid subgroups. *J Am Acad Child Adolesc Psychiatry*, 40, 147–58.

Kaplan, B., Crawford, S., Cantell, M., Kooistra, L. & Dewey, D. 2006. Comorbidity, co-occurrence, continuum: What's in a name? *Child Care Health Dev*, 32, 723–731.

Katzman, A., Bilkey, S., Chokka, R., Fallu, A. & Klassen, L. J., 2017. Adult ADHD and comorbid disorders: Clinical implications of a dimensional approach. *BMC Psychiatry*, 17, 302.

Kessler, C., Adler, L., Barkley, R., et al., 2006. The prevalence and correlates of adult ADHD in the United States: Results from the National Comorbidity Survey Replication. *Am J Psychiatry*, 163, 716–723.

Klein, N. & Riso, P., 1993. Psychiatric disorders: Problems of boundaries and comorbidity. In: Costello, G. (ed.) *Basic issues in psychopathology*. New York: Guilford.

Kok, M., Groen, Y., Fuermaier, M. & Tucha, O. 2020. The female side of pharmacotherapy for ADHD-A systematic literature review. *PLoS One*, 15, e0239257.

Kooij, S., Bejerot, S., Blackwell, et al., 2010. European consensus statement on diagnosis and treatment of adult ADHD: The European Network Adult ADHD. *BMC Psychiatry*, 10, 67.

Kooij, S., Bijlenga, D., Salerno, L., et al., 2019. Updated European consensus statement on diagnosis and treatment of adult ADHD. *Eur Psychiatry*, 56, 14–34.

Koyuncu, A., Ayan, T., Ince-Guliyev, E., Erbilgin, S., & Deveci, E., 2022. ADHD and anxiety disorder comorbidity in children and adults: Diagnostic and therapeutic challenges. *Curr Psychiatry Rep*, 24, 129–140.

Koyuncu, A., Ince, E., Ertekin, E., Çelebi, F., & Tükel, R., 2019. Is there a prodrom period in patients with social anxiety disorder? A discussion on the hypothesis of social anxiety disorder development secondary to attention-deficit/hyperactivity disorder. *ADHD Atten Deficit Hyperact Disord*, 11, 343–351.

Leung, M. & Chan, F., 2017. A cross-sectional cohort study of prevalence, co-morbidities, and correlates of attention-deficit hyperactivity disorder among adult patients admitted to the Li Ka Shing psychiatric outpatient clinic, Hong Kong. *East Asian Arch Psychiatry*, 27, 63–70.

Lilienfeld, O., 2003. Comorbidity between and within childhood externalizing and internalizing disorders: Reflections and directions. *J Abnorm Child Psychol*, 31, 285–291.

Lin, C., Long, Y., Ko, H. & Yen, Y., 2024. Comorbid attention deficit hyperactivity disorder in women with premenstrual dysphoric disorder. *J Womens Health (Larchmt)*, 33, 1267–1275.

Mauer, S., Ghazarian, G., & Ghaemi, N., 2023. Affective Temperaments misdiagnosed as adult attention deficit disorder: Prevalence and treatment effects. *J Nerv Ment Dis*, 211, 504–509.

McIntyre, S., Kennedy, H., Soczynska, K., et al., 2010. Attention-deficit/hyperactivity disorder in adults with bipolar disorder or major depressive disorder: Results from the international mood disorders collaborative project. *Prim Care Companion J Clin Psychiatry,* 12.

Milberger, S., Biederman, J., Faraone, V., Murphy, J. & Tsuang, T., 1995. Attention deficit hyperactivity disorder and comorbid disorders: Issues of overlapping symptoms. *Am J Psychiatry,* 152, 1793–1799.

Nageye, F. & Cortese, S., 2019. Beyond stimulants: A systematic review of randomised controlled trials assessing novel compounds for ADHD. *Expert Rev Neurother,* 19, 707–717.

Nordgaard, J., Nielsen, M., Rasmussen, R. & Henriksen, G., 2023. Psychiatric comorbidity: A concept in need of a theory. *Psychol Med,* 53, 5902–5908.

Ómarsdóttir, S., Kjartansdóttir, H., Magnússon, P., Ólafsdóttir, H., Sigurðsson, F., 2021. Adults referred to a national ADHD clinic in Iceland: Clinical characteristics and follow-up status. *Nord J Psychiatry,* 75, 559–567.

Plana-Ripoll, O., Pedersen, B., Holtz, Y., et al., 2019. Exploring comorbidity within mental disorders among a danish national population. *JAMA Psychiatry,* 76, 259–270.

Polanczyk, V., Willcutt, G., Salum, A., Kieling, C. & Rohde, A., 2014. ADHD prevalence estimates across three decades: An updated systematic review and meta-regression analysis. *Int J Epidemiol,* 43, 434–442.

Regnart, J., Truter, I. & Meyer, A., 2017. Critical exploration of co-occurring attention-deficit/ hyperactivity disorder, mood disorder and substance use disorder. *Expert Rev Pharmacoecon Outcomes Res,* 17, 275–282.

Reimherr, W., Marchant, K., Gift, E., Steans, A., 2017. ADHD and anxiety: Clinical significance and treatment implications. *Curr Psychiatry Rep,* 19, 109.

Roberts, B., Eisenlohr-Moul, T. & Martel, M., 2018. Reproductive steroids and ADHD symptoms across the menstrual cycle. *Psychoneuroendocrinology,* 88, 105–114.

Robinson, J., Krimsky, M., Lieberman, L., Allen, P., Vytal, K. & Grillon, C., 2014. Towards a mechanistic understanding of pathological anxiety: The dorsal medial prefrontal-amygdala 'aversive amplification' circuit in unmedicated generalized and social anxiety disorders. *Lancet Psychiatry,* 1, 294–302.

Salvi, V., Ribuoli, E., Servasi, M., Orsolini, L. & Volpe, U., 2021. ADHD and bipolar disorder in adulthood: Clinical and treatment implications. *Medicina (Kaunas),* 57.

Sandstrom, A., Perroud, N., Alda, M., Uher, R. & Pavlova, B., 2021. Prevalence of attention-deficit/hyperactivity disorder in people with mood disorders: A systematic review and meta-analysis. *Acta Psychiatr Scand,* 143, 380–391.

Schatz, D. B. & Rostain, A. L., 2006. ADHD with comorbid anxiety: A review of the current literature. *J Atten Disord,* 10, 141–149.

Schiweck, C., Arteaga-Henriquez, G., Aichholzer, M., et al., 2021. Comorbidity of ADHD and adult bipolar disorder: A systematic review and meta-analysis. *Neurosci Biobehav Rev,* 124, 100–123.

Schram, T., Frijters, D., Van-De Lisdonk, H., et al., 2008. Setting and registry characteristics affect the prevalence and nature of multimorbidity in the elderly. *J Clin Epidemiol,* 61, 1104–1112.

Simon, V., Czobor, P., Balint, S., Meszaros, A. & Bitter, I., 2009. Prevalence and correlates of adult attention-deficit hyperactivity disorder: Meta-analysis. *Br J Psychiatry,* 194, 204–211.

Tillfors, M., Mörtberg, E., Van-Zalk, N. & Kerr, M., 2013. Inhibited and impulsive subgroups of socially anxious young adults: Their depressive symptoms and life satisfaction. *Open Journal of Psychiatry,* 3, 195–201.

Trifu, C., Kohn, B., Vlasie, A. & Patrichi, E., 2020. Genetics of schizophrenia. *Exp Ther Med,* 20, 3462–3468.

Tyrer, P., 2017. Comorbidity, consanguinity and co-occurrence. *BJPsych Advances,* 23(3), 167–168. https://doi.org/10.1192/apt.bp.116.016444

Unal, A., 2024. Does temperament constitute a risk factor for adult attention deficit hyperactivity disorder? *Cureus,* 16, e70915.

Valderas, M., Starfield, B., Sibbald, B., Salisbury, C. & Roland, M., 2009. Defining comorbidity: Implications for understanding health and health services. *Ann Fam Med,* 7, 357–363.

Van Ameringen, M., Mancini, C., Simpson, W. & Patterson, B., 2011. Adult attention deficit hyperactivity disorder in an anxiety disorders population. *CNS Neurosci Ther,* 17, 221–226.

Van Emmerik-Van-Oortmerssen, K., Van-de Glind, G., van den Brink, W., et al., 2012. Prevalence of attention-deficit hyperactivity disorder in substance use disorder patients: A meta-analysis and meta-regression analysis. *Drug Alcohol Depend,* 122, 11–19.

Van Hulzen, E., Scholz, J., Franke, B., et al., 2017. Genetic overlap between attention-deficit/ hyperactivity disorder and bipolar disorder: Evidence from genome-wide association study meta-analysis. *Biol Psychiatry,* 82, 634–641.

Weiss, M., Gibbins, C. & Hunter, D., 2011. Attention-deficit hyperactivity disorder and anxiety disorder in adults. In: Buitelaar, J., Kan, C. & Asherson, P (eds.) *ADHD in adults: Characterization, diagnosis, and treatment.* New York: Cambridge University Press.

Westreich, D., 2012. Berkson's bias, selection bias, and missing data. *Epidemiology,* 23, 159–164.

Woon, C. & Zakaria, H., 2019. Adult attention deficit hyperactivity disorder in a Malaysian Forensic Mental Hospital: A cross-sectional study. *East Asian Arch Psychiatry,* 29, 118–123.

Chapter 6

Bendy Bodies, Bendy Brains
Neurodiversity and Brain–Body Interactions

*Jessica A. Eccles, Lisa Quadt, and
Hugo D. Critchley*

Introduction

Most of the patients we see in our adult neurodevelopmental service, covering assessments for adult ADHD, autism, and Tourette syndrome, and participants who take part in our research studies, face both mental and physical health challenges. Furthermore, a significant number are hypermobile and experience pain and fatigue and associated issues. Moreover, mental health challenges such as anxiety are also experienced. Hypermobility refers to the ability of a person's joints to move beyond the normal range of motion. People with hypermobility may experience joint pain, instability, or even dislocations, but not everyone with hypermobile joints experiences symptoms. It can be present in both children and adults. While hypermobility isn't inherently considered neurodivergence, there's a strong connection and often significant shared characteristics. Hence the need for holistic, integrated healthcare that addresses both neurodevelopmental, mental, and physical health aspects in individuals with complex conditions.

We know both neurodivergent and hypermobile individuals are often dismissed and struggle within the medical system (Halverson et al., 2023). This negative experience can impact psychological well-being and outcomes for individuals. This highlights the importance of understanding the connection between the brain, body, and care as a means of improving individual lived experience. Such issues have been underscored by a survey from *Embracing Complexity* (a coalition of neurodevelopmental charities), which found that nearly half of neurodivergent respondents felt their mental or physical health treatment was worse due to their neurodivergence. Indeed, our own previous patient and public involvement work highlights recurring challenges faced by neurodivergent individuals and their families, with years-long struggles to obtain assessments and diagnoses for both mental and physical health issues; a persistent sense of being dismissed, disbelieved, or overlooked by professionals and institutions; and frequent encounters with poor understanding and a lack of accommodations in healthcare and educational settings. The short- and long-term impact of such challenges should not be downplayed as the ripple effect impacts both individuals and their families, and can be

DOI: 10.4324/9781003495949-7

detrimental to how neurodivergent persons engage with society and, indeed, how society responds to them.

Different Brains: What Is Neurodivergence?

As Legault et al. argue, diversity is an undeniable fact of nature. Within this context, the concept of neurodivergence becomes particularly relevant (Legault et al., 2021). Although "neurodiversity" and "neurodivergence" are sometimes used interchangeably, this can create confusion.

To clarify, *neurodiversity* refers to the natural variation in cognitive functioning that applies to everyone, while *neurodivergence* specifically describes individuals whose cognitive profiles differ significantly from societal norms (Legault et al., 2021). Neurodivergent individuals may be identified as having differences such as autism, ADHD, or Tourette syndrome. However, the term *neurodivergence* moves beyond the deficit-based medical model (American Psychiatric Association, 2013) of neurodevelopmental traits and conditions, such as autism and ADHD to acknowledge a broader range of characteristics and strengths (Fletcher-Watson and Happé, 2019). In this chapter, we aim to align our language with guidance from the neurodiversity movement (Bottema-Beutel et al., 2021).

Despite this strength-based perspective, neurodivergent individuals often experience various mental health challenges (Pantazakos, 2025, Shaw et al., 2022). The concept of bodily prediction errors is particularly useful in explaining heightened anxiety in neurodivergent individuals (Garfinkel et al., 2016) and serves as a target for effective interventions (Quadt et al., 2021). The concept of bodily prediction errors comes from the field of neuroscience and refers to the mismatch between the brain's expectations of sensory input related to the body and the actual sensory information received. Essentially, the brain constantly makes predictions about the state of the body, such as movement, posture, or sensations like touch or pain. When there is a discrepancy between the prediction and the sensory feedback (e.g., the body's actual position or state), this is considered a "prediction error". In the context of hypermobility or neurodivergent conditions, the brain's predictions about bodily movements or sensations may not align with the actual experience. For example, in hypermobility, a person might experience an unexpected feeling of discomfort or instability because the brain did not predict how the joints or muscles would react to certain movements, leading to a prediction error. Over time, this mismatch might contribute to issues with proprioception (the sense of the body's position and movement in space), coordination, or the experience of pain. Understanding bodily prediction errors is particularly useful when looking at conditions like ADHD or autism, as they can involve altered processing of sensory and motor information, potentially affecting movement, sensory perception, or motor control.

Moreover, autonomic and interoceptive processes remain key to understanding emotional experiences and vulnerabilities in neurodivergent people. Autonomic processes refer to the functions of the autonomic nervous system, which controls involuntary bodily functions that regulate vital processes such as heart rate, blood pressure, digestion, respiration, and temperature regulation. The autonomic nervous system operates automatically, without conscious control, and is divided into two branches:

1. *Sympathetic Nervous System:* Often referred to as the "fight or flight" system, it prepares the body for stressful or emergency situations by increasing heart rate, dilating pupils, and redirecting blood flow to essential organs and muscles.
2. *Parasympathetic Nervous System:* Known as the "rest and digest" system, it calms the body down after a stressful event by slowing the heart rate, promoting digestion, and conserving energy.

Interoceptive processes, on the other hand, refer to the perception of internal bodily sensations. These processes allow us to sense and interpret signals from within our body, such as hunger, thirst, temperature, pain, and the need to breathe. Interoception plays a key role in emotional regulation and overall well-being, as it provides the brain with information about the internal state of the body. It helps us maintain homeostasis (balance) by detecting changes in the body and triggering appropriate responses, such as feeling thirsty when dehydrated or feeling discomfort when in pain. Both autonomic and interoceptive processes are deeply intertwined in maintaining bodily functions and regulating emotional and physical states. Disruptions in these processes are linked to various conditions/differences, such as anxiety, autism, or dysregulation of bodily functions. For example, someone with heightened interoceptive sensitivity may become more aware of bodily sensations, leading to emotional reactions, while autonomic dysfunction might cause issues like difficulty regulating heart rate or blood pressure.

However, developmental differences in proprioception – such as dyspraxia – are also significant. Proprioception is the sense that allows individuals to perceive the position, movement, and orientation of their body parts in space, without needing to rely on sight. It involves sensory receptors located in muscles, tendons, and joints that send signals to the brain about the body's position and movement. This sense is crucial for coordinating movements, maintaining balance, and performing tasks that require fine motor skills, such as walking, typing, or even writing. For example, proprioception helps you touch your nose with your eyes closed or adjust your posture without consciously thinking about it. It enables smooth and coordinated movement by providing feedback on how the body is moving, its position, and how much force is being applied during those movements. Proprioception is especially important in activities that require precise body control, such as sports, dancing, and even basic daily tasks. Issues with proprioception can occur in various conditions like joint hypermobility, sensory processing disorders, or neurological disorders, leading to challenges with balance, coordination, and body awareness. Proprioception, therefore, lies at the interface between the internal self and the external world and is commonly associated with neurodivergence, as outlined in the ESSENCE framework (Gillberg, 2010). This area is gaining research attention (e.g., Li et al., 2023).

Different Bodies: What Is Hypermobility?

As outlined above, joint hypermobility refers to the ability of joints to move beyond typical limits, often due to lax ligaments, as seen in connective tissue disorders or other genetic conditions (Clinch et al., 2011). While relatively common in the general population, estimating its prevalence is challenging due to the variety of criteria, assessment methods, definitions, and cut-off points used across different studies on hypermobility. For instance, one study estimates that approximately 20% of the UK population exhibits joint hypermobility (Mulvey et al., 2013). Another study of 6,022 children found generalised joint hypermobility in 28% of girls and 11% of boys (Clinch et al., 2011). Joint hypermobility can present both strengths and challenges (Dondin and Baeza-Velasco, 2023).

When joint hypermobility is accompanied by other symptoms, such as pain or autonomic dysfunction, healthcare professionals may diagnose it as *hypermobility spectrum disorder* (HSD), previously known as *joint hypermobility syndrome*, or *Ehlers–Danlos Syndrome* (EDS). There are 13 recognised types of EDS, with *hypermobile EDS* (hEDS, formerly EDS-III or EDS-HT) being the most common. The 2017 hEDS diagnostic criteria incorporate age- and sex-specific cut-offs for generalised joint hypermobility (GJH). It is important to recognise that the clinical features of HSD and hEDS extend beyond musculoskeletal and skin-related symptoms. They are associated with:

- Cardiovascular autonomic dysfunction
- Gastrointestinal difficulties
- Fatigue
- Pain syndromes
- Gynaecological and obstetric problems
- Mental health issues

What Is the Hypermobile Neurodivergent Experience

The link between psychological vulnerability and hypermobile joints may seem counterintuitive to many clinicians and readers. However, a consistent relationship with anxiety has been confirmed across multiple studies worldwide (Sharp et al., 2021). Evidence is also growing for associations between hypermobility and neuropsychiatric conditions throughout the lifespan, including neurodevelopmental and stress-sensitive medical conditions.

The mind is embodied; thoughts and emotions interact with physiological arousal and the body's physical integrity. Increasing evidence suggests a link between psychiatric conditions and variations in connective tissue, often recognised as joint hypermobility (Sharp et al., 2021). Joint hypermobility is common but frequently under-recognised, significantly impacts quality of life, and may occur in isolation or as part of hypermobility spectrum disorders (HSD), including joint hypermobility syndrome and hypermobile Ehlers–Danlos syndrome (hEDS).

We have evaluated current evidence linking psychiatric disorders to hypermobility across the lifespan, starting with the well-established connection to anxiety. In this study, we explored emerging associations with affective disorders, eating disorders, and less-researched links with personality disorders, substance misuse, and psychosis (Sharp et al., 2021). Additionally, we have demonstrated the relationship between neurodivergence, hypermobility and physical problems, such as dysautonomia and pain (Csecs et al., 2022). We found that hypermobility was observed in 51% of neurodivergent adults, compared to 20% in the general population and 17.5% in the comparison group. The odds ratio (OR)[1] for hypermobility in the neurodivergent group compared to the general population was 4.51 (95% CI 2.17–9.37), with higher odds in females than males. Using age-specific cut-offs, the OR for hypermobility in the neurodivergent group versus the comparison group was 2.84 (95% CI 1.16–6.94). Therefore, we concluded that, in neurodivergent adults, joint hypermobility is strongly associated with dysautonomia and pain, more so than in the general population or comparison group. Additionally, joint hypermobility mediates the link between neurodivergence and these physical symptoms.

Increased awareness of this association can improve the management of core symptoms and co-occurring physical issues in neurodivergent individuals, guiding more effective service delivery and holistic care strategies in the future (Csecs et al., 2022).

With growing knowledge of mind–body interactions, the potential underlying mechanisms, including dysautonomia, abnormal interoceptive processing, immune dysregulation, and proprioceptive impairments, all within the context of psychosocial stressors and genetic predisposition, are becoming increasingly clear. We will discuss later in this chapter the clinical implications of these findings and emphasise the importance of recognising the transdiagnostic nature of hypermobility and related disorders.

We advocate for early screening and detection of hypermobility in individuals presenting with mental health or somatic symptoms, aiming to facilitate preventive measures and long-term holistic management strategies. Future research needs to elucidate the fundamental interactions between the mind, body, and brain. This chapter describes three of our empirical studies demonstrating the relevance of the brain–body link between neurodivergence and hypermobility.

Hypermobility, Neurodivergence, and the Role of Sensation in Emotional Experience

Embodied Feeling

Influential theories suggest that emotions are closely tied to the state of the body, with feeling and sensing inherently connected. Research in basic and clinical neuroscience, such as the work by Damasio and colleagues (Damasio and Carvalho, 2013), has reframed key ideas initially proposed by William James and Carl Lange. These theories link affective feelings and related motivational behaviours to changes in interoceptive representations, which interact with perceived changes in the external environment.

Emotional experiences often have distinct physical sensations, such as a "racing heart", "stomach churning", "blood draining", or feeling "hot-headed", or "tense". Uncertainty plays a significant role in emotional salience. For instance, interoceptive changes like increased cardiovascular arousal can heighten feelings of anxiety, even when there is no clear external cause, for example, physical exertion (Khalsa et al., 2018, Paulus and Stein, 2006).

Predictive coding models suggest that unexpected bodily responses, or interoceptive surprises, generate prediction error signals. These signals drive emotional learning and behaviour by amplifying physiological sensations, forming the basis of affective experience (Critchley and Garfinkel, 2017). Individual differences in how reliably and strongly the body signals these changes influence the emotional weight assigned to bodily prediction errors (Critchley et al., 2013). Consequently, the precision of sensory regulation becomes a key factor in shaping emotional experiences.

The relationship between proprioception – the sense of the body's position and movement in space – and emotion remains largely unexplored. This contrasts with interoception, where viscerosensory signals like cold or hunger are well-recognised as triggers for motivational and emotional behaviours and feelings. The connection between emotion and proprioception appears to be bidirectional: emotions, as states of action-readiness, influence posture (Lelard et al., 2019), making posture a channel for emotional communication (de Gelder, 2006).

There is growing interest in variant connective tissue structures, such as joint hypermobility, as models for studying brain–body interactions (Csecs et al., 2022). Hypermobility is associated with interoceptive and autonomic differences and is linked to variations in anxiety and related emotional states across diagnostic groups (Sharp et al., 2021). In hypermobile individuals, differences in neural function and structure have been observed in brain regions involved in emotional experience (e.g., amygdala and insular cortices) and proprioception (e.g., inferior parietal lobule volume) (Eccles et al., 2012, Mallorqui-Bague et al., 2014).

Hypermobility is also tied to developmental proprioceptive differences (Baeza-Velasco et al., 2018a, 2018b). Altered sensation due to exaggerated joint range of motion is associated with developmental dyspraxia, coordination difficulties, gait differences, and increased risk of joint pathology, such as osteoarthritis, from wear and tear. Hypermobility may predispose individuals to proprioceptive imprecision, though this may be mitigated through muscle strengthening and movement training, such as in dance, gymnastics, and sports, which utilise the aesthetic and functional benefits of hypermobility.

We hypothesised that imprecise, and thus poorly predicted, proprioceptive signals enhance the generation of bodily prediction errors, translating these into emotional feelings and affective experiences. This relationship was explored in the context of neurodivergence, where developmental differences in the interaction between physical and psychological states are likely established early.

Role of Sensation

In previous research, we explored the relationship between body-based sensory signals, emotions, and neurodivergence, focusing on the role of proprioception (body position sensing) and connective tissue variation (e.g., joint hypermobility) (Eccles et al., 2024). Influential theories propose that emotions arise from bodily states, with interoceptive signals (e.g., heart rate) and proprioceptive feedback influencing emotional experiences. Neurodivergence (e.g., autism and ADHD) often involves sensory and emotional regulation differences, potentially linked to these bodily processes.

Key findings from this study reveal that individuals with joint hypermobility frequently exhibit proprioceptive imprecision, leading to heightened emotional dysregulation. Neurodivergent traits amplify this relationship, with the study suggesting that "proprioceptive surprise" (unexpected body sensations) plays a pivotal role. Mediation models showed hypermobility and neurodivergence interact to impact emotional regulation through proprioception. This association emphasises how body-based prediction errors contribute to emotional states, aligning with predictive coding theories.

The study's innovative conceptual model combines brain–body interactions, emphasising the importance of recognising neurodivergence and hypermobility for understanding emotional and physical health. Joint hypermobility often goes undiagnosed, despite its links to anxiety, depression, and sensory differences. Improved recognition of its overlap with neurodivergence could enhance medical outcomes.

Despite limitations, such as reliance on self-reports, a predominantly white female sample, and lack of direct proprioceptive measures, the research offers a foundation for future studies. Further exploration of how proprioceptive differences influence emotions could inform new therapies, particularly for neurodivergent individuals. The findings highlight potential shortcomings of traditional treatments like cognitive behavioural therapy (CBT) for such populations and suggest alternative approaches that consider embodied sensory experiences. This research contributes to a deeper understanding of the intertwined nature of sensory, emotional, and neurodevelopmental processes.

Mental Health Crises

A second study conducted by the team in this area described the prevalence of autistic traits among adults accessing acute mental health services in the UK and their association with quality of life (QoL) and physical health conditions, particularly hypermobility. Using validated tools such as the RAADS-14, MHQoL, and 5PQ, the study assessed 55 participants, predominantly white, with a mean age of 35.7 years. Most were referred to crisis services due to low mood or suicide attempts. Results showed that 78% of participants scored above the RAADS-14 threshold for autism, with 41% estimated to meet the diagnostic criteria. Only 15% had a prior autism diagnosis.

The study found significant associations between higher RAADS-14 scores, reduced QoL, and hypermobility. A third of participants screened positive for hypermobility, which may link physical symptoms to mental health challenges in neurodivergent individuals. These findings suggest a high prevalence of undiagnosed autism in crisis services, highlighting the need for tailored approaches to care.

Key limitations include the small, predominantly white sample size, which limits generalisability, and potential self-selection bias. The low specificity of the RAADS-14 was also acknowledged. Despite these challenges, the findings underline the importance of adapting services to address the needs of neurodivergent individuals. Recommendations include recruiting staff with expertise in autism, improving diagnostic clarity, and incorporating frameworks like SPACE (see Chapter 3 of this book for further information on the framework, Csecs et al., 2021) to design multidisciplinary care.

Future research should investigate the prevalence of autism on a larger scale, examine co-occurring conditions such as ADHD, and explore the lived experiences of autistic individuals with mental health challenges. Collecting diverse demographic data and improving understanding of hypermobility's role in mental and physical health are also essential. These insights have significant implications for improving healthcare services and addressing the complex needs of autistic individuals in crisis.

Bipolar Disorder

The third study conducted by this team that will be included in this chapter explored joint hypermobility and its association with bipolar affective disorder (bipolar disorder), a chronic psychiatric condition characterised by fluctuating mood states such as mania, hypomania, and depression. Bipolar disorder typically emerges in late adolescence or early adulthood, affecting approximately 1–2.4% of the population. Neurodevelopmental conditions, including ADHD and autism, frequently co-occur with bipolar disorder. Up to 30% of adults with bipolar disorder also have ADHD, compared to 3–6% of the general population. Autism is similarly prevalent in individuals with bipolar disorder, with rates six times higher than in non-autistic individuals. Shared genetic factors underlie these connections, as seen in familial clustering of bipolar disorder, ADHD, and autism.

In this study we explored the interconnected roles of joint hypermobility, neurodivergent traits, and bipolar disorder. Findings demonstrated that individuals with bipolar disorder exhibit higher rates of hypermobility (55.8%) compared to controls (18.5%). Neurodivergent characteristics (autistic and ADHD traits) are also more common in the bipolar disorder group, with mediation analyses revealing that these traits partially explain the relationship between hypermobility and bipolar disorder.

These results suggest a brain–body model linking hypermobility to bipolar disorder through neurodivergent traits, potentially driven by shared developmental pathways involving connective tissue variability, sensory processing differences, and autonomic dysregulation. This highlights the importance of integrating physical and mental health care, as many individuals remain undiagnosed or misdiagnosed.

This study provides a foundation for future research to explore longitudinal and causal relationships, emphasising the need for dimensional approaches to diagnosis and treatment. Improved understanding of these associations could refine clinical practices, promote earlier recognition of co-occurring conditions/differences, and enhance therapeutic outcomes by addressing both neurodevelopmental and affective components of bipolar disorder. This integrative approach represents a significant step toward more holistic care for individuals with complex mental and physical health profiles.

Conclusions

In conclusion, this chapter emphasises the need for more holistic, integrated healthcare that addresses both neurodevelopmental and physical health aspects in individuals with complex conditions like joint hypermobility and neurodivergence. We underscore the complex brain–body relationship between neurodivergence and joint hypermobility, highlighting their profound impact on both mental and physical health. Individuals with neuro-differences such as ADHD, autism, and bipolar disorder often experience co-occurring challenges related to joint hypermobility, including pain, fatigue, and mental health vulnerabilities like anxiety and depression. The studies presented demonstrate how proprioception, sensory regulation, and autonomic dysregulation contribute to emotional and physical health difficulties. The chapter advocates for a holistic, integrated approach to healthcare that recognises the interplay between neurodevelopmental and physical conditions. It stresses the importance of early screening and tailored care for neurodivergent and hypermobile individuals and the need for further research into the underlying mechanisms at play.

By improving diagnostic clarity and treatment approaches, healthcare systems can provide more effective and comprehensive care for these underserved people navigating these complex and often undiagnosed health challenges. This will require a collaborative effort between healthcare professionals, researchers, funders and individuals with these conditions to ensure holistic, optimal care, and improved quality of life.

Acknowledgements

We are indebted to the assistance of Professor Sarah Garfinkel, Dr Jenny Csecs, Georgia Savage, Rebecca Dew, Dr Christopher Muller-Pollard, Dr Alessandro Colasanti, Professor James Stone, Dr Lisa Page, and Dr Samuel Cowley.

Note

1 In research, the odds ratio (OR) is a measure of association used to quantify the relationship between two events, particularly in cases of binary outcomes (e.g., yes/no, success/failure, presence/absence). It compares the odds of an event occurring in one group to the odds of it occurring in another group.

References

American Psychiatric Association. 2013. *Diagnostic and statistical manual of mental disorders* (5th ed.). Arlington, VA: American Psychiatric Association.

Baeza-Velasco, C., Cohen, D., Hamonet, C., Vlamynck, E., Diaz, L., Cravero, C., Cappe, E. & Guinchat, V. 2018a. Autism, joint hypermobility-related disorders and pain. *Frontiers in Psychiatry*, 656.

Baeza-Velasco, C., Sinibaldi, L. & Castori, M. 2018b. Attention-deficit/hyperactivity disorder, joint hypermobility-related disorders and pain: Expanding body-mind connections to the developmental age. *ADHD Attention Deficit and Hyperactivity Disorders*, 10, 163–175.

Bottema-Beutel, K., Kapp, S. K., Lester, J. N., Sasson, N. J. & Hand, B. N. 2021. Avoiding ableist language: Suggestions for autism researchers. *Autism Adulthood*, 3, 18–29.

Clinch, J., Deere, K., Sayers, A., Palmer, S., Riddoch, C., Tobias, J. H. & Clark, E. M. 2011. Epidemiology of generalized joint laxity (hypermobility) in fourteen-year-old children from the UK: A population-based evaluation. *Arthritis Rheum*, 63, 2819–2827.

Critchley, H. D., Eccles, J. & Garfinkel, S. N. 2013. Interaction between cognition, emotion, and the autonomic nervous system. *Handbook of Clinical Neurology*, 117, 59–77.

Critchley, H. D. & Garfinkel, S. N. 2017. Interoception and emotion. *Current Opinion in Psychology*, 17, 7–14.

Csecs, J. L., Dowell, N. G., Savage, G. K., Iodice, V., Mathias, C. J., Critchley, H. D. & Eccles, J. A. 2021. Variant connective tissue (joint hypermobility) and dysautonomia are associated with multimorbidity at the intersection between physical and psychological health. *American Journal of Medical Genetics Part C: Seminars in Medical Genetics*, 187, 500–509.

Csecs, J. L. L., Iodice, V., Rae, C. L., Brooke, A., Simmons, R., Quadt, L., Savage, G. K., Dowell, N. G., Prowse, F., Themelis, K., Mathias, C. J., Critchley, H. D. & Eccles, J. A. 2022. Joint hypermobility links neurodivergence to dysautonomia and pain. *Frontiers in Psychiatry*, 12.

Damasio, A. & Carvalho, G. B. 2013. The nature of feelings: Evolutionary and neurobiological origins. *Nat Rev Neurosc*, 14, 143–152.

De Gelder, B. 2006. Towards the neurobiology of emotional body language. *Nature Reviews Neuroscience*, 7, 242–249.

Dondin, M. & Baeza-Velasco, C. 2023. Joint hypermobility and fatigue are associated with injuries in a group of preprofessional ballet dancers. *J Dance Med Sci*, 27, 80–86.

Eccles, J. A., Beacher, F. D., Gray, M. A., Jones, C. L., Minati, L., Harrison, N. A. & Critchley, H. D. 2012. Brain structure and joint hypermobility: Relevance to the expression of psychiatric symptoms. *Br J Psychiatry*, 200, 508–509.

Eccles, J. A., Quadt, L., Garfinkel, S. N. & Critchley, H. D. 2024. A model linking emotional dysregulation in neurodivergent people to the proprioceptive impact of joint hypermobility. *Philosophical Transactions of the Royal Society of London B Biological Sciences*, 379, 20230247.

Fletcher-Watson, S. & Happé, F. 2019. *Autism: A new introduction to psychological theory and current debate*, Routledge.

Garfinkel, S. N., Tiley, C., O'Keeffe, S., Harrison, N. A., Seth, A. K. & Critchley, H. D. 2016. Discrepancies between dimensions of interoception in autism: Implications for emotion and anxiety. *Biological Psychology,* 114, 117–126.

Gillberg, C. 2010. The ESSENCE in child psychiatry: Early symptomatic syndromes eliciting neurodevelopmental clinical examinations. *Research in Developmental Disabilities,* 31, 1543–1551.

Halverson, C. M. E., Penwell, H. L. & Francomano, C. A. 2023. Clinician-associated traumatization from difficult medical encounters: Results from a qualitative interview study on the ehlers-danlos syndromes. *SSM – Qualitative Research in Health,* 3, 100237.

Khalsa, S. S., Adolphs, R., Cameron, O. G., Critchley, H. D., Davenport, P. W., Feinstein, J. S., Feusner, J. D., Garfinkel, S. N., Lane, R. D., Mehling, W. E., Meuret, A. E., Nemeroff, C. B., Oppenheimer, S., Petzschner, F. H., Pollatos, O., Rhudy, J. L., Schramm, L. P., Simmons, W. K., Stein, M. B., Stephan, K. E., Van Den Bergh, O., Van Diest, I., Von Leupoldt, A. & Paulus, M. P. 2018. Interoception and mental health: A roadmap. *Biol Psychiatry Cogn Neurosci Neuroimaging,* 3, 501–513.

Legault, M., Bourdon, J.-N. & Poirier, P. 2021. From neurodiversity to neurodivergence: The role of epistemic and cognitive marginalization. *Synthese,* 199, 12843–12868.

Lelard, T., Stins, J. & Mouras, H. 2019. Postural responses to emotional visual stimuli. *Neurophysiologie Clinique,* 49, 109–114.

Li, J., Wang, W., Cheng, J., Li, H., Feng, L., Ren, Y., Liu, L., Qian, Q. & Wang, Y. 2023. Relationships between sensory integration and the core symptoms of attention-deficit/hyperactivity disorder: The mediating effect of executive function. *Eur Child Adolesc Psychiatry,* 32, 2235–2246.

Mallorqui-Bague, N., Garfinkel, S. N., Engels, M., Eccles, J. A., Pailhez, G., Bulbena, A. & Critchley, H. D. 2014. Neuroimaging and psychophysiological investigation of the link between anxiety, enhanced affective reactivity and interoception in people with joint hypermobility. *Frontiers in Psychology,* 5, 1162.

Mulvey, M. R., Macfarlane, G. J., Beasley, M., Symmons, D. P., Lovell, K., Keeley, P., Woby, S. & McBeth, J. 2013. Modest association of joint hypermobility with disabling and limiting musculoskeletal pain: Results from a large-scale general population-based survey. *Arthritis Care and Research (Hoboken),* 65, 1325–1333.

Pantazakos, T. (2025). Neurodiversity and psychotherapy—Connections and ways forward. *Counselling and Psychotherapy Research, 25*(1), e12675.

Paulus, M. P. & Stein, M. B. 2006. An insular view of anxiety. *Biol Psychiatry,* 60, 383–387.

Quadt, L., Garfinkel, S. N., Mulcahy, J. S., Larsson, D. E., Silva, M., Jones, A.-M., Strauss, C. & Critchley, H. D. 2021. Interoceptive training to target anxiety in autistic adults (ADIE): A single-center, superiority randomized controlled trial. *EClinicalMedicine,* 39, 101042.

Sharp, H. E. C., Critchley, H. D. & Eccles, J. A. 2021. Connecting brain and body: Transdiagnostic relevance of connective tissue variants to neuropsychiatric symptom expression. *World Journal of Psychiatry,* 11, 805–820.

Shaw, S. C., Doherty, M., McCowan, S. & Eccles, J. A. 2022. Towards a neurodiversity-affirmative approach for an over-represented and under-recognised population: Autistic adults in outpatient psychiatry. *Journal of Autism and Developmental Disorders,* 52, 4200–4201.

Chapter 7

Supporting Neurodivergent Mental Health in Education

Claire O'Neill

Introduction

Schools are increasingly recognised as organisations that develop children and young people holistically by cultivating a balanced set of cognitive, social, and emotional skills in all learners (OECD, 2017). Attention to the role of schools in supporting mental health and well-being is growing. For example, The World Health Organisation recognises that schools can promote good mental health and well-being through interventions that promote competence and psychological strengths (WHO, 2021). Furthermore, well-being research indicates that multi-component, preventative, whole organisation approaches at both universal and targeted levels are the most beneficial approaches for schools and centres of education (Department of Education and Skills, Ireland, 2019). However, these research findings need to be carefully considered when it comes to reflecting on the mental health of neurodivergent learners in our schools. For instance, there is well-established research highlighting that neurodivergent people are at disproportionate risk for experiencing mental health difficulties like depression (Hudson et al., 2019) and suicide (Royal College of Psychiatry, 2022) yet to date there is a dearth of high-quality research on effective mental health supports for neurodivergent people within the schooling/education environment (Lei et al., 2024).

Education is central to supporting and nurturing good mental health in learners, teachers, staff, and the wider school community (Weare, 2010). It can facilitate learners in how to be agentic in nourishing mental health and shape lifelong learners who can critically appraise what works best in terms of self-care practices. An understanding that a one-size-fits-all approach does not work in our neurodiverse classrooms extends to the school-based strategies aimed at mental health promotion. Indeed, schools when supporting neurodivergent learners need to be vigilant that they do not cause iatrogenic harm, that is, harm arising from health-promoting efforts themselves. To avoid harm, a consideration of the specific barriers and facilitators of good mental health in neurodivergent school students is essential. At a rudimentary level, teachers need to be self-aware and check for unconscious bias and ableism relating to understanding and supporting neurodivergent mental health. Meaningful reflection on attitudes and an evidence-based framework of

DOI: 10.4324/9781003495949-8

practice in terms of supporting neurodivergent students mental health can facilitate human flourishing and thriving for learners of all neurotypes. It is essential that schools are ambitious and evidence based when setting well-being goals for neurodivergent learners; it is not sufficient for this cohort of learners to merely cope within an ableist and neurotypically designed education system. Neurodivergent learners deserve to thrive within schools and a school-wide awareness that neurodivergent flourishing is not only possible but already exists is fundamental (Chapman and Carel, 2022; Pellicano and Heyworth, 2023). This chapter explores the significant role schools and education play in the mental health of neurodivergent learners.

What We Know about Neurodivergent Mental Health in School-Age Learners

Studies indicate that many neurodivergent school-age learners encounter negative experiences that can have an adverse effect on mental health (Connolly, Constable and Mullally, 2023; Kelly et al., 2024; Quinton et al., 2024). These effects are multifactorial and have been attributed to bullying (Fink et al., 2015; Novin et al. 2019; Rowley et al., 2012), stigma and discrimination (Araujo et al., 2023; Han et al., 2022; Turnock et al., 2022), and barriers to attending school (Granieri et al., 2023; Hamilton, 2024; Paget et al., 2018). These difficulties occur across several neurodivergent neurotypes, including ADHD (Schilpzand et al., 2018), dyslexia (Georgiou et al., 2024), dyspraxia (O'Dea et al., 2021), and autism (Holmes, 2024).

Given these findings and the link between poor mental health amongst neurodivergent learners and school-associated phenomena like bullying, stigma, and difficulties in school attendance, a crucial question for educators must be the following: What can we do to support, plan, evaluate, improve, and reimagine brighter and healthier futures for neurodivergent learners? This question poses a Herculean task, and robust theoretical underpinnings and adaptable frameworks can help schools fathom how to achieve better mental health for this cohort of learners.

One such framework is the Continuum of Support (DES, 2007). This framework provides a pragmatic and evidence-based framework for educational contexts. Although originating in the Irish context, this model holds relevance to education systems internationally. Indeed, frameworks like the Continuum of Support have been recommended for use in schools since at least the Salamanca Statement (UNESCO, 1994). The model is grounded in several theoretical perspectives, including the biosocial model of support (Grinker, 1953; Engel, 1977; Lugg, 2022), Input-Process-Outcome Models (Elasra, 2017), and Multi-Tiered Systems of Support (MTSS) (Stoiber and Gettinger, 2015). Not only does the Continuum help organise support at school level, it is also a transparent tool that can incorporate external systems that may become involved in supporting a young person's mental health. Furthermore, and of relevance to neurodivergent learners, the Continuum recognises that learners will have different needs and the goal is to match available support to individual needs while considering constraints like resourcing and expertise (Moran, 2022). In this sense, the Continuum moves beyond generic models and frameworks and considers the unique needs of the young person. This is particularly important when engaging with neurodivergent students who may have multiple and complex needs. The Continuum of Support is a flexible and systematic model suitable for schools aiming to address the mental health of learners. The model operates on three progressive levels to scaffold, plan, track, and evaluate mental health support in schools (Donnelly and Kyriazopoulou, 2014).

Level 1 of the Continuum of Support

Level 1 corresponds to support at a whole school and classroom level. It is sometimes called support for all or universal support (Weare and Nind, 2011; Werner-Seidler et al., 2017). Level 1 also encompasses whole-school culture and climate and phenomena such as positive relationships, sense of belonging, and inclusive pedagogy, all of which are protective factors for mental health (Butler et al., 2022). Many programmes are taught at a level 1 tier of support and can include health and well-being curricula and social and emotional education programmes. Studies indicate that such programmes improve learners' social and emotional skills, attitudes, and learning outcomes (Durlak et al., 2011). Many programmes taught in schools are a universal support, equating to level 1 of the Continuum of Support. Level 1 supports are generally the easiest and most cost effective to implement. However, the needs of the learner should always be the primary driver of the support offered and not what is most convenient for the school and support services. Whilst level 1 can offer important supports through a broader application, some students, particularly neurodivergent students, are likely to require more tailored supports and this type of approach would not meet these needs. However, having a whole-school and more macro-based approach is the first step in developing a supportive school culture which can then be implemented at a more micro-level such as 1:1 supports in the classroom.

Level 2 of the Continuum of Support

The middle tier of the Continuum of Support is known as level 2. This refers to school-level support provided for some learners. At this level, teachers identify needs and provide more targeted support and early interventions. Sometimes level 1 or universal supports are adapted to deliver more targeted support that equates more accurately to level 2 of the model (Weare and Nind, 2011; Werner-Seidler et al., 2017). Research calls for the inclusion of both universal and targeted approaches and there is evidence that both universal (level 1) and more bespoke group support (level 2) in schools can effectively prevent and manage anxiety and low mood for many learners (Ahlen et al., 2015; Das et al., 2016; Werner-Seidler et al., 2017). Indeed, as outlined above more universal approaches are key to generating a supportive school culture which is imperative for level 2, more targeted supports, to be implemented in any meaningful way. Therefore, whilst level 1 and level 2 are applied differently, each is reliant upon the other to facilitate meaningful implementation. Moreover, such approaches are even more necessary when referring to neurodivergent students. For example, a school culture that facilitates universal support for students is key to developing an inclusive culture which supports the various needs of its students. In addition, expanding beyond the universal to a more targeted approach allows for those who would otherwise get lost in the education system, to be identified as requiring additional supports to reach their full potential. This is particularly important for neurodivergent students whose needs may not be recognised within a time frame that allows them to reach their potential.

Level 3 of the Continuum of Support

Many neurodivergent learners are placed at level 3 of the Continuum of Support. Learners at level 3, who are struggling with their mental health, ideally receive individualised support, preferably in partnership with specialist services like external mental health professionals or specialist agencies like child and adolescent mental health services (CAMHS). Learners at level 3 are generally considered to have what are termed as complex and enduring needs. Effective implementation of the Continuum of Support is augmented by having a sound theoretical base and rationale for support, specific, well-defined goals, and direct and explicit focus on outcomes for each component of a whole-school approach (Weare and Nind, 2011). Lack of access to professional development and support from outside agencies can be a barrier to effectively supporting learners needing level 3 support (Gee et al., 2021). Therefore, level 3 is key to multiagency support that goes beyond education. This is an important level as it recognises that the neurodivergent students often require engagement beyond the schooling system and having a schooling system operating in isolation from other services limits positive life outcomes for students. Providing schools with the support systems to link in with other services is key to good outcomes for students and ensures that the supports provided by the school do not cease at the end of the school day but rather reach out into all areas of the young person's life. This more holistic approach is key to ensuring follow on support and interagency collaboration in terms of meeting a young person's needs.

The above framework highlights the importance of developing an inclusive and caring school culture that allows for flexibility within the school environment but also holistic connections beyond the school walls.

Operationalising Neurodiversity to Support Neurodivergent Flourishing and Avoid Iatrogenic Harm

However, even when using an evidence-informed framework like the Continuum of Support, there is a need for educators to appreciate that not all approaches are equal, and some may potentially cause harm. This is described in research as iatrogenic harm (Foulkes and Stringaris, 2023; Foulkes et al., 2024). Given that neurodivergent learners belong to a minority group, there is oftentimes inadequate research to guide practice and in the context of such limited resources, it is imperative that further research is conducted to ensure effective use of resources and to reduce the risk of iatrogenic harm for these learners. This being so, many factors including an evidence-based neurodiversity-informed approach need to be considered when planning for the mental health support needs of these learners. Educators should be involved in mental health promotion and support, and collaborative approaches with clinical and therapeutic partners is essential.

In tandem with a collaborative approach, operationalising the core principles of the Neurodiversity Paradigm supports neurodivergent flourishing. Ne'eman and Pellicano (2022) have outlined a number of key evaluative questions to explore when implementing an intervention or programme. They suggest exploring whether it enhances well-being. What evidence is available related to it? Could it cause distress? Is it meaningful to the individual? Have the voices and autonomy of the individuals it is being directed at been incorporated? Does it encourage masking? Does it align with values and ethical codes? And is there neurodivergent input into the design? Completing these actions is a powerful way to avoid causing harm through unsuitable supports. An awareness of the Neurodiversity Paradigm is a foundational and effective perspective to operationalise practice and enhance the process of supporting the mental health of neurodivergent learners.

Some Approaches that Can Potentially Cause Iatrogenic Harm to Neurodivergent Learners

Neurodiversity-Lite

Neurodiversity-lite, a phenomenon linked to performative neurodiversity and in essence a watering down and appropriation of the principles of neurodiversity (Roberts, 2021)), has been outlined as having the potential to cause harm. Whereas a school might be well-intentioned in efforts to be neurodiversity-affirmative, there is a risk of harm to neurodivergent learners if the approach is based on unstable foundations like poor understanding or even misunderstanding of the principles of the Neurodiversity Paradigm. Examples of neurodiversity-lite include incorrect use of terminology associated with the paradigm, for example, referring to a neurodivergent learner as a neurodiverse learner. School-based supports can also fall into the realm of neurodiversity-lite, for example, commercially produced resources that rely on overly simplified tropes like superpower narratives. Also, resources that appropriate the language of the Neurodiversity Paradigm without adopting its core philosophy and principles have the potential to be harmful.

Harm can also occur at a pedagogic level. For instance, schools that conceptualise fairness as everyone being treated the same, demonstrate a lack of understanding of the recognition of difference at the core of the Neurodiversity Paradigm. Schools that embrace an inclusive pedagogy, focusing on the value of equity and that all learners need different supports to thrive, are more aligned with the Paradigm. Neurodiversity-lite is more likely to be in existence when the leadership and staff of a school lack a deep understanding of concepts central to a neurodivergent learner's way of being. Pedagogical approaches built on a flimsy foundation of neurodiversity-lite can be detrimental to the mental health of neurodivergent learners and thus have a high risk of causing harm to the student/s. For schools to be truly Neurodiversity Paradigm-informed, a sound knowledge and understanding of phenomena, like monotropism, double empathy, masking, burnout, and minority stress, is fundamental.

Mindfulness-Based Interventions (MBIs)

Mindfulness-based interventions (MBIs) continue to be popular in educational settings and there is a growing evidence base to support their efficacy (Jennings, 2015; Weare, 2018; Zenner et al., 2014). In any quality training in MBIs, for example, the Mindfulness in Schools Project (MISP), the main purpose of cultivating a mindful practice, such as meditation, is simply to enhance awareness in the present moment. However, when MBIs are introduced without adequate professional training and/or a lack of understanding of mindfulness, there is the potential for iatrogenesis, where the MBI can cause an adverse effect (Brito et al., 2021). MBIs when poorly understood or misapplied are sometimes referred to as "McMindfulness" (Purser, 2019). Examples of this include scenarios when MBIs are introduced ostensibly as a well-being intervention and have unsuitable support goals attached, for example, to improve regulation or academic performance (Reveley, 2016). Another example of where harm may be caused is where MBIs are viewed as a panacea to be universally applied to support a wide range of mental health difficulties (Purser, 2019).

When it comes to neurodivergent learners, an understanding of the potential harms of MBIs as they relate to this cohort of learners is essential. For example, there is potential for traumatic memories to be triggered in some MBI practices (Lee et al., 2024). It is of relevance to this cohort of learners that increased anxiety is a potential adverse effect of some mindfulness practices (Cebolla et al., 2017). Furthermore, care must be taken with neurodivergent learners with sensory profile differences as research reports changes to perception of sensory inputs such as light, sound, and body sensations after some MBIs (Lindahl and Britton, 2019).

MBIs, especially when introduced as mindfulness infused into broader educational practices, have the potential to be of benefit to neurodivergent learners. In addition to having a sound knowledge of neurodiversity, it is essential that MBIs are supported by a teacher who is experienced and trained in the teaching of individual, authentic, and holistic versions of mindfulness (Brito et al., 2021; Sellman and Buttarazzi, 2020). The enduring enthusiasm for MBIs in schools suggests that there is merit in further research into the risks and benefits of MBIs for neurodivergent learners.

Cognitive Behavioural Interventions (CBIs)

CBIs are often recommended to schools by external professionals and agencies as they are an evidence-based universal support that can be taught to whole classes.

Unfortunately, the demands placed on a neurodivergent learner engaging in a whole class-based CBI can be significant. *Friends for Life* (Barrett, 2004; Barrett et al., 2006) is one example of CBI that is popular with schools and well-researched internationally. The National Centre for Health and Care Excellence (NICE) Guidelines (2022) recommend that Autistic people should receive therapeutic support that has been adapted to take account of their neurodivergence. Autism-specific research suggests that Friends for Life is effective in supporting anxiety in Autistic learners when the programme is adapted for the individual (Burke et al., 2017; Slack, 2013). To date, there is a lack of research on the efficacy of CBIs with other neurominorities.

It is possible, however, for neurodivergent individuals to be harmed by poorly adapted CBI approaches. Nicholls (2021) identifies components of CBIs that are potentially challenging and even harmful for neurodivergent individuals. For example, tasks and home school links commonly associated with CBIs can be challenging and confusing, resulting in much cognitive and emotional load to learners. These tasks can be counterproductive, particularly if the neurodivergent young person is already struggling with their mental health.

The nature of CBI-based tasks is often designed with the neuro-normative learner in mind. For example, tasks identifying, exploring, and describing emotions in detail abound in CBIs. Phenomena associated with neurodivergence like alexithymia and interception differences can make it more difficult for neurodivergent learners to identify their emotions, mood, and feelings. These tasks, especially without skilled adaptation, can be difficult and even counterproductive for neurodivergent learners. When goal setting in CBIs, it is important to consider any externally observed behaviour in the context of a neurodivergent way of being. Teachers supporting neurodivergent learners with CBIs might find the growing field of research into working therapeutically with neurodivergent learners helpful (Grant and Wethers, 2024; Wilson and Gullon-Scott, 2024).

The Neurodiversity Paradigm and the Key Areas of Health Promotion

The four Key Areas of Health Promotion as outlined in the Irish Department of Education and Skill's Wellbeing Policy Statement (2019) offers schools a comprehensive framework to plan, action, and evaluate mental health education and support for neurodivergent learners. The framework is an especially helpful tool to support neurodivergent mental health when synthesised with Ne'eman and Pellicano's Operationalising Neurodiversity Framework. Combining these models not only provides a clear roadmap for mental health support, but can also help avoid iatrogenic harm. By exploring each area of health promotion, it becomes more apparent how schools can support the mental health of neurodivergent learners.

Key Area 1: Culture and Environment

School culture and environment are key determinants of successful health promotion in schools. In the broader sense, the school environment incorporates concepts like connectedness, climate, and culture and these have been found to be a key driver of successful well-being promotion in schools (Viner et. al, 2012). Evidence suggests that these concepts are central to neurodivergent well-being (Farahar, 2022; Najeeb and Quadt, 2024; Slagus and Kitchin, 2024). When considering culture and environment and the mental health of neurodivergent learners, it is helpful to follow the lead of Viner et al. and take a broad view of what school culture and environment encompasses. Tools like the LEARNING Framework can help schools evaluate their culture and environment in terms of how supportive they are for neurodivergent learners. The Learning Framework explores the environment, agency, relationships, nature, inclusion, neurodiversity informed, goals, and language (O'Neill, 2024).

It is well established that the built environment of schools can be hostile for neurodivergent learners (Finnigan, 2024; Tufvesson and Tufvesson, 2009). Culture and environment, as a key area, however, encompasses more than the built environment. A school environment that supports mental health is one that commits to fostering strong relationships, encourages authentic and meaningful participation, and develops learner autonomy. A culture based on a cohesive whole-school approach is important when it comes to well-being and supporting mental health (Weare, 2010). A whole-school approach helps integrate strategies and systems throughout the whole-school environment. This creates the capacity to be reflective and responsive to the needs of the school and the individuals who are part of the school community (Department of Education and Skills, Ireland, 2019).

Key Area 2: Relationships and Partnerships

A teacher's role extends beyond facilitating learning, and high-quality learner–teacher relationships are considered paramount to children and young people's well-being (OECD, 2017). Research into positive relationships in educational settings and neurodivergent learners outline factors like educators needing to question neuronormative-based assumptions and adopting more inclusive approaches like Universal Design for Learning (UDL) (Spaeth and Pearson, 2023). Although there is a dearth of neurodiversity-related studies exploring the one good adult concept, there is copious more generalised research outlining the importance of one good adult as a strong protective factor for vulnerable learners (Dooley and Fitzgerald, 2012; Frederick et al., 2023). It would be beneficial to see more research exploring the one good adult concept with neurodivergent learners.

Besides the concept of one good adult, other approaches can be taken to developing strong school-based relationships. Approaches that are practised by schools that actively promote strong and nurturing relationships include Restorative Practices (Zakszeski and Rutherford, 2021), Nel Nodding's ethics of care (Adhikari et al., 2023), and cultivating relationships that foster a sense of belonging (Porter et al., 2024).

For a neurodiversity-specific approach to relationships, McGreevy et al. (2024) recommend an experience sensitive approach and offer a framework that can help teachers and other caring professionals support neurodivergent young people. An experience-sensitive approach to supporting neurodivergent young people includes fostering a sense of togetherness in the learning environment, acknowledging the uniqueness of each individual, an awareness of neurodivergence, and the putting of effort into making sense of neurodivergent experiences.

These recommendations are consistent with research about neurodivergent learners who, in terms of authentic school inclusion, value feelings of safety and belonging in their relationships with peers and teachers (Lebenhagen, 2024). Peer relationships are also central to good mental health and a sense of belonging in schools. Relationships based on peer support can promote a sense of belonging and provide a space for neurodivergent learners to explore their neurodivergent identity and experience an insider perspective (Crompton et al., 2024).

Key Area 3: Policy and Planning

Organisation management factors are as essential to a successful whole-school approach to well-being promotion as curricular and extracurricular factors (NICE, 2022). School-level policy and planning is often shaped by wider system influences. Wider system influences relevant to the promotion of good mental health in neurodivergent learners include Goal 4 of the United Nations Sustainable Development Goals (UN, 2015) and the United Nations Convention on the Rights of People with Disabilities (UN, 2006). These international policies in turn shape national policies that influence school-level policy and planning. Coherent policy and planning at school level can greatly influence the educational experiences of neurodivergent learners. Effective policy development and planning occurs in schools that foster collaborative and professional practices like reflection and school-wide evaluation (Hargreaves and O'Connor, 2019). School-based structures like learner support teams and supportive collaborative models help school leadership and staff to professionally reflect on how well policies and planning are serving the school community (Department of Education and Skills, Ireland, 2019).

Schools need to consider the implications of policy and planning from the perspective of neurodivergent learners more generally, taking into consideration their mental health, specific school context, and the supporting systems available to the school and learners. Several planning tools exist for supporting schools wishing to enhance their planning from a neurodiversity perspective and include the UK AET School Competency Framework (Autism Education Trust, 2024). Consideration must also be given to supporting wellness and mental health of neurodivergent students as their needs in these areas are typically different than their neurotypical peers.

A key consideration is the professional capacity of school staff to implement, sustain, and evaluate well-being policy and planning. At the kernel of effective school-based mental health, support must be the use of evidence-based policy and planning to aid the promotion of school-based protective factors and the reduction of school-based risk factors (Spencer et al., 2022).

Key Area 4: Curriculum (Learning and Teaching)

Health promotion permeates all aspects of teaching and learning. Children and young people spend most of their day in classrooms and, consequently, their daily experience of teaching and learning contributes to their well-being. The teaching and learning must be democratic, inclusive, engaging, and differentiated, fostering expectations of high achievement and providing opportunity for success. The importance of having a deliberate focus on the development of emotional and social competencies is also highlighted by research (WHO, 2021). Supporting neurodivergent mental health can and should happen across the wider curriculum. An example of this is the meaningful representation of neurodivergence in the curriculum. This can include exposure to resources that have accurate portrayals of neurodivergent ways of being and use neurodivergent role models in curricular areas. Besides curricular resources, pedagogic practices can be impactful too. For example, inclusive approaches like Universal Design for Learning (UDL) can support the mental health of neurodivergent learners by reducing barriers to learning and offering more choice in action and expression (Spaeth and Pearson, 2023). The promotion of good mental health can be supported through learning and teaching practices. The idea of discrete learning styles has been debunked (Newton and Miah, 2017); however, many neurodivergent learners demonstrate different attention styles. One such example is a monotropic attention patterns. With an understanding of monotropism, learner interests can be used very effectively as a catalyst and motivation for learning. Moreover, monotropism is closely related to the concept of flow and flow states are considered especially beneficial to well-being (Heasman et al., 2024; Rapaport et al., 2023; Wood, 2022). More recently, there has been an increase of neurodiversity-specific approaches, programmes, and curricula. Learning about Neurodiversity in School (LEANS) in one such example. LEANS, a rigorously designed and researched curriculum, is designed as a universal support for all learners from 8 to 11 years of age. It is flexible to map onto the learning priorities of many education systems (Alcorn et al., 2023).

Undoubtedly, there are several permutations in how to frame this topic. The 4 Key Areas of Health Promotion demonstrate that health promotion in schools is a complex process. One valuable aspect of this model is its adaptability and the ease with which educators can combine the model with other useful frameworks and approaches. Moreover, the 4 Key Areas framework is flexible enough to map onto approaches used in other education systems. Clearly, supporting the mental health of neurodivergent learners is multifaceted and the 4 Key Areas of Health Promotion support the assertion that curricular, extracurricular management and organisational factors are essential to a successful whole-school approach to well-being promotion (NICE, 2022).

A valuable output from research from Lei et al. (2024) consists of a list of assessment questions designed for use by clinicians. These questions cover general neurodiversity questions, questions around assessment, identity, well-being, and school. They are designed to be adapted, and it is noteworthy how the 4 Key Areas of Health Promotion are infused throughout the guiding questions.

Conclusion

This is an ever-evolving area, and new challenges always arise. What remains constant is that schools play a pivotal role in supporting the mental health of all learners, especially given that learners spend so much of their day in school. However, it is imperative that a partnership and collaborative approach, that is steeped in evidence-based approaches, is taken when supporting the mental health of neurodivergent learners. Uniformly delivered universal approaches might not always be effective and, as discussed, have the potential to cause iatrogenic harm. Actively cultivating a positive school culture and climate, listening to and acting upon learner voice, reflective practice, and rigorous professional development and collaboration are essential actions for educationalists supporting the mental health of neurodivergent learners.

The Neurodiversity Paradigm is a promising perspective that offers potential for schools supporting the mental health of neurodivergent learners. Operating within a new paradigm however exciting tasks stakeholders to be both reflective and responsive in their navigation of this paradigmatic shift. As a concluding reflective exercise, some future-focused guidelines are offered here to help with this change process.

1. Listen more to neurodivergent voices and interdisciplinary neurodivergent expertise.
2. Take a collaborative and partnership approach.
3. Put the neurodivergent learner at the centre of this process.

References

Adhikari, A., Saha, B. and Sen, S., 2023. Nel Noddings' theory of care and its ethical Components. *International Research Journal of Education and Technology*, 5(8), pp. 198–206. ISSN 2581–7795

Ahlen, J., Lenhard, F. and Ghaderi, A., 2015. Universal prevention for anxiety and depressive symptoms in children: A meta-analysis of randomized and cluster-randomized trials. *The Journal of Primary Prevention*, 36(6), pp. 387–403. https://doi.org/10.1007/s10935-015-0405-4

Alcorn, A.M., McGeown, S., Mandy, W., Aitken, D. and Fletcher-Watson, S., 2023. Learning about neurodiversity at school (LEANS): Evaluation of the LEANS resource pack in mainstream primary schools. *Preprint.*https://doi.org/10.31219/osf.io/fhc2k

Araujo, A.G.R., Silva, M.A.D. and Zanon, R.B., 2023. Autism, neurodiversity and stigma: Political and inclusive perspectives. *Psicologia Escolar e Educacional*, 27, p. e247367. https://doi.org/10.1590/2175-35392023-247367-T

Autism Education Trust, 2024. *Autism education trust competency framework*. Available at: School-Competency-Framework_T-HUB-Sc-Mt.pdf – (autismeducationtrust.org.uk) (Accessed 15 August 2024).

Barrett, P.M., 2004. *FRIENDS for Life! For Children. Participant Workbook and Leaders Manual*. Australian Academic Press.

Barrett, P.M., Farrell, L.J., Ollendick, T.H. and Dadds, M., 2006. Long-term outcomes of an Australian universal prevention trial of anxiety and depression symptoms in children and youth: An evaluation of the friends program. *Journal of Clinical Child and Adolescent Psychology*, 35(3), pp. 403–411. https://doi.org/10.1207/s15374424jccp3503_5

Brito, R., Joseph, S. and Sellman, E., 2021. Mindfulness "in" Education as a Form of Iatrogenesis. *Journal of Transformative Education*, *19*(3), pp. 261–283. https://doi.org/10.1177/15413446209872

Burke, M.K., Prendeville, P. and Veale, A., 2017. An evaluation of the "FRIENDS for Life" programme among children presenting with autism spectrum disorder. *Educational Psychology in Practice*, *33*(4), pp. 435–449. https://doi.org/10.1080/02667363.2017.1367648

Butler, N., Quigg, Z., Bates, R., Jones, L., Ashworth, E., Gowland, S. and Jones, M., 2022. The contributing role of family, school, and peer supportive relationships in protecting the mental wellbeing of children and adolescents. *School Mental Health*, *14*(3), pp. 776–788. https://doi.org/10.1007/s12310-022-09502-9

Cebolla, A., Demarzo, M., Martins, P., Soler, J. and Garcia-Campayo, J., 2017. Unwanted effects: Is there a negative side of meditation? A multicentre survey. *PLoS One*, *12*(9), p. e0183137. https://doi.org/10.1371/journal.pone.0183137

Chapman, R. and Carel, H., 2022. Neurodiversity, epistemic injustice, and the good human life. *Journal of Social Philosophy*. https://doi.org/10.1111/josp.12456

Connolly, S.E., Constable, H.L. and Mullally, S.L., 2023. School distress and the school attendance crisis: A story dominated by neurodivergence and unmet need. *Frontiers in Psychiatry*, *14*, p. 1237052. https://doi.org/10.3389/fpsyt.2023.1237052

Crompton, C.J., Fotheringham, F., Cebula, K., Webber, C., Foley, S. and Fletcher-Watson, S., 2024. Neurodivergent-designed and neurodivergent-led peer support in school: A feasibility and acceptability study of the neurodivergent peer support toolkit (NEST). https://doi.org/10.31219/osf.io/6eayd

Das, J.K., Salam, R.A., Lassi, Z.S., Khan, M.N., Mahmood, W., Patel, V. and Bhutta, Z.A., 2016. Interventions for adolescent mental health: An overview of systematic reviews. *Journal of Adolescent Health*, *59*(4), pp. S49–S60. https://doi.org/10.1016/j.jadohealth.2016.06.020

Department of Education and Science (DES), Ireland. 2007. *Special Educational Needs: A Continuum of Support, Guidelines for Teachers*. Stationary Office.

Department of Education and Skills (DES), Ireland. (2019). *Wellbeing Policy Statement and Framework for Practice*. Stationary Office.

Donnelly, V. and Kyriazopoulou, M., 2014. *Organisation of provision to support inclusive education – summary report*. European Agency for Special Needs and Inclusive Education. Available at: www.european-agency.org (Accessed 28 June 2024).

Dooley, B.A. and Fitzgerald, A., 2012. *My world survey: National study of youth mental health in Ireland*. Headstrong and UCD School of Psychology. Available at: https://researchrepository.ucd.ie/server/api/core/bitstreams/19fedd09-447f-4913–88d9–6306318d01e0/content (Accessed 27 June 2024).

Durlak, J.A., Weissberg, R.P., Dymnicki, A.B., Taylor, R.D. and Schellinger, K.B., 2011. The impact of enhancing students' social and emotional learning: A meta-analysis of school-based universal interventions. *Child Development*, *82*(1), pp. 405–432. https://doi.org/10.1111/j.1467-8624.2010.01564.x

Elasra, A., 2017. School process and educational outcomes in England. *Investigaciones de Economía de la Educación volume 12*, pp. 223–262.

Engel, G.L., 1977. The need of a new medical model: A challenge for biomedicine. In: Leon Wurmser, Ellen McDaniel, eds. *Dimensions of behavior: The psychiatric foundations of medicine*. Boston: Butterworth-Heinemann.

Farahar, C., 2022. Autistic identity, culture, community, and space for well-being. In: D. Milton, S. Ryan, eds. *The Routledge International Handbook of Critical Autism Studies*. Routledge, pp. 229–241. https://doi.org/10.4324/9781003056577

Fink, E., Deighton, J., Humphrey, N. and Wolpert, M., 2015. Assessing the bullying and victimisation experiences of children with special educational needs in mainstream schools: Development and validation of the bullying behaviour and experience scale. *Research in Developmental Disabilities*, *36*, pp. 611–619. https://doi.org/10.1016/j.ridd.2014.10.048

Finnigan, K.A., 2024. Sensory responsive environments: A qualitative study on perceived relationships between outdoor built environments and sensory sensitivities. *Land, 13*(5), p. 636. https://doi.org/10.3390/land13050636

Foulkes, L., Andrews, J.L., Reardon, T. and Stringaris, A., 2024. Research recommendations for assessing potential harm from universal school-based mental health interventions. *Nature Mental Health, 2*(3), pp. 270–277. https://doi.org/10.1038/s44220-024-00208-2

Foulkes, L. and Stringaris, A., 2023. Do no harm: Can school mental health interventions cause iatrogenic harm?. *British Journal of Psychiatry Bulletin, 47*(5), pp. 267–269. https://doi.org/10.1192/bjb.2023.9

Frederick, J., Spratt, T. and Devaney, J., 2023. Supportive relationships with trusted adults for children and young people who have experienced adversities: Implications for social work service provision. *The British Journal of Social Work, 53*(6), pp. 3129–3145. https://doi.org/10.1093/bjsw/bcad107

Gee, B., Wilson, J., Clarke, T., Farthing, S., Carroll, B., Jackson, C., King, K., Murdoch, J., Fonagy, P. and Notley, C., 2021. Delivering mental health support within schools and colleges–a thematic synthesis of barriers and facilitators to implementation of indicated psychological interventions for adolescents. *Child and Adolescent Mental Health, 26*(1), pp. 34–46. https://doi.org/10.1111/camh.12381

Georgiou, G.K., Parrila, R. and McArthur, G., 2024. Dyslexia and mental health problems: Introduction to the special issue. *Annals of Dyslexia, 74*(1), pp. 1–3. https://doi.org/10.1007/s11881-024-00300-3

Granieri, J.E., Morton, H.E., Romanczyk, R.G. and Gillis Mattson, J.M., 2023. Profiles of school refusal among neurodivergent youth. *European Education, 55*(3–4), pp. 186–201. https://doi.org/10.1080/10564934.2023.2251013

Grant, R.J. and Wethers, R., 2024. Trauma-informed considerations with neurodivergent children and adolescents. *Trauma Impacts: The Repercussions of Individual and Collective Trauma*, p. 111.

Grinker, R.R., 1953. *Psychosomatic Research*. New York: W. W. Norton & Co.

Hamilton, L.G., 2024. Emotionally based school avoidance in the aftermath of the COVID-19 pandemic: Neurodiversity, agency and belonging in school. *Education Sciences, 14*(2), p. 156.https://doi.org/10.3390/educsci14020156

Han, E., Scior, K., Avramides, K. and Crane, L., 2022. A systematic review on autistic people's experiences of stigma and coping strategies. *Autism Research, 15*(1), pp. 12–26. https://doi.org/10.1002/aur.2652

Hargreaves, A. and O'Connor, T.M., 2019. The 4 B's. *The Learning Professional, 40*(3), pp. 54–62. ISSN: 2476194X

Heasman, B., Williams, G., Charura, D., Hamilton, L.G., Milton, D. and Murray, F., 2024. Towards autistic flow theory: A non-pathologising conceptual approach. *Journal for the Theory of Social Behaviour*. https://doi.org/10.1111/jtsb.12427

Holmes, S.C., 2024. Inclusion, autism spectrum, students' experiences. *International Journal of Developmental Disabilities, 70*(1), pp. 59–73. https://doi.org/10.1080/20473869.2022.2056403

Hudson, C.C., Hall, L. & Harkness, K.L., 2019. Prevalence of depressive disorders in individuals with autism spectrum disorder: A meta-analysis. *Journal of Abnormal Child Psychology 47*, 165–175. https://doi.org/10.1007/s10802-018-0402-1

Jennings, P., 2015. *Mindfulness for Teachers: Simple Skills for Peace and Productivity in the Classroom*. New York, NY: W. W. Norton. https://doi.org/10.1007/s12671-015-0470-z

Kelly, C., Martin, R., Taylor, R. and Doherty, M., 2024. Recognising and responding to physical and mental health issues in neurodivergent girls and women. *British Journal of Hospital Medicine, 85*(4), pp. 1–12. https://doi.org/10.12968/hmed.2023.0337

Lebenhagen, C., 2024. Autistic students' views on meaningful inclusion: A Canadian perspective. *Journal of Education (Boston, Mass.), 204*(1), pp. 13–28. https://doi.org/10.1177/00220574221101378

Lee, W., McCaw, C.T. and Van Dam, N.T., 2024. Mindfulness in education: Critical debates and pragmatic considerations. *British Educational Research Journal*. https://doi.org/10.1002/berj.3998

Lei, J., Cooper, K., and Hollocks, M.J., 2024. Psychological interventions for autistic adolescents with co-occurring anxiety and depression: Considerations linked to autism social identity and masking. *Autism in Adulthood*. https://doi.org/10.1089/aut.2024.0005 (Ahead of Print).

Lindahl, J.R. and Britton, W.B., 2019. 'I have this feeling of not really being here': Buddhist meditation and changes in sense of self. *Journal of Consciousness Studies*, 26(7–8), pp. 157–183.

Lugg, W., 2022. The biopsychosocial model–history, controversy, and Engel. *Australasian Psychiatry*, 30(1), pp. 55–59. https://doi.org/10.1177/10398562211037333

McGreevy, E., Quinn, A., Law, R., Botha, M., Evans, M., Rose, K., Moyse, R., Boyens, T., Matejko, M., & Pavlopoulou, G., 2024. An experience sensitive approach to care with and for autistic children and young people in clinical services. *Journal of Humanistic Psychology*, 0(0). https://doi.org/10.1177/00221678241232442

Moran, L., 2022. *The utility of the continuum of support framework in supporting class teachers and special education teachers in the identification and monitoring of pupils.* Available at: https://dspace.mic.ul.ie/handle/10395/3035 (Accessed 24 June 2024).

Najeeb, P. and Quadt, L., 2024. Autistic well-being: A scoping review of scientific studies from a neurodiversity-affirmative perspective. *Neurodiversity*, 2, p. 27546330241233088. https://doi.org/10.1177/27546330241233088

National Institute for Health and Care Excellence (NICE), 2022. *Social, emotional, and mental wellbeing in primary and secondary education, NICE guideline [NG223].* Available at: Overview | Social, emotional and mental wellbeing in primary and secondary education | Guidance | NICE (Accessed 29 June 2024).

Ne'eman, A. and Pellicano, E., 2022. Neurodiversity as politics. *Human Development*, 66(2), pp. 149–157. https://doi.org/10.1159/000524277

Newton, P.M. and Miah, M., 2017. Evidence-based higher education–is the learning styles 'myth' important? *Frontiers in Psychology*, 8, p. 241866. https://doi.org/10.3389/fpsyg.2017.00444

Nicholls, A., 2021. *Why doesn't standard talking therapy work for autistic people?* Articles – Dr Alice Nicholls (Accessed 28 June 2024).

Novin, S., Broekhof, E. and Rieffe, C., 2019. Bidirectional relationships between bullying, victimization and emotion experience in boys with and without autism. *Autism*, 23(3), pp. 796–800. https://doi.org/10.1177/1362361318787446

O'Dea, Á., Stanley, M., Coote, S. and Robinson, K., 2021. Children and young people's experiences of living with developmental coordination disorder/dyspraxia: A systematic review and meta-ethnography of qualitative research. *Plos One*, 16(3), p. e0245738. https://doi.org/10.1371/journal.pone.0245738

OECD, 2017. *PISA 2015 results (volume III): Students' well-being.* Paris: OECD Publishing. https://doi.org/10.1787/9789264273856-en

O'Neill, C., 2024. *An inclusive school culture. Inclusion Ireland webinar series.* An Inclusive School Culture. youtube.com (Accessed 28 June 2024).

Paget, A., Parker, C., Heron, J., Logan, S., Henley, W., Emond, A. and Ford, T., 2018. Which children and young people are excluded from school? Findings from a large British birth cohort study, the A von Llongitudinal Study of Parents and Children (ALSPAC). *Child: Care, Health, and Development*, 44(2), pp. 285–296. DOI: https://doi.org/10.1111/cch.12525

Pellicano, E. and Heyworth, M., 2023. The foundations of autistic flourishing. *Current Psychiatry Reports*, 25(9), pp. 419–427. https://doi.org/10.1007/s11920-023-01441-9

Porter, J., McDermott, T., Daniels, H. and Ingram, J., 2024. Feeling part of the school and feeling safe: Further development of a tool for investigating school belonging. *Educational Studies*, 50(3), pp. 382–398. https://doi.org/10.1080/03055698.2021.1944063

Purser, R., 2019. *McMindfulness: How indfulness became the new capitalist spirituality.* London: Repeater. ISBN: 9781912248315

Quinton, A., Happé, F., Fazel, M., Skripkauskaite, S. and Soneson, E., 2024. How is being neurodivergent associated with negative experiences and mental health in young people? https://doi.org/10.17605/OSF.IO/BY5N2

Rapaport, H., Clapham, H., Adams, J., Lawson, W., Porayska-Pomsta, K. and Pellicano, E., 2023. "In a state of flow": A qualitative examination of autistic adults' phenomenological experiences of task immersion. *Autism in Adulthood.* https://doi.org/10.1089/aut.2023.0032

Reveley, J., 2016. Neoliberal meditations: How mindfulness training medicalizes education and responsibilizes young people. *Policy Futures in Education, 14*(4), pp. 497–511. https://doi.org/10.1177/1478210316637 9

Roberts, J., 2021. *Performative neurodiversity – the appropriation and watering down of a human rights movement for profit. Therapist neurodiversity collective.* Available at: https://therapistndc.org/performative-neurodiversity-the-appropriation-and-watering-down-of-a-human-rights-movement-for-profit/ (Accessed 27 June 2024).

Rowley, E., Chandler, S., Baird, G., Simonoff, E., Pickles, A., Loucas, T. and Charman, T., 2012. The experience of friendship, victimization and bullying in children with an autism spectrum disorder: Associations with child characteristics and school placement. *Research in Autism Spectrum Disorders, 6*(3), pp. 1126–1134. https://doi.org/10.1016/j.rasd.2012.03.004

Royal College of Psychiatry, 2022. *Suicide and Autism, a National Crisis.* Available at: https://www.rcpsych.ac.uk/docs/default-source/improving-care/nccmh/suicide-prevention/workshops-(wave-4)/wave-4-workshop-2-suicide-and-autism---slides.pdf?sfvrsn=bf3e0113_2 (Accessed 15 August 2024).

Schilpzand, E.J., Sciberras, E., Alisic, E., Efron, D., Hazell, P., Jongeling, B., Anderson, V. and Nicholson, J.M. 2018. Trauma exposure in children with and without ADHD: Prevalence and functional impairment in a community-based study of 6–8-year-old Australian children. *European Child and Adolescent Psychiatry, 27,* 811–819. https://doi.org/10.1007/s00787-017-1067-y

Sellman, E.M. and Buttarazzi, G.F., 2020. Adding lemon juice to poison–raising critical questions about the oxymoronic nature of mindfulness in education and its future direction. *British Journal of Educational Studies, 68*(1), pp. 61–78. https://doi.org/10.1080/00071005.2019.1581128

Slack, G., 2013. *An evaluation of the FRIENDS for Life intervention with an autistic spectrum population: Evaluating the impact on children's anxiety.* Doctoral dissertation, University of Nottingham. www.eprints.nottingham.ac.uk/14520/

Slagus, J. and Kitchin, A., 2024. Welcoming the weird and wonderful: Creating classroom environments that support neurodiversity. *Understanding Mental Health Across Educational Contexts: Promoting Wellness in Classrooms,* p. 248.

Spaeth, E. and Pearson, A., 2023. A reflective analysis on how to promote a positive learning experience for neurodivergent students. *Journal of Perspectives in Applied Academic Practice, 11*(2). https://doi.org/10.56433/jpaap. v11i2.517

Spencer, L. P., Flynn, D., Johnson, A., Maniatopoulos, G., Newham, J. J., Perkins, N., Wood, M., Woodley, H., & Henderson, E. J., 2022. The implementation of whole-school approaches to transform mental health in UK schools: A realist evaluation protocol. *International Journal of Qualitative Methods, 21.* https://doi.org/10.1177/16094069221082360

Stoiber, K.C. and Gettinger, M., 2015. Multi-tiered systems of support and evidence-based practices. In: *Handbook of response to intervention: The science and practice of multi-tiered systems of support.* Boston, MA: Springer US, pp. 121–141.

Tufvesson, C. and Tufvesson, J., 2009. The building process as a tool towards an all-inclusive school. A Swedish example focusing on children with defined concentration difficulties such as ADHD, autism, and Down's syndrome. *Journal of Housing and the Built Environment, 24,* pp. 47–66. https://doi.org/10.1007/s10901-008-9129-6

Turnock, A., Langley, K. and Jones, C.R., 2022. Understanding stigma in autism: A narrative review and theoretical model. *Autism in Adulthood, 4*(1), pp. 76–91. https://doi.org/10.1089/aut.2021.000

UNESCO, 2004. *The Salamanca statement and framework for action on special needs education.* World Conference on Special Needs Education: Access and Quality, Salamanca, Spain, 1994 Available at: The Salamanca Statement and Framework for Action on Special Needs Education – UNESCO Digital Library (Accessed 8 June 2024).

United Nations, 2006. The UN convention on the rights of persons with disabilities. *Treaty Series, 2515,* 3. Available at: https://www.ohchr.org/ (Accessed 29 June 2024).

United Nations, 2015. *The UN sustainable development goals.* New York: United Nations. Available at: http://www.un.org/sustainabledevelopment/summit/ (Accessed 28 June 2024).

Viner, R.M., Ozer, E.M., Denny, S., Marmot, M., Resnick, M., Fatusi, A. and Currie, C., 2012. Adolescence and the social determinants of health. *The Lancet, 379*(9826), pp. 1641–1652. https://doi.org/10.1016/S0140–6736(12)60149–4

Weare, K., 2010. Promoting mental health through schools. In: P. Aggleton, C. Dennison & I. Warwick, eds. *Promoting health and wellbeing through schools.* Routledge, pp. 36–53. https://doi.org/10.4324/9780203860090

Weare, K., 2018. *The evidence for mindfulness in schools for children and young people.* Mindfulness in Schools Project. Available at: Microsoft Word - 5 Evidence for mindfulness in schools.docx (ave-institut.de) (Accessed 28 June 2024).

Weare, K. and Nind, M., 2011. Mental health promotion and problem prevention in schools: What does the evidence say?. *Health Promotion International, 26*(suppl_1), pp. i29–i69. https://doi.org/10.1093/heapro/dar075

Werner-Seidler, A., Perry, Y., Calear, A.L., Newby, J.M. and Christensen, H., 2017. School-based depression and anxiety prevention programs for young people: A systematic review and meta-analysis. *Clinical Psychology Review, 51,* pp. 30–47. https://doi.org/10.1016/j.cpr.2016.10.005

Wilson, A.C. and Gullon-Scott, F., 2024. 'It's not always textbook social anxiety': A survey-based study investigating the nature of social anxiety and experiences of therapy in autistic people. *Autism.* https://doi.org/10.1177/13623613241251513

Wood, R., 2022. From disempowerment to well-being and flow: Enabling autistic communication in schools. In: *The Routledge international handbook of critical autism studies.* Routledge, pp. 277–287. ISBN: ISBN9781003056577

World Health Organisation, 2021. *WHO guideline on school health services.* Geneva. Available at: Who-shs-guideline_web_v28.pdf (Accessed 29 June 2024).

Zakszeski, B. and Rutherford, L., 2021. Mind the gap: A systematic review of research on restorative practices in schools. *School Psychology Review, 50*(2–3), pp. 371–387. https://doi.org/10.1080/2372966X.2020.1852056

Zenner, C., Herrnleben-Kurz, S. and Walach, H., 2014. Mindfulness-based interventions in schools – a systematic review and meta-analysis. *Frontiers in Psychology, 5,* p. 603. https://doi.org/10.3389/fpsyg.2014.00603

Chapter 8

Understanding College Students and Mental Health through the Neurodiversity Paradigm

Jessica Monahan

Introduction

As the term neurodiversity gains popularity and momentum, those in higher education must grapple with what it means to be neurodiversity-affirming. In this chapter, I will discuss neurodivergent college students and mental health, focusing on unpacking how systems impact student identity and mental health. I will make recommendations at the institutional and individual levels that are grounded in research and lived experience. To do this well, I need to disclose my identities, as they have shaped how I view neurodivergent college students and mental health. I am a white, middle-class, queer, first-generation college student with ADHD and complex PTSD. Some of these identities have afforded me great privilege, while some have created challenges due to stigma and societal expectations. In this chapter, I have attempted to address the complexity of intersectionality. While my identities are complex and intersecting, I cannot (and do not wish to) speak on behalf of groups outside my identity. However, I draw on research from other oppressed college student identities.

Throughout this chapter, I will primarily use identity-first language (e.g., disabled) instead of person-first language (person with a disability). Many adults in the disabled community prefer identity-first language (Galinsky *et al.*, 2003; Best *et al.*, 2022; Smith *et al.*, 2023; Taboas *et al.*, 2023), which is also my preference and what I have chosen to use. I also use the term "bodymind" to explicitly acknowledge that the body and the mind are intertwined and should be referenced together, especially when discussing disability (Price, 2011; Ranon Nachman and Brown, 2024).

Theoretical Background

Becoming neurodiversity-affirming requires fundamental shifts in our thinking. It is more complex than reading a number of resources and consulting a checklist. It is about acknowledging the oppressive systems that we exist in, challenging those systems, and creating a resilient and supportive community. Identities are socially constructed (Jones and Stewart, 2016), and the experiences of individuals with

DOI: 10.4324/9781003495949-9

historically marginalized identities must be examined within the context of these systems. Exploring issues through a critical lens allows for the opportunity for genuine change (hooks, 1994). Therefore, I will begin our discussion with a brief overview of Critical Disability Theory (CDT) and the Neurodiversity Paradigm. Next, we will explore the higher education context, Student Development Theory (SDT), and end with recommendations that align with the Disability Justice Framework.

Critical Disability Theory

Minich (2016) defines CDT as involving "the scrutiny of normative ideologies [that] should occur not for its own sake but with the goal of producing knowledge in support of justice for people with stigmatized bodies and minds" (p. 5). That is, we must critically examine disability within the context of our cultures, social norms, and the systems within which we learn, work, and live. One of the main goals of CDT is to identify, expose, and dismantle ableism (Hall, 2019). At its very core, ableism is the belief and behaviors that enforce the idea that a non-disabled bodymind is the "correct" way of being (Campbell, 2009). Ableism exists in systems, legislation, policies, and interpersonal and intrapersonal interactions. Like many forms of prejudice and stereotypes, ableism can be internalized and exist within each of us, including the disabled, at no fault of our own. We live in societies that believe there is one right way to be, and after years of hearing these messages, we must actively work to undo and challenge this thinking.

Neurodiversity Paradigm

The Neurodiversity (ND) Paradigm considers that there is natural and normal variation in how brains develop and adapt to their environment (Walker, 2021). The ND Paradigm situates disability as morally neutral, in that being disabled is not inherently bad or good, it just *is*. As such, the ND paradigm is in direct opposition to the medical model of disability, which assumes that there is something wrong with the brain and it must be fixed. The medical model posits that biological abnormalities, such as genetic defects, pathogens, or biochemical imbalances primarily cause diseases. It emphasizes the role of biological processes in the pathophysiology and course of illness (Deacon, 2013; Gillick, 1985; Tamm, 1993). The medical model typically places the need for change with the disabled bodymind. Not only does the ND Paradigm shift the focus to systems of oppression, but it also reframes mental health disabilities as reactions or responses to the experiences we have as human beings. For example, for most people like me with a diagnosis of dissociative identity disorder (DID), there is an extensive history of trauma. Our brains are actively trying to protect us from reliving trauma, which looks very different from a brain that has not had the same experience. However, people with DID have brains that deviate from how the majority of brains (neurotypical, or neuromajority) experience the world. I require support to meet the demands of daily life, and in alignment with the ND paradigm, that need for support is morally neutral.

The Diagnostic and Statistical Manual of Mental Disorders (DSM) is the primary tool that is used in the United States to diagnose mental health disorders. While the complete history of the DSM is outside of the scope of this chapter, it is important to acknowledge that it has deep roots in capitalism. Scholars have argued that over the years, the DSM was influenced heavily by the pharmaceutical industry and began to focus on the ability to work as part of the criteria for many disorders (Wise, 2024). The medical model heavily relies on pharmacological treatments. This approach has led to the widespread use of medications, particularly in the treatment of mental disorders, where conditions are often viewed as brain diseases caused by chemical imbalances (Deacon, 2013; Massoud et al., 1998). However, the DSM-I mentioned work 10 times (Meadows, 2022) and the current iteration of the DSM (5th edition) mentions a person's ability to work 385 times. The increased emphasis upon work has become intertwined with a person's ability to contribute to the workforce. To be quite blunt, my brain does not work within the constraints of capitalism, and therefore is considered and/or labelled as disordered. To be successful in my employment and to fit within the current expectations of my employment role, I require a diagnosis and medication. Within this understanding, it is me who is required to adapt to the system and to engage with the medical model. Yet, society has little onus to adapt to me or those like me, as we typically do not fit within the narrow understanding of being economically useful. Further to this, receiving a diagnosis and medication requires medical insurance, another economic framework that underpins the life of folx like me. Ironically, for many people in the United States, access to medical insurance is contingent upon employment and if employment is contingent upon access to diagnosis and medication, and indeed any other supports required, where does that leave us? It is beyond this chapter to delve into this any more deeply, but these are very important considerations and further critical discussion is required in this area.

This is a complex area as I acknowledge the complexity of identifying a system as ableist and the need to dismantle it while also needing to participate in it for survival. While we work to tear down and rebuild the broken systems, we must also lean into the beauty of our brains, learn about the ND Paradigm, and consider how we can shift our thinking to benefit ourselves. The ND paradigm allows each of us to make decisions for ourselves around the type of support (if any) that we require. The medical model would suggest that I should always be on medication, and always trying to "fix" my ADHD or complex PTSD. The ND paradigm allows me to make my own decisions about the support I need, while removing the shame of how my brain works.

Considering the Context: Higher Education

Higher education, as defined by any formalized education after secondary school, is a common "next step" for many students, and every student has their own reasons for taking that path. Many students see higher education as an opportunity to gain specialized knowledge and become competitive in the job market. Others have been told it is necessary to ensure financial stability. However, for many students, college is also an opportunity to explore their identity. Understanding the holistic experience of a student has been a goal for higher education as far back as the 1930s when scholars began studying college student development (Jones and Stewart, 2016).

Student Development Theory (SDT)

SDT aims to understand the experiences of college students, which should then, in turn, provide professionals at institutions of higher education (IHEs) with the valuable information necessary to provide support. Jones and Stewart (2016) categorize SDT into three distinct waves. In the earliest writings of SDT (first wave), scholars attempted to understand the development of college students and how the unique environment influenced their development (Jones and Stewart, 2016). These fundamental questions posed by Knefelkamp and colleagues (1978) serve as the building blocks for SDT through to the present day. However, the first wave of SDT focused on white men who could afford college (Jones and Stewart, 2016). There was little to no focus on oppressed identities – those that are historically marginalized based on race, gender, sexuality, class, and disability.

The second wave of SDT began to address these complex identities, acknowledging that these students have different experiences than the white male students who were the focus of the first wave (Jones and Stewart, 2016). During this time, scholars emphasized that identity is socially constructed, and institutions of oppression play an integral role in developing these identities (Jones and Abes, 2013). The most recent SDT literature (third wave) emphasizes the importance of understanding that identity is fluid, ever-changing, and heavily influenced by the social context in which an individual exists (Jones and Stewart, 2016). In addition, scholars like Weber (2010) discuss intersectionality and how oppressive systems of power impact students. Students who are in college are influenced by the social norms and expectations that exist within these settings. The third wave also encourages rethinking the systems within IHEs that actively continue to oppress students, including those with disabilities (Shpigelman et al., 2022).

Disability in Higher Education

While it is incredibly difficult to identify the exact number of disabled students who attend some form of postsecondary education, there have been several studies in the United States that provide some context. According to the National Center for Education Statistics, in the 2020–2021 academic year, approximately 20% of college students reported having a disability (National Center for Education Statistics, 2023). This number is likely much higher as many students choose not to disclose their disabilities, or do not have formal diagnoses which prevents them from accessing disability services (Moriña, 2024).

Disabled students who choose to attend college may face difficulty in navigating systems that were designed for non-disabled bodyminds. Despite many individuals who act with good intentions, IHEs are riddled with ableist policies and a community with deeply ingrained internalized ableism. In higher education, the indirect message sent to students (and to faculty and staff) is that there is one correct way to be and that the correct way is non-disabled. A prime example is the need for students to use accommodations to ensure access to the academic curriculum, instead of the curriculum being designed and delivered according to how disabled students may experience the world. IHEs are designed to support and develop non-disabled students, and those deviating outside of the majority or "norm" determined by the institution are othered, with the onus of access relying squarely on their shoulders.

For legal context, in the United States, college students with disabilities are protected under Section 504 of the Rehabilitation Act of 1973 and the Americans with Disabilities Act (ADA) of 1990, which was reauthorized in 2008 to include a more robust definition of disability and its impact on daily life. These federal laws prohibit discrimination based on disability and require that IHEs in America provide reasonable accommodations to students, so they may access the curriculum and college campus. When a student would like to use an accommodation to access the content in the United States, they must locate and contact the correct office or person on campus. They must then schedule and attend an intake appointment, at which time most IHEs require the student to provide medical documentation of a disability. This is despite national professional organizations encouraging the acceptance and use of a student's lived experience and personal report of why accommodations are necessary (AHEAD, 2012).

It is problematic that IHEs require medical or professional documentation for access given the barriers that many students face in accessing a formal diagnosis. In the United States, there is no universal healthcare, which places evaluations for disabilities like ADHD, autism, or learning disabilities out of reach for those who cannot afford them. While many college students can access health insurance through their IHE, coverage may not be comprehensive. For those who can access evaluations, many providers are not trained to identify disabilities in women or those who have spent a lifetime masking (suppressing) their neurodivergent traits (Lewis, 2017). This dynamic, when viewed through CDT, places access to support and learning in the hands of medical providers and individuals in the IHE who decide and enforce accommodation policies (Ranon Nachman and Brown, 2024).

Disabled students who choose to navigate the ableist systems of higher education must use cognitive energy that non-disabled students do not need to. The irony is that many disabled students do not have an unlimited capacity for cognitive load. Within the ND Paradigm, limited capacity for anything, including cognitive load, is not inherently bad. It is morally neutral. However, in spaces created for and by non-disabled bodyminds, having a limited capacity for cognitive load can be detrimental. As many advocates will argue, navigating these systems as a disabled bodymind can be physically and mentally exhausting.

College Students and Mental Health

College campuses are dealing with a major mental health crisis. In the United States, students continue to access college counseling centers at high rates (Center for Collegiate Mental Health (CCMH)). They are seeking support for a wide variety of mental health concerns with anxiety, depression, and stress being reported most frequently. It is well-documented that discrimination and oppressive systems create mental health concerns in people who have historically marginalized identities, like disabilities (Temple *et al.*, 2019; Hackett *et al.*, 2020; Brown and Ciciurkaite, 2022). In the 2021–2022 academic year, one in three LGBTQIA+ college students had seriously considered death by suicide and an alarming 7% had attempted death by suicide (Trevor Project, 2022). These rates were even higher for LGBTQIA+ students of color (Trevor Project, 2022). This is not surprising given that microaggressions toward students of color are associated with higher levels of depression (Torres-Harding *et al.*, 2020) and perceived stigma based on racial identity is associated with higher rates of suicidal ideation, planning, and attempts (Goodwill and Zhou, 2020).

During the 2022–2023 academic year in the United States, almost 20% of students who accessed college counseling centers reported experiencing discrimination (within the last six months) based on disability, gender, nationality/country of origin, race/ethnicity/culture, religion, or sexual orientation. Students who experienced discrimination in at least one of these areas had higher rates of general distress, social isolation, and suicidal thoughts than students who had not experienced discrimination. More concerning is that students who experienced discrimination in more than one of these areas had even higher rates of these issues than students who experienced discrimination based on one identity (Center for Collegiate Mental Health, 2022).

Across studies, students with disabilities report more mental health concerns than their non-disabled peers (Aguilar and Lipson, 2021; Solís García *et al.*, 2024). For students with mental health disabilities, accessing support and accommodations may be more difficult, as faculty and staff are less likely to believe that they require accommodations (Kain *et al.*, 2019). Not only is this a form of discrimination, but it is also an example of ableism preventing students from accessing support that they are entitled to by law. Unsurprisingly, students with mental health disabilities are more likely to drop out of college than their peers (Koch *et al.*, 2017). As is seen time and time again, many of these mental health concerns for college students stem from "attitudinal barriers and prejudices within the environment" (Solís García *et al.*, 2024).

Reframing Mental Health in the ND Paradigm

Within the ND paradigm, there is no "normal" brain, simply a "majority." Therefore, when someone experiences mental health concerns, their brains are not broken or abnormal. They are in the neuro-minority. As we discussed, discrimination impacts college student's mental health. It is reasonable to hypothesize that student mental health would improve if systems and those in our communities acknowledged, addressed, and challenged ableist behaviors and policies.

For many, neurodivergence is an important part of their identity. Of course, many times these divergences from the majority *are* perceived as disabilities because they are not able within the long-standing and preexisting societal structures. As a result, at a very minimum additional support may be required; or more comprehensively a more inclusive system needs to be designed. However, when we begin to see disability and mental health disabilities as part of a person's identity, we can create more explicit spaces for neurodivergent folx to connect, build community, and collectively support one another. As outlined above, it is reasonable, from the data, to hypothesize that a change to a system that appears to have a causal effect on mental health difficulties is necessary. Perpetuating neurotypical hegemony through upholding the same old system and at the same time expecting change is simply not good enough. We can create more explicit spaces for neurodivergent folx to connect, build community, and collectively support one another, but this cannot be done in isolation of wider systemic changes. Examining neurodiversity and mental health for college students is more than just an exercise in how to best support these students. It is an opportunity to critically examine the structures and the systems that we exist in. To push back. To say no to the ways in which these systems continue to oppress us simply because our brains are in the neuro-minority.

Recommendations

The Disability Justice Framework seeks to push against oppressive norms by building power in the disability community and our allies. The creators of the Disability Justice Framework have outlined ten key principles: intersectionality, leadership of those most impacted, anti-capitalist politics, cross-movement solidarity, recognizing wholeness, sustainability, commitment to cross-disability solidarity, interdependence, collective access, and collective liberation (Berne *et al.*, 2018). Ultimately, the Disability Justice Framework focuses on the resiliency and resistance of individuals and our communities. When thinking about how to create neurodiversity-affirming spaces for those at IHEs, I preach the importance of the "sweet spot". We need to be encouraging and fighting for systemic change at the institutional level. Simultaneously, we need to be supporting disabled individuals so that they can thrive in the systems that currently exist.

This approach is highlighted in an article by Hoffman et al. (2019) that explores the experiences of students of color in traditionally white IHEs. They argue that to support students of color, institutions need assimilative spaces, which "facilitate the integration of students of color into the broader campus culture" (Hoffman *et al.*, 2019). For students with disabilities or mental health needs, this translates into ensuring that this population has access to the services and supports that they need to succeed in the ableist systems of IHE. Currently, a disabled student's success in higher education is defined by societal expectations and institutions created by non-disabled bodyminds. Therefore, students must also have access to subversive spaces, which "are positioned as counterspaces or potential counterspaces where minoritized identities can be centered and success is not predefined from an institutional standpoint" (Hoffman *et al.*, 2019). For disabled students, this may look like spaces where disabled identities are celebrated, and success is defined by disabled bodyminds. Therefore, the recommendations that follow focus on systemic changes and practical things that individuals can do to become more neurodiversity-affirming. These recommendations are guided by the principles of CDT, the ND paradigm, and many of the principles of the Disability Justice Framework.

Reforming the Systems

Before any IHE considers systemic changes to become more neurodiversity-affirming, the administration must engage in meaningful discussion and collaboration with the neurodivergent population on campus. Decisions should not be made without the leadership of those who are impacted by the policies and practices being discussed. IHEs must acknowledge disability as a possible part of someone's identity by intentionally including it in Diversity, Equity, and Inclusion (DEI) efforts (Dwyer *et al.*, 2022). The Center for Collegiate Mental Health explicitly calls on IHEs to prioritize DEI (including belonging) as a preventative measure against poor college student mental health (CCMH, 2022). IHEs should consider creating positions within DEI offices that focus on disability. Examining this recommendation through the Disability Justice Framework, this person should identify as disabled, be willing to act collaboratively with disabled students on campus (leadership of those most impacted), and commit to working with other cultural groups on campus (intersectionality, commitment to cross-movement organizing).

Reflecting the Disability Justice Framework principles of "collective access and interdependence", IHEs should consider how they can create spaces for groups on campus to support one another, allowing for a shared connection and meeting one another's access needs collaboratively. Many IHEs have cultural centers that act as safe spaces and advocacy centers for historically marginalized groups on campus. IHEs should work to establish disability cultural centers, as these spaces provide an important resource for students where they can subvert the "norm" or the majority expectations (Hoffman *et al.*, 2019; Dwyer *et al.*, 2022). Many students on campuses do not disclose their disability identities because of stigma, fear of negative consequences, or wanting to break free from the negatively viewed disabled identity that was formed in secondary schools (Moriña, 2024). Normalizing disability as part of someone's cultural identity may make students feel more comfortable disclosing. Not only do these spaces allow students to explore their identities and feel a sense of belonging (Hoffman et al., 2019), for some, they may act as important preventative mental health care. For example, when students had access to LGBTQIA+ services on campuses, they were less likely to consider death by suicide, highlighting the role that services and support at a university can play in the mental health of students (Trevor Project, 2022). Similarly, IHEs should work with the folx on campus with mental health concerns to develop and implement mental health initiatives that are sensitive to the complexities of intersectionality, mental health, and the college experience (Solís García *et al.*, 2024).

Many neurodiversity advocates discuss the need for more inclusive spaces to reduce forced disclosure (needing to disclose a disability when someone does not want to) and promote access by removing the need for formal accommodations. Ideally, IHEs would convert to a "needs-based system", where access to support is not dependent on a person's ability to provide a formal diagnosis (Wise, 2024). Disability offices should revise their policies, so that they align more closely with the AHEAD[1] guidelines, which center student's lived experiences and expertise as the most important documentation. Policies should explicitly state what students can do when they cannot access a medical or formal diagnosis but still need support and accommodations. IHEs should consider ways to streamline the accommodation process for students, faculty, and staff. For example, having a one-page guide to "what to expect" when requesting disability services would increase access for many disabled folx.

Finally, IHEs should focus their energy and resources on professional development and events that share information about neurodiversity, led by neurodivergent folx on campus. Professional development opportunities should include identifying and dismantling disability and mental health discrimination at the individual and institutional levels (Thornicroft *et al.*, 2022). In co-production with disabled folx, IHEs should focus professional development on defining and recognizing ableism, along with ways in which individuals can be anti-ableist. Faculty should be trained and supported in Universal Design for Learning (UDL), which is a framework for instructors to develop their courses that reduces the need for accommodations and increase access to the content for all students (Fornauf and Erickson, 2020). While UDL is not perfect, it is a means to begin the discussion of exploring ways to make classrooms more inclusive with faculty who may otherwise not consider the access needs of disabled students.

Recommendations for Individuals

In their book on neurodiversity, Sonny Jane Wise says, "Any kind of paradigm shift or change within society starts with small steps, quiet questions, and hopeful ideas" (Wise, 2024, p. 191). To infuse the ND paradigm into the higher education setting, each of us must begin to unpack our deep-rooted and internalized ableism. This work is difficult and for many, they may not realize that internalized ableism is something they need to contend with. Individuals who work in higher education and college students must seek out opportunities to learn about anti-ableism and actively work to be anti-ableist both in the higher education setting and in their personal lives (Wise, 2024).

While this work is happening, we must also be considering ways that we can push against the systems that continue to oppress. In academia, there is no reward or incentive for faculty and staff to share disability or mental health concerns publicly. In fact, it carries risk due to how disabled people and those with mental health concerns are stigmatized (Friedman and Owen, 2017; Dammeyer and Chapman, 2018; Thornicroft *et al.*, 2022). However, when students feel like they belong and have supportive faculty, their mental health improves and they are more engaged in their academic work (Linley *et al.*, 2016; Drum *et al.*, 2017; Busby *et al.*, 2020). One way to let students know that faculty are supportive and safe is to be vulnerable with them. Faculty who are disabled can share that with students. While this may feel like an overwhelming idea, in a 2017 study, Price and colleagues found that when faculty disclosed mental health disabilities to groups on campus, 90% of those faculty reported that students responded the most positively. Not only does sharing disability or mental health concerns with students normalize disability on campus, but it also increases disabled representation across professional fields. It sends the message to students that their oppressed identities are welcomed and safe with disclosers. This is a powerful way to push against the established norm that there is one correct bodymind.

Faculty can engage in professional development to learn how to create more inclusive classrooms, exploring ways in which they can reduce the need for formal accommodations within their work (like UDL). Additionally, faculty can allow for informal accommodations, without requiring students to request formal accommodations through the disability office. In their book, Sonny Jane Wise offers suggestions for accommodations in workplace and educational settings. A few examples of these accommodations include allowing the use of a recording device (communication differences), sunglasses or tinted glasses in the classroom (sensory differences), additional time to process questions and provide answers (communication differences), and breaks when needed (time management and focusing). In addition to accommodations, Wise recommends normalizing different ways in which students may need to regulate themselves. For example, I always have a small assortment of fidgets available to students in my classroom. I also use a fidget, which normalizes this practice in my classroom.

Students can speak loudly about how their brains work and organize to demand that IHEs examine policies for ableist language and practices, rewriting them in meaningful collaboration with the disabled community. Students should consider developing registered student organizations or clubs that support the disability community on campus. Drawing from the Disability Justice Framework, students are well-equipped to provide natural support to one another. Through the use of social media, students can share information about how to access specific centers on their campuses with a focus on what others can expect when they attempt to use services.

Conclusion

Disabled college students and those with mental health concerns will continue to advocate in higher education spaces. IHEs will need to listen because they play an important role in students' identity development. It is imperative to explicitly acknowledge and include disability in DEI initiatives. Individuals embedded in IHEs who strive to create inclusive and welcoming environments for all college students must invest time and energy into understanding the ND paradigm and encouraging these fundamental shifts in their thinking. Research should focus on changing the perceptions, attitudes, and behaviors of folx who work in IHE with a focus on interventions that support people in identifying and dismantling internalized ableism. Additionally, scholars must consider studies that encourage policymakers and IHEs to develop more inclusive policies to make genuine change on their campuses.

Clearly, there is so much work to be done in neurodiversity, mental health, and with college students. At times, the dramatic change that needs to take place can feel overwhelming and difficult. However, we do not need to tear down the systems in one fell swoop. We may be more successful if we start within the systems that exist and push against them. Challenge them. Stretch them. When the systems are oppressive, we can look to one another, the humans within the systems for support, compassion, and connection.

Note

1 https://www.ahead.ie/udl-practice

References

Aguilar, O. and Lipson, S.K. (2021) 'A public health approach to understanding the mental health needs of college students with disabilities: Results from a national survey', *Journal of Postsecondary Education and Disability*, 34(3), pp. 273–285.
AHEAD (2012) *Supporting accommodation requests: Guidance on documentation practices.* Huntersville, NC. Available at: https://www.ahead.org/professional-resources/accommodations/documentation.
Berne, P. *et al.* (2018) 'Ten principles of disability justice', *WSQ: Women's Studies Quarterly*, 46(1–2), pp. 227–230. Available at: https://doi.org/10.1353/wsq.2018.0003.
Best, K.L. *et al.* (2022) 'Language matters! The long-standing debate between identity-first language and person first language', *Assistive Technology*, 34(2), pp. 127–128. Available at: https://doi.org/10.1080/10400435.2022.2058315.
Brown, R.L. and Ciciurkaite, G. (2022) 'Disability, discrimination, and mental health during the covid-19 pandemic: A stress process model', *Society and Mental Health*, 12(3), pp. 215–229. Available at: https://doi.org/10.1177/21568693221115347.
Busby, D.R. *et al.* (2020) 'Suicide risk among gender and sexual minority college students: The roles of victimization, discrimination, connectedness, and identity affirmation', *Journal of Psychiatric Research*, 121, pp. 182–188. Available at: https://doi.org/10.1016/j.jpsychires.2019.11.013.
Campbell, F.K. (2009) *Contours of ableism: The production of disability and abledness.* London, UK: Palgrave Macmillan. Available at: https://doi.org/10.1057/9780230245181.
Center for Collegiate Mental Health (2022) *2023 annual report. STA 24–147.* Center for Collegiate Mental Health.
Dammeyer, J. and Chapman, M. (2018) 'A national survey on violence and discrimination among people with disabilities', *BMC Public Health*, 18(1), p. 355. Available at: https://doi.org/10.1186/s12889-018-5277-0.

Deacon, B. (2013) 'The biomedical model of mental disorder: A critical analysis of its valid-ity, utility, and effects on psychotherapy research', *Clinical Psychology Review*, 33(7), pp. 846–861. https://doi.org/10.1016/j.cpr.2012.09.007.

Drum, D.J. *et al.* (2017) 'College students' sense of coherence and connectedness as predic-tors of suicidal thoughts and behaviors', *Archives of Suicide Research: Official Journal of the International Academy for Suicide Research*, 21(1), pp. 169–184. Available at: https://doi.org/10.1080/13811118.2016.1166088.

Dwyer, P. *et al.* (2022) 'Building neurodiversity-inclusive postsecondary campuses: Rec-ommendations for leaders in higher education', *Autism in Adulthood*, p. aut.2021.0042. Available at: https://doi.org/10.1089/aut.2021.0042.

Fornauf, B.S. and Erickson, J.D. (2020) 'Toward an inclusive pedagogy through universal design for learning in higher education: A review of the literature', *Journal of Postsecond-ary Education and Disability*, 33(2), pp. 183–199.

Friedman, C. and Owen, A.L. (2017) 'Defining disability: Understandings of and attitudes towards ableism and disability', *Disability Studies Quarterly*, 37(1). Available at: https://doi.org/10.18061/dsq.v37i1.5061.

Galinsky, A.D. *et al.* (2003) 'The reappropriation of stigmatizing labels: Implications for social identity'. In *Research on managing groups and teams*. Bingley: Emerald (MCB UP), pp. 221–256. Available at: https://doi.org/10.1016/S1534–0856(02)05009–0.

Gillick, M. (1985) 'Common-sense models of health and disease', *The New England Jour-nal of Medicine*, 314(10), pp. 652–653. https://doi.org/10.1056/NEJM198509123131120.

Goodwill, J.R. and Zhou, S. (2020) 'Association between perceived public stigma and sui-cidal behaviors among college students of color in the U.S.', *Journal of Affective Disor-ders*, 262, pp. 1–7. Available at: https://doi.org/10.1016/j.jad.2019.10.019.

Hackett, R.A. *et al.* (2020) 'Disability discrimination and well-being in the United King-dom: A prospective cohort study', *BMJ Open*, 10(3), p. e035714. Available at: https://doi.org/10.1136/bmjopen-2019–035714.

Hall, M., C. (2019) Critical disability theory. In E. N. Zalta (Eds.), *The Stanford Ency-clopedia of Philosophy*. Stanford University. https://plato.stanford.edu/entries/disability-critical/#toc

Hoffman, G.D. *et al.* (2019) 'Assimilation and subversion on campus: A critical discourse analysis of students' experiences of race and institutional resources', *Journal of Diver-sity in Higher Education*, 12(3), pp. 230–241. Available at: https://doi.org/10.1037/dhe0000093.

hooks, bell (1994) *Teaching to transgress: Education as the practice of freedom*. New York/London: Routledge/Taylor & Francis Group.

Jones, S.R. and Abes, E.S. (2013) *Identity development of college students: Advancing frameworks for multiple dimensions of identity*. 1st ed. San Francisco: Jossey-Bass.

Jones, S.R. and Stewart, D. (2016) 'Evolution of student development theory', *New Direc-tions for Student Services*, 2016(154), pp. 17–28. Available at: https://doi.org/10.1002/ss.20172.

Kain, S., Chin-Newman, C. and Smith, S. (2019) '"It's all in your head": Students with psychiatric disability navigating the university environment', *Journal of Postsecondary Education and Disability*, 32(4), pp. 411–425.

Knefelkamp, L., Widick, C. and Parker, C.A. (1978) 'Editors' notes: Why bother with the-ory?', *New Directions for Student Services*, 1978(4). Available at: https://doi.org/10.1002/ss.37119780402.

Koch, L.C., Mamiseishvili, K. and Wilkins, M. (2017) 'Integrated postsecondary services and supports for college students with psychiatric disabilities', *Journal of Applied Reha-bilitation Counseling*, 48(1), pp. 16–51.

Lewis, L.F. (2017) 'A mixed methods study of barriers to formal diagnosis of autism spec-trum disorder in adults', *Journal of Autism and Developmental Disorders*, 47(8), pp. 2410–2424. Available at: https://doi.org/10.1007/s10803-017-3168-3.

Linley, J.L. *et al.* (2016) 'Faculty as sources of support for LGBTQ college students', *College Teaching*, 64(2), pp. 55–63. Available at: https://doi.org/10.1080/87567555.2015.1078275.

Massoud, T., Hademenos, G., Young, W., Gao, E., Pile-Spellman, J., & Viñuela, F. (1998). 'Principles and philosophy of modeling in biomedical research', *FASEB Journal: Official Publication of the Federation of American Societies for Experimental Biology*, 12(3), 275–285. https://doi.org/10.1096/FASEBJ.12.3.275.

Meadows, J. (2022, 5 July) *Would you still have ADHD without capitalism?* Available at: https://www.sluggish.xyz/p/would-you-still-have-adhd-without (Accessed 1 October 2024).

Minich, J.A. (2016) 'Enabling whom? Critical disability studies now', *Lateral*, 5(1). Available at: https://doi.org/10.25158/L5.1.9.

Moriña, A. (2024) 'When what is unseen does not exist: Disclosure, barriers and supports for students with invisible disabilities in higher education', *Disability & Society*, 39(4), pp. 914–932. Available at: https://doi.org/10.1080/09687599.2022.2113038.

National Center for Education Statistics (2023) *Number and percentage distribution of students enrolled in postsecondary institutions, by level, disability status, and selected student characteristics: Academic year 2019–20 [data table]*. U.S. Department of Education, Institute of Education Sciences. Available at: https://nces.ed.gov/programs/digest/d22/tables/dt22_311.10.asp.

Price, M. (2011) *Mad at School: Rhetorics of mental disability and academic life*. Ann Arbor, MI: University of Michigan Press. Available at: https://doi.org/10.3998/mpub.1612837.

Price, M. *et al.* (2017) 'Disclosure of mental disability by college and university faculty: The negotiation of accommodations, supports, and barriers', *Disability Studies Quarterly*, 37(2). Available at: https://dsq-sds.org/index.php/dsq/article/view/5487/4653.

Ranon Nachman, B. and Brown, K.R. (2024) 'Crip places: Dismantling disability discourse in the 2-year college literature', *Journal of Diversity in Higher Education*, 17(4), pp. 634–647.

Shpigelman, C.-N. *et al.* (2022) 'Supporting the development of students with disabilities in higher education: Access, stigma, identity, and power', *Studies in Higher Education*, 47(9), pp. 1776–1791. Available at: https://doi.org/10.1080/03075079.2021.1960303.

Smith, M., Horton, R. and Fitzgibbons, M. (2023) 'Preferences for person-first language and identity-first language in autistic communities', *Journal of Critical Study of Communication and Disability*, pp. 106–140. Available at: https://doi.org/10.48516/JCSCD_2023VOL1ISS2.13.

Solís García, P., Real Castelao, S. and Barreiro-Collazo, A. (2024) 'Trends and challenges in the mental health of university students with disabilities: A systematic review', *Behavioral Sciences*, 14(2), p. 111. Available at: https://doi.org/10.3390/bs14020111.

Taboas, A., Doepke, K. and Zimmerman, C. (2023) 'Preferences for identity-first versus person-first language in a US sample of autism stakeholders', *Autism*, 27(2), pp. 565–570. Available at: https://doi.org/10.1177/13623613221130845.

Tamm, M., (1993). Models of health and disease. *The British Journal of Medical Psychology*, 66(Pt 3), pp. 213–228. https://doi.org/10.1111/J.2044–8341.1993.TB01745.X.

Temple, J.B., Kelaher, M. and Williams, R. (2019) 'Disability discrimination and avoidance in later life: Prevalence, disability differentials and association with mental health', *International Psychogeriatrics*, 31(9), pp. 1319–1329. Available at: https://doi.org/10.1017/S1041610218001722.

Thornicroft, G. *et al.* (2022) 'The Lancet commission on ending stigma and discrimination in mental health', *The Lancet*, 400(10361), pp. 1438–1480. Available at: https://doi.org/10.1016/S0140–6736(22)01470–2.

Torres-Harding, S., Torres, L. and Yeo, E. (2020) 'Depression and perceived stress as mediators between racial microaggressions and somatic symptoms in college students of color', *American Journal of Orthopsychiatry*, 90(1), pp. 125–135. Available at: https://doi.org/10.1037/ort0000408.

Trevor Project. (2022). *2022 National survey on LGBTQ youth mental health*. https://www.thetrevorproject.org/survey-2022/assets/static/trevor01_2022survey_final.pdf

Walker, N. (2021) *Neuroqueer heresies: Notes on the neurodiversity paradigm, autistic empowerment, and postnormal possibilities*. Fort Worth: Autonomous Press.

Weber, L. (2010) *Understanding race, class, gender, and sexuality: A conceptual framework*. 2 ed. New York, NY: Oxford University Press.

Wise, S.J. (2024) *We're all neurodiverse: How to build a neurodiversity-affirming future and challenge neuronormativity*. London: Jessica Kingsley Publishers.

Chapter 9

Immigrant Population, Neurodiversity, and Mental Health in New Zealand

Rachel Mukwezwa-Tapera

Introduction

Neurodiversity is a complex phenomenon that is becoming increasingly recognised worldwide. However, the social impact of this phenomenon on African migrants is not well documented. This chapter draws on research that sought to understand the social effects of neurodiversity among Indigenous African migrants in Aotearoa New Zealand (hereafter Aotearoa NZ). Whilst this study focuses on African migrants in Aotearoa NZ, it is likely that the findings apply equally to other migrants in other parts of the world. Interviews were held with parents of neurodivergent children, African community leaders, and child and health specialists. Through this study, several gaps in understanding neurodiversity in Aotearoa NZ have been identified. One of the critical issues found was the overlap between neurodiversity, mental health, and disability, and the intersection of race and class. In this chapter, we will explore the experiences of neurodivergent African migrants in Aotearoa NZ, to discuss the challenges in understanding neurodiversity, its overlap with mental illness and the related stigma, the impact of intersectionality, and the complex realities of being a neurodivergent African[1] migrant in Aotearoa NZ.

Understanding Neurodiversity beyond the Eurocentric Worldview

Neurodiversity and neurodivergence are terms used to describe the complex phenomenon of variations in brain functioning (Chapman, 2020a; Dwyer, 2022; Walker, 2014). Defining these terms is challenging and not always straightforward (Dwyer, 2022). Every brain is unique, and the infinite variation in the functioning of minds and brains is called neurodiversity (Chapman, 2020a; Walker, 2014). That said, society has a dominant standard of what typical development, intellectual or cognitive functioning should look like (Exceptional Individuals, 2020), and any deviation of the brain from these dominant societal conventions is perceived as abnormal and often labelled as a disorder. It is important to note that the dominant standard of 'normal' or neurotypical is based on a Eurocentric worldview and excludes diverse understandings.

DOI: 10.4324/9781003495949-10

Defining neurodiversity for Africans, as with other Indigenous communities, considers their ways of knowing and being. Neurodiversity is perceived differently across diverse African communities. Having migrated from other countries and having diverse cultures, religions, histories, and lived realities means African migrants' perspectives and understandings of neurodiversity are different. Often, conflict arises when African families seek support for their children, and their knowingness and realities of how they can best support their children are dismissed in favour of strategies informed by the Western medical model. African families experience challenges explaining their children's conditions and how they thought these could be managed. They express sentiments of being unheard, sometimes resulting in disengagement with service providers and practitioners (Mukwezwa-Tapera, 2022).

Neurodiversity has increasingly become a growing movement for learning and disability, attracting interest worldwide (Ne'eman and Pellicano, 2022). The notion that diversity is natural and valuable is recognised and acknowledged by the neurodiversity paradigm (Dwyer, 2022; Kapp, 2020; Russell, 2020). As with social dynamics with ethnicity, culture, or other forms of human diversity, to claim a standard is fictitious (Walker, 2014). As such, claiming a standard for neurocognitive functioning is not valid. Instead, it adds another layer of othering and discrimination, evident in ethnicity, culture, and other forms of human diversity. Although the neurodiversity paradigm explicitly includes every neurodivergent person regardless of the level of support they require (Den Houting, 2019), it is concentrated mainly in English-speaking countries (Cascio, 2015), reflecting predominantly Western perspectives, overlooking and excluding Indigenous worldviews and diverse cultural perspectives (Strand, 2017). As such, current understandings of neurodiversity are primarily based on Western populations and provide a limited perspective that does not adequately capture the diverse experiences of neurodivergent individuals across different regions globally (Gillespie-Lynch et al., 2020).

The ethos of 'nothing about us without us' ensures the inclusion of neurodivergent people. However, it is unfortunate that not all voices and perspectives are included, particularly those of Indigenous communities and other minoritised groups. The intersectionality of neurodivergence with other aspects of identity, such as ethnicity, language, and migration, is often not considered, resulting in culturally insensitive approaches to neurodiversity (Mukwezwa-Tapera, 2022). It is evident that no matter the good intentions or how noble movements perceive themselves to be, the likelihood of harming and excluding minoritised communities is always high because of the imperial core that underpins global systems.

For minoritised groups who have always been othered, the language associated with grouping people is always concerning as it is likely to lead to more discrimination. Moreover, colonised language alienates minoritised people (Ngwagwa, 2021), thus perpetuating long-standing discriminatory practices. African American disability advocates encourage the use of the term 'neuroexpansive' as they reject the term 'neurodivergent' and the ideology underpinning it (Ngwagwa, 2021). They argue that this terminology is centred around whiteness and that Black people's experiences do not divert from the white definition of 'standard' (Ngwagwa, 2021). It is from these dominant societal conventions of 'normal' or 'standard' that misdiagnosis and underdiagnosis occur. Because of these societal definitions of normality, some parents interviewed in this research thought cultural differences were sometimes perceived as unfavourable and met with hostility, not help. Diverse worldviews and perspectives on neurodiversity therefore impact the understanding of neurodiversity (Mukwezwa-Tapera, 2022). The lack of appreciation of cultural diversity is evident in practitioners' tools to assess neurocognitive conditions and the strategies used to manage certain conditions (Mukwezwa-Tapera, 2022). The development of most of these tools is informed by the Western medical model, which is deeply rooted in racist ideologies and systems of oppression (Ngwagwa, 2021).

The Neurodiversity and Mental Illness Nexus

In the previous section, neurodiversity was described as the natural variations of brain function. From the research exploring the experiences of neurodivergent African migrants in Aotearoa NZ, there is a perceived unclear delineation between neurodiversity and mental illness, especially if attempting to differentiate neurodiversity and mental health illness by translating the English definitions of these complex phenomena to languages other than English. Mental illness describes a range of mental health conditions that affect the mood, thinking, and behaviour of an individual. Because the term 'mental' describes anything to do with the mind, intellect, or the brain, it is easy to see how and why there is an overlap in how people view or understand neurodiversity outside of the Eurocentric framework.

Findings from this study highlighted that narratives of African community leaders, parents, and caregivers suggested an overlap between neurodiversity and mental illness in that both phenomena seemed to have something to do with the brain. This overlap means that the stigma and stereotypes attached to mental illness were also attached to neurodiversity, making the experiences of affected people complex. The co-occurrence of neurodiversity and disability also emerged as challenging, with disability being either physical (affecting physical function and mobility), intellectual (affecting intellectual functioning and adaptive behaviour), or both. The overlap between neurodiversity and mental illness and their co-occurrence with disability made the experiences of African migrants complex and challenging. On further analysis, experiences of stigma and discrimination were common in the nexus of neurodiversity, mental illness, and disability. Stigma is a multidimensional social construct that involves feelings, attitudes, and behaviours (Penn and Martin, 1998) and has helped spell out the experiences of 'shame, social awkwardness, rejection, misunderstanding and exclusion' suffered by people in certain situations (Link and Stuart, 2017, pg. 3). Stigma has been applied to a range of situations that include incontinence, incarceration, sexual minority status, HIV/AIDS, tribal identities, and physical abnormalities (Koschorke et al., 2017; Link and Stuart, 2017; Overton and Medina, 2008; Sheehan et al., 2016). Stigmatised people are often labelled and ostracised and become outcasts (Johnstone, 2001; Overton and Medina, 2008; Penn and Martin, 1998). The labelled individuals are considered unfit to meet society's ideal standards and ultimately impair the collective identity (Corrigan and Watson, 2002; Overton and Medina, 2008; Penn and Martin, 1998). Historical attitudes continue to influence contemporary perceptions of mental illness and related stigmatised conditions, such as neurodivergence, which is frequently misunderstood as a mental health disorder. Stigma, therefore, has seeped into how society often holds negative stereotypes about mental illness, and these were also extended to neurodiversity and any form of disability, resulting in the prejudice and discrimination of those affected. There is often an unclear delineation between neurocognitive conditions and mental illness. Under the medical model, both are pathologised and perceived as disorders, negatively deviating from normal functioning, and, as such, require treatment to correct the deficits and functional limitations (Dwyer, 2022; Russell, 2020; Savulescu and Kahane, 2011). Often, the medical model's focus on deficits fails to acknowledge strengths, perpetuating the stigma and shame associated with diagnoses (Shaw et al., 2021). Distinguishing between neurodiversity and mental illness proves challenging, given the fine line between human genetic diversity – resulting in sensory, cognitive, and developmental variations – and ingrained responses to distressing experiences (Chapman, 2020a, 2020b). Conditions like autism, which exhibit neurocognitive variations, can be seen as both natural diversity and a disability (Den Houting, 2019).

Neurodiversity, mental illness, and disability are often stigmatised conditions, with negative societal attitudes emanating from misunderstanding and lack of awareness about these conditions (Botha and Frost, 2020; Corrigan and Watson, 2002). Stigma in Western and non-Western contexts varies (Koschorke et al., 2017), with the same behaviour eliciting different reactions in different societies. The reactions to stigma take a whole new dimension for neurodivergent African migrants living in a foreign society and this was a significant point to note in this research. Again, bringing back the intersectionality lens, stigma is attached differently to the same circumstance in different contexts, meaning for African migrants, there could be differences in the stigma they experience in a foreign country compared to their home countries, often being compounded by the impact of racism, othering, and the discriminatory nature of socially constructed attributes. The scenario becomes even more complex for migrants, who often lack social networks and experience other challenges related to migration and adaptation. Being a migrant in itself carries a certain stigma resulting from discrimination-based narratives against them (Cabieses et al., 2024). Coupling this with societal stereotypes and misconceptions attached to neurodiversity and mental illness results in the affected people often being criminalised and punished (Ngwagwa, 2021) rather than being heard and receiving the support they require.

Intersectionality

Understanding neurodiversity for African migrants is not just defining terms; it extends beyond. Understanding the social effects of neurodiversity for minoritised communities calls for recognising and acknowledging how multiple forms of disadvantage aggregate and create hurdles that are not easily understood (Crenshaw, 2013). Intersectionality is an intricate concept that recognises that socially constructed identity markers do not exist independently of others (Crenshaw, 2013), are informed by social, historical, and cultural contexts (Botha and Gillespie-Lynch, 2022; Strand, 2017), and result in oppression, discrimination, or privilege (Botha and Gillespie-Lynch, 2022; Crenshaw, 2013). For African migrants, the convergence of a Black body, neurocognitive condition(s), and being a migrant was challenging to navigate.

The intersectionality of ethnicity and neurodiversity, in this instance, compounds the experiences of Black body racism and ethnic bias, amongst other disadvantages. Societal misconceptions and stereotypes are compounded in this intersectionality, often resulting in the affected people being criminalised and punished (Ngwagwa, 2021). From the experiences shared by the parents, caregivers, and community leaders in this study, negotiating these identities is complex on multiple levels (Mukwezwa-Tapera, 2022). The realities of African migrants who are neurodivergent are multidimensional. They cannot be fully understood by looking at the social tenets in isolation, as socially constructed categories are fluid and shaped by social processes (Hankivsky, 2012), which can be biased, discriminatory, and/or misinformed in terms of a person's lived reality. As a result of this, intersectionality significantly impacts the access to and utilisation of services. This will be discussed further below.

In summary, the above highlights that the intersection of a Black body, being a migrant, and the stigma and discrimination attached to neurodiversity, mental illness, and disability create challenging and complex experiences for neurodivergent African migrants. Moreover, the above underlines that intersectionality has a significant impact on the access and utilisation of services by neurodivergent African migrants and their families, compounding the challenges experienced. The following sections of this chapter will look at the complexity of neurodiversity for African migrants, and the challenges faced as a result of a combination of the intersecting attributes.

Neurodiversity Is Complex

The experiences shared by the participants in this research showed that most aspects of their lived realities and contexts while navigating neurodiversity were complex. It is crucial to remember that the intersections of the different socially constructed attributes discussed in the preceding section were also evident and integrated into the factors below.

Diverse Understandings

Different peoples and communities have unique perceptions and understandings of neurodivergent-related conditions and how they could be managed. The differences in understanding neurodiversity were not always acknowledged when parents engaged with healthcare professionals or their children's teachers. The American Psychiatric Association (APA) (2013) acknowledges the importance of cultural, ethnic, religious, or geographical differences when making the diagnosis; however, this research highlighted that these were not always considered. Indeed, this was reported as a shared experience of the parents of neurodivergent African migrants and was discussed in terms of creating tensions between the family and the practitioner. The resulting tension caused some parents to disengage from seeking services causing them to rely more on the support of their peers who had similar experiences or seeking advice from their families and communities overseas. This suggests a cultural difference between the family and practitioner in terms of the interpretation of some neuro differences and a rigidity of the host country's practitioner in having a culturally narrow perspective of the family's needs, leading to alienation and disengagement.

Moreover, diverse understandings of child behaviour should also be considered when working with migrant families whose children are undergoing diagnosis. Defining 'normal' child behaviour is impossible when we are looking at children coming from culturally diverse communities. Growth milestones may be a more appropriate option. However, it is essential to note that child growth milestones were developed with specific population groups and contexts, and although being used in most places across the world, they may not be the best index to measure child growth for some communities, especially so for children with neurodisabilities (Gladstone et al., 2010; Kelly et al., 2006). Thus, using such an approach may indeed result in Eurocentric interpretation of whether a child has reached a growth milestone, thus ingraining structural inequalities and institutional discrimination. Given some of these complicated aspects, it becomes very challenging to establish 'normal' child behaviours, especially for migrants in foreign countries who have entirely different ways of perceiving child development and where their ways of understanding child behaviour are often not considered valuable or indeed correct.

The lack of appreciation of the diverse understandings of neurodiversity has resulted in misdiagnosis and lack of diagnosis for some children. Sometimes, cultural attributes have been mistaken as signs of neurocognitive conditions. For example, when migrant children are being assessed in a Western host country, failing to make eye contact is perceived as a sign of autism. However, in some cultures, making eye contact is a sign of disrespect (de Leeuw et al., 2020; Zhang et al., 2006). The assessment tools used to determine neurocognitive conditions are developed from a Western perspective, with some questions not applicable to non-Western communities. For example, a question that asks whether a child can use a fork and knife to eat or if a child can sit at the dinner table and complete their meal without getting up would not apply to families and communities who do not use forks and knives or eat their meals while sitting at a dinner table. So, trying to make a diagnosis of a neurocognitive condition in a person from the Global Majority[2] using a Western tool will not always give a correct diagnosis. This research highlighted that these types of failures, to acknowledge diverse understandings and perspectives of neurodiversity, impacted the experiences of neurodivergent children at school and made their lived realities challenging.

Language

Language is an essential connector between people. In Western countries like Aotearoa NZ, a level of proficiency in English is necessary for navigating everyday living and for most migrants, who are often speakers of other languages, this can be very challenging. In this research the importance of language was evident. This was from both the perspective of the family and the practitioner. For example, for the family, describing the presentation of a child; and for the practitioner, when describing complex neurodiversity concepts in simple language and, in some instances through an interpreter. Furthermore, explaining the complicated medical concepts in everyday English was discussed as very challenging. These communication barriers heightened the risk of misdiagnosis and underdiagnosis.

Limitations in English competency impede access to healthcare, and interpretation is vital in connecting health professionals and clients (Flores, 2005; Gartley and Due, 2017; Latif et al., 2022). This research highlighted that in cases where interpretation was provided, the information-sharing process was lengthened, requiring more time and perhaps additional appointments to communicate information to families. English is often the second or third language for most African migrants who speak many other languages and thus the use of interpreters is not uncommon. Although this research did not ascertain the quality of interpretation parents received at their appointment, the likelihood of complex information being lost or information leading to misdiagnosis or omitting important information during interpretation was relatively high (Cassim et al., 2022; Karliner et al., 2007).

Racism and Marginalisation

African migrants experience racism. Institutional racism is ingrained in the systems of Western countries, making it very easy to push African migrants to the margins. Racism is a deeply ingrained system within societal structures that typically confers advantages to white individuals while systematically disadvantaging people of colour (Eddo-Lodge, 2020; Kendi, 2019). This pervasive issue extends its reach into various aspects of society, including healthcare. The presence of racism within health systems is a well-documented phenomenon in Aotearoa NZ and other Western nations, with numerous studies highlighting its persistent and detrimental effects (Clarke, 2006; Durey and Thompson, 2012; Harris et al., 2006; Paradies, 2016; Talamaivao et al., 2021).

African migrants are discriminated against at face value because skin colour and Black body racism, as briefly discussed above, impacts all dimensions of survival. African migrants are affected by discriminatory practices when accessing social services (Butcher et al., 2006), jobs (Tuwe, 2018; Udah et al., 2019; Weichselbaumer, 2017), education (Arar, 2021; Molla, 2021; Saiti and Chletsos, 2020), and healthcare (Anderson, 2008; Kanengoni-Nyatara et al., 2020, 2023). Stereo-typing of African migrants increases racial profiling, which has negative conse-quences on multiple aspects of their lived realities. Coupling all of these challenges with neurodiversity results in even more complex realities for individuals and their families.

African migrant parents in this research highlighted the challenges their neu-rodivergent children faced in schools and when seeking healthcare and support. These difficulties were often complex for the parents to articulate due to two main factors. Firstly, the lack of language to verbalise experiences of racism and discrim-ination, and secondly, because of the normalisation of racism that made discrimi-natory experiences seem ordinary. Linguistic barriers and unfamiliarity with the specific terminology to describe discriminatory practices make it challenging for African migrants to express encounters with racism (Crenshaw, 2013). The omni-presence and subtlety of systemic racism in Aotearoa NZ enables environments where discriminatory practices are perceived as expected occurrences. As a result, African migrants may struggle to recognise and report these experiences (Atiba Goff and Barsamian Kahn, 2012) and the multiple layers of discrimination expe-rienced by African migrants complicate the ability to pinpoint and communicate distinct occurrences of unfair treatment (Bowleg, 2008; Crenshaw, 2013).

The racialised context in Aotearoa NZ, significantly impacted the sense of belonging for neurodivergent African migrants and their families. Participants recounted experiences of racial microaggressions while interacting with services and society at large. Racial microaggressions, defined as subtle forms of racism occurring without intent to harm (Almond, 2019), are pervasive in various settings, including interactions with service providers (Cormack et al., 2018; Flett et al., 2020), and these experiences can lead to diminished self-esteem in some individu-als (Cénat et al., 2024). For Black people in Western settings, racial microaggres-sions and discrimination are commonplace occurrences. In this study, parents and community leaders emphasised how the diminished self-esteem negatively influ-enced the willingness to seek services, support, and participate in society. This is in line with the literature which outlines that racial microaggressions are harm-ful and negatively impact self-esteem (D'hondt et al., 2024; Nadal et al., 2014; Wong-Padoongpatt et al., 2017). The harm was amplified for the neurodivergent African migrants in the margins, navigating exceptionally complex realities at the intersection of being a Black body, being a migrant and being neurodivergent, amongst other attributes. As Gillborn et al., 2012 note, the intersectionality of race and disability in education can lead to unique forms of disadvantage that are often overlooked by traditional approaches to equality – and even more so for neurodi-versity support, which is often inadequate.

The harm highlighted above also extends to the family. While this research did not explicitly explore the impacts on immediate family members, these effects were likely significant, particularly in educational and work settings. The impact of racism and marginalisation is significant in further complicating the lived realities of neurodivergent African migrants. As discussed in the next section, it permeates most aspects of daily life, including accessing services.

Accessing Services

Access to adequate medical care is a fundamental human right (United Nations, 2015); however, the exceptionally complex experiences of neurodivergent African migrants and their families indicate significant violations of this fundamental human right. While neurodivergent African migrants and their families generally benefited from accessing services and support, obtaining these resources proved challenging. Levesque et al. (2013) define access as the opportunity to fulfil healthcare needs. However, various barriers, including lack of information, complex health system navigation, and discrimination, hindered these families from acquiring desirable services. These obstacles effectively denied them the chance to utilise available support systems fully and thus led to a breach of their human rights under the UN Convention.

For migrants who come from different places with different health systems, it is overwhelming to learn a new system and how to navigate it. These circumstances are worsened when the host country has gaps in national policies supporting migrant health (Mladovsky et al., 2012). Western health systems are challenging to navigate due to the lack of integration of intercultural healthcare strategies. Such strategies embrace diverse cultural practices, comprehend individual perspectives, and adapt their approaches accordingly to optimise the quality of care delivered (Anand and Lahiri, 2009). The Western-dominated health system does not reflect the rich diversity of Aotearoa NZ. Aotearoa NZ's health system, like other institutions, suffers from a lack of diversity representation, leading to inequitable experiences for Māori (the Indigenous Peoples of Aotearoa NZ) and ethnic migrant communities (McSweeney-Novak, 2021; Simon-Kumar, 2019). Parents in this research unanimously reported encountering culturally inappropriate practices within the Western biomedical services they accessed. This reflects a broader issue of colour and cultural blindness in the health system, stemming from universalist concepts that prioritise a single dominant standard at the expense of cultural and ethnic diversity (DiAngelo, 2018; Rosenthal and Levy, 2010; Virgona and Kashima, 2021). The rampant nature of colour and cultural blindness is enabled by institutional racism, as discussed in the preceding section. The dominance of these systems leaves no room for diverse understandings of health to grow. It perpetuates forms of racism and discrimination like ethnic bias and increases stigma and stereotypes, further pushing neurodivergent African migrants and their families into the fringes of society. The absence of intercultural healthcare in Aotearoa NZ impacts significantly on inequitable access to services for neurodivergent African migrants. Addressing these disparities requires a fundamental shift in how health services are designed and delivered, ensuring that they recognise and are culturally responsive and inclusive of the diverse needs of all communities in Aotearoa NZ and beyond.

The health system in Aotearoa NZ is fragmented (Goodyear-Smith and Ashton, 2019), and the challenges associated with navigating it are recognised (Htut et al., 2019). A striking agreement emerged across participant groups in this research: African migrant parents, African community leaders, and non-migrant health and child specialists emphasised that the health system's complexity posed significant navigational challenges. This intricacy potentially hindered access to essential services and support, highlighting a critical barrier in healthcare provision for neurodivergent African migrants and their families. Services and support for neurodiversity in Aotearoa NZ are spread across different sectors, and there were challenges involved with accessing these by the participants in this research. While parents appreciated the variety of available services, the multitude of agencies and their complex interrelationships created navigational challenges. This complexity, exacerbated by inter-agency politics, risked neurodivergent African migrants falling through the cracks of support systems. Research emphasises that multi-sector partnerships and collaboration can enhance patient engagement and improve health equity (Knox et al., 2016; Towe et al., 2016). However, this may be unlikely for the neurodivergent African migrants in this research. A focus on improving inter-agency complementarity and collaboration to streamline service provision is essential in improving access to services. Integrating services and coordinating functions could simplify navigation, enhance equity, and improve service quality (Goodyear-Smith and Ashton, 2019) while considering broader systemic factors (Alderwick et al., 2021).

Access to relevant information was a concerning recurrence in the participants' experiences. For all the parents in this research, information on services and support was not always available. Moreover, efficient information timeliness has been reported to promote patient engagement (Li et al., 2022); however, some organisations' lack of responsiveness and delay resulted in parents disengaging from those services and seeking alternatives. Social media was discussed as being the best alternative to access quick information in real time. No service provider provided information as efficiently and most parents identified frustrating experiences in terms of seeking information from service providers. This frustration often led parents to search the internet and social media for answers to their questions and information. Social media can be a useful tool for disseminating information to the public, whereby institutions and practitioners can utilise it for communicating important information and disseminating health knowledge (Chen and Wang, 2021; Moorhead et al., 2013; Zhou et al., 2018) in a timely manner (Li et al., 2022). Although the internet can be a reliable source of information, it can also provide mis- and dis-information on health-related matters. Moreover, other downsides reported were information overload (Khaleel et al., 2020; Lee et al., 2016; Swar et al., 2017), the time required to sieve through the vast web, which could lead to exhaustion and fatigue (Fu et al., 2020), information anxiety, and information avoidance (Soroya et al., 2021). All the parents in this research experienced mental overload at some point in their search for information, exacerbating the risk of the negative consequences of information anxiety and avoidance for the caregivers and families. This resulted in increased stress and possibly fuelled denial or complicated their journey to acceptance of their neurodivergent diagnosis. Access to timely and relevant information emerges as a significant enabler to improved outcomes for neurodivergent African migrants.

Aotearoa NZ has a publicly funded health system; however, the system is overburdened. Several scholars have reported concern about underfunding of the health sectors in Aotearoa NZ (Bagshaw et al., 2022; Barnett and Bagshaw, 2020; Cumming, 2021; Goodyear-Smith and Ashton, 2019; Keene et al., 2016). Some child and health specialists in this research echoed similar sentiments. They identified insufficient funding as a critical barrier to effective neurodivergent services and support. They suggested increased, equity-focused funding could streamline assessments and appointments, leading to more comprehensive sessions and faster diagnoses. While this study could not definitively connect funding deficits to a shortage of child and health specialists, it is probable that the well-documented scarcity of healthcare staff in Aotearoa NZ (Gorman and Brooks, 2009; Rees et al., 2018; Zurn and Dumont, 2008) affects numerous services. The widespread nature of these staffing shortages suggests that specialised services are also impacted, potentially limiting support available for neurodivergent individuals, resulting in concerning outcomes like wait times as long as 18 months for some services.

Alternative options would be private healthcare, which is very expensive and out of reach for most migrants. Fasani et al. (2022) highlight the extended time frame – sometimes up to 15 years – required for economic migrants and migrants with a refugee experience in Europe to attain financial stability. This economic challenge is compounded for families with neurodivergent children from diverse cultural and linguistic backgrounds who frequently experience poverty (Papoudi et al., 2021). Although comparative studies specific to Aotearoa NZ are absent, research from various contexts (Anderson, 2008; Badu et al., 2018; Lebano et al., 2020; Norredam, 2011) suggests that access disparities likely exist among minoritised population groups more generally. Consequently, this may imply that many of the African families with neurodivergent children interviewed in this study may have faced or continue to face economic hardship, impacting their ability to pay privately to access services and support.

Conclusion

Neurodiversity, mental illness, and disability are complex conditions that intersect in complex ways, leading to significant challenges for individuals and families. These pose similar societal challenges. The lived realities of neurodivergent African migrants in Aotearoa NZ were explored to understand the complexities better. Recognising the diverse understanding and perspectives of neurodiversity is essential to consider in contexts like Aotearoa NZ that are richly diverse. Embracing these diverse understandings is crucial in informing appropriate decisions, recommending the most suitable services and support, and improving accessibility for neurodivergent individuals belonging to minoritised communities, as highlighted by the research with African migrants.

The intricate web of intersecting attributes of being a Black body, being a migrant, and being neurodivergent, among many other socially constructed attributes, further complicates the realities of neurodivergent African migrants and their families. The intersectionality of these attributes converges disadvantages for neurodivergent African migrants and further marginalises them. The range of socially constructed attributes individually and cumulatively brings disadvantages, and it is challenging to tell which one of these attributes is causing a disadvantage at any given point. The negative impact of intersectionality is evident in the complex realities of neurodivergent African migrants and their families that extend across all dimensions of their lives – from school to health services and participation in society. Acknowledging that all these consequences are rooted in racism is the first step to addressing most, if not all, of these challenges.

Opportunities to improve the experiences of neurodivergent communities in Aotearoa NZ are vast. The genuine engagement and inclusion of the perspectives of neurodivergent people from diverse backgrounds in the formulation of services is crucial. This enables their voices to be heard and improvements made on what is working and what is not. Recognising the rich diversity of Aotearoa NZ and having it reflected in policy and service provision is an enabler for access to services by marginalised communities who struggle to navigate the health system and feel unseen and unheard. Innovative strategies for community sensitisation and improving awareness, diagnosis, and care related to neurodiversity are essential for all Aotearoa NZ communities and further afield. Community awareness is crucial to combat social stigma, which is a critical driver in pushing marginalised communities further into the fringes. Increased awareness promotes cultural safety and opportunities to advocate for equitable access to care for neurodivergent people. More rights-based community-led initiatives are needed to address inequitable access to services.

Notes

1 In this project, we acknowledge the diversity of African communities and the differences in their ways of being.
2 It refers to non-white persons who are racialised (and minoritised) as Black, African, Asian, Brown, dual-heritage, and Indigenous to the Global South and/or racialised as 'ethnic minorities' (Campbell-Stephens, 2020).

References

Alderwick H, Hutchings A, Briggs A and Mays N (2021) The impacts of collaboration between local health care and non-health care organisations and factors shaping how they work: A systematic review of reviews. *BMC Public Health* 21.
Almond AL (2019) Measuring racial microaggression in medical practice. *Ethnicity & Health* 24(6): 589–606.

American Psychiatric Association (2013) *Diagnostic and statistical manual of mental disorders: DSM–5*. Arlington, VA: American Psychiatric Association, c2013.

Anand R and Lahiri I (2009) Intercultural competence in health care: Developing skills for interculturally competent care. *The SAGE Handbook of Intercultural Competence*: 387–402.

Anderson A (2008) Understanding migrants' primary healthcare utilisation in New Zealand through an ethnographic approach. *Diversity and Equality in Health and Care* 5(4).

Arar KH (2021) Research on refugees' pathways to higher education since 2010: A systematic review. *Review of Education* 9(3): e3303.

Atiba Goff P and Barsamian Kahn K (2012) Racial bias in policing: Why we know less than we should. *Social Issues and Policy Review* 6(1): 177–210.

Badu E, Mpofu C and Farvid P (2018) Towards TB elimination in Aotearoa/New Zealand: Key informant insights on the determinants of TB among African migrants. *Tropical Medicine and Infectious Disease* 3(2): 44.

Bagshaw P, Bagshaw S, Barnett P, Nicholls G, Gowland S and Shaw C (2022) The answer is more investment in health and welfare-not more rationing of healthcare! *The New Zealand Medical Journal (Online)* 135(1552): 145–147.

Barnett P and Bagshaw P (2020) Neoliberalism: What it is, how it affects health and what to do about it. *The New Zealand Medical Journal* 133: 76–84.

Botha M and Frost DM (2020) Extending the minority stress model to understand mental health problems experienced by the autistic population. *Society and Mental Health* 10(1): 20–34.

Botha M and Gillespie-Lynch K (2022) Come as you are: Examining autistic identity development and the neurodiversity movement through an intersectional lens. *Human Development* 66(2): 93–112.

Bowleg L (2008) When Black lesbian woman≠ Black lesbian woman: The methodological challenges of qualitative and quantitative intersectionality research. *Sex Roles* 59: 312–325.

Butcher A, Spoonley P and Trlin AD (2006) *Being accepted: The experience of discrimination and social exclusion by immigrants and refugees in New Zealand* (vol. 13). Auckland: New Settlers Programme, Massey University.

Cabieses B, Belo K, Calderón AC, Rada I, Rojas K, Araoz C, et al. (2024) The impact of stigma and discrimination-based narratives in the health of migrants in Latin America and the Caribbean: A scoping review. *The Lancet Regional Health–Americas* 40.

Campbell-Stephens R (2020) *Global majority; Decolonising the language and reframing the conversation about race*. Leeds Beckett University. https://www.leedsbeckett.ac.uk/-/media/files/schools/school-of-education/final-leeds-beckett-1102-global-majority.pdf

Cascio MA (2015) Cross-cultural autism studies, neurodiversity, and conceptualisations of autism. *Culture, Medicine, and Psychiatry* 39: 207–212.

Cassim S, Kidd J, Ali M, Hamid NA, Jamil D, Keenan R, et al. (2022) 'Look, wait, I'll translate': Refugee women's experiences with interpreters in healthcare in Aotearoa New Zealand. *Australian Journal of Primary Health* 28: 296–302.

Cénat JM, Darius WP, Dalexis RD, Kogan CS, Guerrier M and Ndengeyingoma A (2022) Perceived racial discrimination, internalised racism, social support, and self-esteem among Black individuals in Canada: A moderated mediation model. *Cultural Diversity and Ethnic Minority Psychology* 30: 118.

Chapman R (2020a) Defining neurodiversity for research and practice. *Neurodiversity Studies: A New Critical Paradigm*: 218–220.

Chapman R (2020b) Neurodiversity, disability, wellbeing. *Neurodiversity Studies: A New Critical Paradigm*: 57–72.

Chen J and Wang Y (2021) Social media use for health purposes: Systematic review. *Journal of Medical Internet Research* 23(5): e17917.

Clarke I (2006) Essentialising Islam: Multiculturalism and Islamic politics in New Zealand. *New Zealand Journal of Asian Studies* 8(2): 69.

Cormack D, Stanley J and Harris R (2018) Multiple forms of discrimination and relationships with health and wellbeing: Findings from national cross-sectional surveys in Aotearoa/New Zealand. *International Journal for Equity in Health* 17: 1–15.

Corrigan PW and Watson AC (2002) Understanding the impact of stigma on people with mental illness. *World Psychiatry* 1(1): 16.

Crenshaw K (2013) Demarginalizing the intersection of race and sex: A black feminist critique of antidiscrimination doctrine, feminist theory and antiracist politics. In: *Feminist legal theories*. Routledge: 23–51.

Cumming J (2021) Going hard and early: Aotearoa New Zealand's response to Covid–19. *Health Economics, Policy, and Law*: 1–13.

de Leeuw A, Happé F and Hoekstra RA (2020) A conceptual framework for understanding the cultural and contextual factors on autism across the globe. *Autism Research* 13(7): 1029–1050.

Den Houting J (2019) Neurodiversity: An insider's perspective. *Autism* 23(2): 271–273.

D'hondt F, Maene C and Stevens PA (2024) Ethnic microaggressions and adolescents' self-esteem and academic futility: The protective role of teachers. *Youth & Society* 56(1): 193–216.

DiAngelo R (2018) *White fragility: Why it's so hard for white people to talk about racism.* Boston: Beacon Press. https://www.beacon.org/White-Fragility-P1631.aspx

Durey A and Thompson SC (2012) Reducing the health disparities of Indigenous Australians: Time to change focus. *BMC Health Services Research* 12(1): 1–11.

Dwyer P (2022) The neurodiversity approach (es): What are they and What do they mean for researchers? *Human Development* 66(2): 73–92.

Eddo-Lodge R (2020) *Why I'm no longer talking to white people about race.* London: Bloomsbury Publishing. https://www.bloomsbury.com/uk/why-im-no-longer-talking-to-white-people-about-race-9781408870587/

Exceptional Individuals (2020) *Neurodivergent & neurodiversity: Meanings & examples.* Available at: https://exceptionalindividuals.com/neurodiversity/.

Fasani F, Frattini T and Minale L (2022) (The struggle for) refugee integration into the labour market: Evidence from Europe. *Journal of Economic Geography* 22(2): 351–393.

Flett J, Lucas N, Kingstone S and Stevenson B (2020) *Mental distress and discrimination in aotearoa New Zealand: Results from 2015–2018 mental health monitor and 2018 health and lifestyles survey/prepared for Te Hiringa Hauora Health Promotion Agency by Hayde Flett, Natalie Lucas, Sydney Kingstone, and Brendan Stevenson.* Wellington, NZ: Health Promotion Agency Te Hiringa Hauora.

Flores G (2005) The impact of medical interpreter services on the quality of health care: A systematic review. *Medical Care Research and Review* 62(3): 255–299.

Fu S, Li H, Liu Y, Pirkkalainen H and Salo M (2020) Social media overload, exhaustion, and use discontinuance: Examining the effects of information overload, system feature overload, and social overload. *Information Processing & Management* 57(6): 102307.

Gartley T and Due C (2017) The interpreter is not an invisible being: A thematic analysis of the impact of interpreters in mental health service provision with refugee clients. *Australian Psychologist* 52(1): 31–40.

Gillborn D, Rollock N, Vincent C and Ball SJ (2012) 'You got a pass, so what more do you want?': Race, class and gender intersections in the educational experiences of the black middle class. *Race Ethnicity and Education* 15(1): 121–139.

Gillespie-Lynch K, Dwyer P, Constantino C, Kapp SK, Hotez E, Riccio A, et al. (2020) Can we broaden the neurodiversity movement without weakening it? Participatory approaches as a framework for cross-disability alliance building. In: *Disability alliances and allies.* Leeds: Emerald Publishing Limited: 189–223.

Gladstone M, Lancaster GA, Umar E, Nyirenda M, Kayira E, van den Broek NR, et al. (2010) The Malawi developmental assessment tool (MDAT): The creation, validation, and reliability of a tool to assess child development in rural African settings. *PLoS Medicine* 7(5): e1000273.

Goodyear-Smith F and Ashton T (2019) New Zealand health system: Universalism struggles with persisting inequities. *The Lancet* 394(10196): 432–442.

Gorman DF and Brooks PM (2009) On solutions to the shortage of doctors in Australia and New Zealand. *Medical Journal of Australia* 190(3): 152–156.

Hankivsky O (2012) Women's health, men's health, and gender and health: Implications of intersectionality. *Social Science & Medicine* 74(11): 1712–1720.

Harris R, Tobias M, Jeffreys M, Waldegrave K, Karlsen S and Nazroo J (2006) Racism and health: The relationship between experience of racial discrimination and health in New Zealand. *Social Science & Medicine* 63(6): 1428–1441.

Htut M, Ho E and Wiles J (2019) A study of Asian children who are diagnosed with autism spectrum disorder and available support services in Auckland, New Zealand. *Journal of Autism and Developmental Disorders*: 1–11.

Johnstone M (2001) Stigma, social justice and the rights of the mentally ill: Challenging the status quo. *Australian and New Zealand Journal of Mental Health Nursing* 10(4): 200–209.

Kanengoni-Nyatara B, Andajani-Sutjahjo S and Holroyd E (2020) Improving health equity among the African ethnic minority through health system strengthening: A narrative review of the New Zealand healthcare system. *International Journal for Equity in Health* 19: 1–14.

Kanengoni-Nyatara B, Watson K, Galindo C, Charania NA, Mpofu C and Holroyd E (2023) Barriers to and recommendations for equitable access to healthcare for migrants and refugees in Aotearoa, New Zealand: An integrative review. *Journal of Immigrant and Minority Health*: 1–17.

Kapp SK (2020) *Autistic community and the neurodiversity movement: Stories from the frontline*. Berlin: Springer Nature: 330.

Karliner LS, Jacobs EA, Chen AH and Mutha S (2007) Do professional interpreters improve clinical care for patients with limited English proficiency? A systematic review of the literature. *Health Services Research* 42(2): 727–754.

Keene L, Bagshaw P, Nicholls MG, Rosenberg B, Frampton CM and Powell I (2016) Funding New Zealand's public healthcare system: Time for an honest appraisal and public debate. *The New Zealand Medical Journal* 129(1435): 10–20.

Kelly Y, Sacker A, Schoon I and Nazroo J (2006) Ethnic differences in achievement of developmental milestones by 9 months of age: The millennium cohort study. *Developmental Medicine and Child Neurology* 48(10): 825–830.

Kendi IX (2019) *How to be an antiracist*. London: The Bodley Head. https://www.ibramx kendi.com/how-to-be-an-antiracist

Khaleel I, Wimmer BC, Peterson GM, Zaidi STR, Roehrer E, Cummings E, et al. (2020) Health information overload among health consumers: A scoping review. *Patient Education and Counseling* 103(1): 15–32.

Knox M, Rodriguez H and Shortell S (2016) Multi-sectoral partnerships and patient-engagement strategies in accountable care organizations. *Frontiers in Public Health Services & Systems Research* 5(4): 27–33.

Koschorke M, Evans-Lacko S, Sartorius N and Thornicroft G (2017) Stigma in different cultures. In: *Anonymous the stigma of mental illness-end of the story?* Cham: Springer International Publishing: 67–82.

Latif Z, Makuvire T, Feder SL, Wadhera RK, Garan AR, Pinzon PQ, et al. (2022) Challenges facing heart failure patients with limited English proficiency: A qualitative analysis leveraging interpreters' perspectives. *JACC: Heart Failure* 10(6): 430–438.

Lebano A, Hamed S, Bradby H, Gil-Salmerón A, Durá-Ferrandis E, Garcés-Ferrer J, et al. (2020) Migrants' and refugees' health status and healthcare in Europe: A scoping literature review. *BMC Public Health* 20(1): 1–22.

Lee AR, Son S and Kim KK (2016) Information and communication technology overload and social networking service fatigue: A stress perspective. *Computers in Human Behavior* 55: 51–61.

Levesque J, Harris MF and Russell G (2013) Patient-centred access to health care: Conceptualising access at the interface of health systems and populations. *International Journal for Equity in Health* 12(1): 1–9.

Li K, Zhou C, Luo XR, Benitez J and Liao Q (2022) Impact of information timeliness and richness on public engagement on social media during COVID-19 pandemic: An empirical investigation based on NLP and machine learning. *Decision Support Systems*: 113752.

Link BG and Stuart H (2017) On revisiting some origins of the stigma concept as it applies to mental illnesses. In: *Anonymous the stigma of mental illness-end of the story?* Cham: Springer International Publishing: 3–28.

McSweeney-Novak M (2021) *New Zealanders' attitudes towards biculturalism in Aotearoa New Zealand*. Doctoral dissertation, Open Access Te Herenga Waka-Victoria University of Wellington.

Mladovsky P, Rechel B, Ingleby D and McKee M (2012) Responding to diversity: An exploratory study of migrant health policies in Europe. *Health Policy* 105(1): 1–9.

Molla T (2021) African refugees in Australia: Social position and educational outcomes. *Journal of Immigrant & Refugee Studies* 19(4): 331–348.

Moorhead SA, Hazlett DE, Harrison L, Carroll JK, Irwin A and Hoving C (2013) A new dimension of health care: Systematic review of the uses, benefits, and limitations of social media for health communication. *Journal of Medical Internet Research* 15(4): e1933.

Mukwezwa-Tapera R (2022) *The social effects of neurodiversity amongst indigenous African migrants in Aotearoa, New Zealand*. Doctoral dissertation, University of Auckland. https://hdl.handle.net/2292/65893

Nadal KL, Wong Y, Griffin KE, Davidoff K and Sriken J (2014) The adverse impact of racial microaggressions on college students' self-esteem. *Journal of College Student Development* 55(5): 461–474.

Ne'eman A and Pellicano E (2022) Neurodiversity as politics. *Human Development* 66(2): 149–157.

Ngwagwa (2021) *Neuroexpansive™ thoughts*. https://scribe.rip/@ngwagwa/neuroexpansive-thoughts-9db1e566d361

Norredam M (2011) Migrants' access to healthcare. *Danish Medical Bulletin* 58(10): B4339.

Overton SL and Medina SL (2008) The stigma of mental illness. *Journal of Counseling & Development* 86(2): 143–151.

Papoudi D, Jørgensen CR, Guldberg K and Meadan H (2021) Perceptions, experiences, and needs of parents of culturally and linguistically diverse children with autism: A scoping review. *Review Journal of Autism and Developmental Disorders* 8(2): 195–212.

Paradies Y (2016) Colonisation, racism and indigenous health. *Journal of Population Research* 33(1): 83–96.

Penn DL and Martin J (1998) The stigma of severe mental illness: Some potential solutions for a recalcitrant problem. *Psychiatric Quarterly* 69(3): 235–247.

Rees GH, Crampton P, Gauld R and MacDonell S (2018) New Zealand's health workforce planning should embrace complexity and uncertainty. *The New Zealand Medical Journal* 131(1477): 109–115.

Rosenthal L and Levy SR (2010) The colorblind, multicultural, and polycultural ideological approaches to improving intergroup attitudes and relations. *Social Issues and Policy Review* 4(1): 215–246.

Russell G (2020) Critiques of the neurodiversity movement. *Autistic Community and the Neurodiversity Movement*: 287.

Saiti A and Chletsos M (2020) Opportunities and barriers in higher education for young refugees in Greece. *Higher Education Policy* 33(2): 287–304.

Savulescu J and Kahane G (2011) Disability: A welfarist approach. *Clinical Ethics* 6(1): 45–51.

Shaw SC, McCowan S, Doherty M, Grosjean B and Kinnear M (2021) The neurodiversity concept viewed through an autistic lens. *The Lancet Psychiatry* 8(8): 654–655.

Sheehan L, Nieweglowski K and Corrigan PW (2016) Structures and types of stigma. In: *Anonymous the stigma of mental illness-end of the story?* Cham: Springer International Publishing: 43–66.

Simon-Kumar R (2019) The multicultural dilemma: Amid rising diversity and unsettled equity issues, New Zealand seeks to address its past and present. *Migration Information Source* 5.

Soroya SH, Farooq A, Mahmood K, Isoaho J and Zara S (2021) From information seeking to information avoidance: Understanding the health information behavior during a global health crisis. *Information Processing & Management* 58(2): 102440.

Strand LR (2017) Charting relations between intersectionality theory and the neurodiversity paradigm. *Disability Studies Quarterly* 37(2).

Swar B, Hameed T and Reychav I (2017) Information overload, psychological ill-being, and behavioral intention to continue online healthcare information search. *Computers in Human Behavior* 70: 416–425.

Talamaivao N, Baker G, Harris R, Cormack D and Paine S (2021) Informing anti-racism health policy in Aotearoa New Zealand. *Policy Quarterly* 17(4): 50–57.

Towe VL, Leviton L, Chandra A, Sloan JC, Tait M and Orleans T (2016) Cross-sector collaborations and partnerships: Essential ingredients to help shape health and wellbeing. *Health Affairs* 35(11): 1964–1969.

Tuwe K (2018) *African communities in New Zealand: An investigation of their employment experiences and the impact on their wellbeing using African oral tradition of storytelling as research methodology. African communities in New Zealand: An investigation of their employment experiences and the impact on their wellbeing using African oral tradition of storytelling as research methodology.* Auckland: Auckland University of Technology.

Udah H, Singh P and Chamberlain S (2019) Settlement and employment outcomes of black African immigrants in Southeast Queensland, Australia. *Asian and Pacific Migration Journal* 28(1): 53–74.

United Nations (2015) *The universal declaration of human rights.* https://www.un.org/en/about-us/universal-declaration-of-human-rights

Virgona A and Kashima ES (2021) Diversity ideologies and flourishing: An Australian study comparing polyculturalism, multiculturalism, and colorblindness. *International Journal of Intercultural Relations* 81: 236–251.

Walker N (2014) *Neurodiversity: Some basic terms and definitions.* https://neuroqueer.com/neurodiversity-terms-and-definitions/

Weichselbaumer D (2017) Discrimination against migrant job applicants in Austria: An experimental study. *German Economic Review* 18(2): 237–265.

Wong-Padoongpatt G, Zane N, Okazaki S and Saw A (2017) Decreases in implicit self-esteem explain the racial impact of microaggressions among Asian Americans. *Journal of Counseling Psychology* 64(5): 574.

Zhang J, Wheeler JJ and Richey D (2006) *Cultural validity in assessment instruments for children with autism from a Chinese cultural perspective.* https://soar.suny.edu/handle/20.500.12648/2223

Zhou L, Zhang D, Yang C and Wang Y (2018) Harnessing social media for health information management. *Electronic Commerce Research and Applications* 27: 139–151.

Zurn P and Dumont JC (2008) *Health workforce and international migration: Can New Zealand compete?* OECD health working papers no. 33. OECD Publishing (NJ1).

Chapter 10

Embracing an Evolving Paradigm of Neurodiversity

Etain Quigley

This book marks a significant step in the ongoing evolution of the neurodiversity field, offering both a foundational exploration and an urgent call to action for systemic change across various sectors, particularly in mental health, health, education, and higher education. As the first in a series, this book sets the stage for an expanding body of work that will continue to address the intersections between neurodiversity, mental health, and systemic inequality. The chapters collectively contribute to a nuanced understanding of the lived experiences of neurodivergent individuals, highlighting the oft-overlooked challenges they face while simultaneously showcasing their resilience and the potential for societal transformation.

At its core, this book exemplifies the principle that we are all learning to live within a paradigm shift. This shift is still ongoing, and as we move forward, our collective understanding of neurodiversity – both as a scientific concept and a lived experience concept – continues to evolve. Neurodiversity is no longer merely a topic of academic interest but a fundamental element of social and cultural discourse, encompassing a broad spectrum of lived experiences, identities, and contributions. It requires a willingness to rethink established norms, confront long-standing biases, and embrace diversity as a core strength rather than a deficiency.

The evolving nature of neurodiversity as both an academic field and a social movement reflects the growing recognition that neurological differences are an inherent part of human diversity. However, this recognition comes with significant challenges. The historical treatment of neurodivergent individuals – rooted in harmful practices, pseudoscientific theories, and the imposition of ableist frameworks – has left a complex residue. The chapters in this volume trace this history, acknowledging past harms while actively engaging in reshaping the present and future through neurodiversity-affirming practices.

A central theme in this volume is the community-led approach, which fosters inclusivity and ensures that those most directly impacted by these issues – neurodivergent individuals – are not only part of the conversation but lead it. This approach reflects the ethos of "nothing about us without us," which has gained momentum in social justice movements worldwide. By centring neurodivergent voices, the book challenges the top-down, authoritative structures of traditional academic writing

DOI: 10.4324/9781003495949-11

and encourages a more inclusive, participatory, and dialogue-based model of scholarship. In embracing this ethos, we acknowledge the complexity and diversity of neurodivergent experiences, affirming that there is no singular "correct" way to be neurodivergent, just as there is no universal blueprint for mental health.

The chapters included in this volume are united by a shared commitment to promoting neurodiversity-affirming language and practices that are rooted in respect, empowerment, and inclusivity. The use of neuro-affirming language has proven essential in dismantling harmful stereotypes and reframing the narrative around neurodivergence. By avoiding pathologising terms and instead focusing on the strengths and contributions of neurodivergent individuals, we are beginning to see a shift in both public perception and institutional support structures. This shift represents a fundamental change in how society perceives neurodivergence – not as an anomaly to be fixed, but as a natural variation in the way the human mind functions.

However, the evolving nature of this movement means that the challenges are far from over. Mental health care systems, education systems, and workplaces continue to grapple with the implications of neurodiversity and how best to support individuals with co-occurring mental health conditions. As the chapters in this book have demonstrated, neurodivergent individuals often face systemic barriers in accessing appropriate support, barriers that are compounded by the lack of tailored interventions and the pervasive stigma surrounding mental health and disability. The experiences shared by the authors underscore the need for ongoing research and the development of evidence-based strategies to support neurodivergent individuals with mental health challenges. These challenges will not be overcome overnight, but through sustained dialogue, policy advocacy, and institutional change, meaningful progress is possible.

As this volume makes clear, the intersection between neurodiversity and mental health is not one of simple causality but one of complexity, where social, biological, and cognitive factors intertwine to create both barriers and opportunities. Neurodivergent individuals are disproportionately affected by mental health challenges such as anxiety, depression, and trauma, but these challenges are not inevitable. They are often exacerbated by environmental factors such as societal stigma, lack of understanding, and inadequate support systems. Yet, as the chapters highlight, embracing neurodivergence as part of one's identity rather than something to be cured or fixed can serve as a powerful protective factor against mental health struggles. This shift in perspective is crucial for fostering environments where neurodivergent individuals can thrive, not just survive.

The importance of systemic change cannot be overstated. Whether in schools, universities, or workplaces, the systems that shape the experiences of neurodivergent individuals must evolve to reflect a deeper understanding of neurodiversity. The chapter on higher education systems, in particular, offers compelling recommendations for making universities more neurodivergent-affirming spaces. These recommendations, ranging from leadership inclusion to the development of flexible support systems and inclusive policies, are crucial for ensuring that neurodivergent students are not left behind in their academic and personal development. However, institutional change must be accompanied by cultural change. Both individuals and institutions must work together to dismantle the ableism that permeates many aspects of society. By fostering greater understanding, empathy, and flexibility, we can create environments that truly support neurodivergent individuals in all their diversity.

This book has only begun to scratch the surface of the complex relationship between neurodiversity and mental health. It offers a starting point for further exploration and action, but the conversation must continue. As we move into the next volume of this series, we must remain committed to the idea that neurodiversity is not a static concept but one that will continue to evolve as we deepen our understanding of the brain, identity, and the intersection of these with societal structures. The paradigm shift we are experiencing is ongoing, and it is one that we all must engage in, whether as scholars, educators, policymakers, or community members.

The future of neurodiversity-affirming practices is one that is rooted in the principles of justice, equity, and inclusion. It requires not just a change in policy but a transformation in how we think about difference, identity, and mental health. This book serves as both a reflection of where we are and a roadmap for where we must go, a place where neurodivergent individuals are fully recognised, supported, and empowered. As we continue to learn, adapt, and evolve within this paradigm shift, it is essential that we do so with humility, compassion, and a shared commitment to creating a more inclusive and equitable world for all.

As we reflect on the diverse contributions within this volume, it is evident that neurodiversity is not merely a conceptual framework but an evolving paradigm that intersects with many aspects of human experience and societal structures. The book presents a rich tapestry of insights, highlighting both the unique challenges faced by neurodivergent individuals and the emerging practices that seek to affirm and support their lived experiences. However, this journey is not without its tensions and challenges. Through a critical lens, we can begin to see how these challenges reflect the complexities and contradictions inherent in the neurodiversity paradigm itself – a paradigm that is still very much in development.

At its heart, the neurodiversity paradigm calls for a fundamental rethinking of how we conceptualise neurological differences. It rejects the medical model, which views conditions such as autism, ADHD, and dyslexia as disorders to be treated or cured, and instead embraces the notion that these conditions are natural variations in human cognitive functioning. This book has consistently engaged with this core idea across the chapters, but as we move through the texts, we begin to see both convergence and divergence in how neurodiversity is understood, applied, and contested. The evolving nature of the neurodiversity paradigm becomes apparent not just in the ideas presented but in the real-world challenges of integrating neurodiversity-affirming practices into systems such as mental health, education, and higher education.

Shared Themes and Collective Movements

A central theme that runs through this volume is the recognition of neurodivergent individuals' unique experiences and needs, as well as the need for structural changes to support their mental health and well-being. The convergence of ideas between the chapters is clear, particularly in the shared commitment to supporting neurodivergent individuals through a rights-based, neurodiversity-affirming approach.

One of the most striking areas of convergence is the emphasis on community-led approaches. Whether discussing the mental health needs of autistic adults, the role of schools in supporting neurodivergent learners, or the challenges faced by neurodivergent students in higher education, the chapters stress the importance of centring the voices of neurodivergent individuals themselves. This approach is consistent with the neurodiversity paradigm's principle of "nothing about us without us," which advocates for neurodivergent individuals' active participation in decision-making processes related to their lives and support systems. Across the board, the authors affirm that genuine inclusion can only occur when neurodivergent individuals are not just subjects of research or care but active agents in shaping the policies, practices, and frameworks that affect them.

Moreover, the chapters share a commitment to neuro-affirming language – language that respects, validates, and honours the experiences of neurodivergent individuals. From the historical overview of neurodiversity to the discussions of co-occurring mental health conditions, the authors underscore the importance of avoiding pathologising language and instead embracing terms that recognise neurodivergence as a natural part of human diversity. This shift in language, while seemingly subtle, has profound implications for how neurodivergent individuals are perceived and treated by society, medical professionals, educators, and their peers. It challenges long-held notions of deficiency and instead invites a broader recognition of diverse cognitive styles as valid and valuable.

Tensions and Critiques within the Neurodiversity Paradigm

While there is much agreement within this volume, there are also points of divergence that reveal the complexity of the neurodiversity paradigm. These divergences, rather than detracting from the overall message, reflect the ongoing development of the paradigm and the need for critical engagement with its application in various contexts.

Mental Health and Neurodiversity: A Delicate Balance

One area where the divergence is most apparent is in the discussion of mental health and neurodivergence. Several chapters discussed the co-occurrence of mental health conditions such as anxiety, depression, and trauma among neurodivergent individuals. For example, the chapter on co-occurring mental health conditions in autistic adults highlights how these individuals are at increased risk for mental health struggles, often exacerbated by external factors such as sensory overload, social rejection, and societal stigma. The chapter on neurodiversity in education also touches on the mental health risks faced by neurodivergent students, such as depression, self-harm, and suicidal ideation, stemming from systemic exclusion and bullying.

Here, the neurodiversity paradigm faces a challenge: while it advocates for accepting neurodivergence as part of the natural spectrum of human cognition, it must also address the significant mental health challenges faced by neurodivergent individuals. This is where tensions arise. Some proponents of the neurodiversity paradigm argue that mental health conditions like anxiety and depression should not be viewed as separate from neurodivergence but as part of the lived experience of neurodivergent individuals, shaped by societal factors such as discrimination and a lack of accommodation. Others, however, caution against collapsing the distinction between neurodivergence and mental illness, particularly when mental health issues are severe or pose a risk to individuals' safety.

This tension is most evident when considering interventions. On one hand, a neurodiversity-affirming approach to mental health challenges emphasises environmental adaptations, strengths-based support, and acceptance. On the other hand, traditional mental health approaches, such as cognitive behavioural therapy (CBT) or mindfulness-based interventions (MBIs), are often seen as inadequate or even harmful when applied to neurodivergent individuals without a nuanced understanding of their needs. For example, CBT may not be effective for individuals with autism or ADHD who struggle with emotional regulation, or MBIs may inadvertently trigger trauma or sensory overload. Thus, while the neurodiversity paradigm provides a framework for affirming neurodivergence, it must also acknowledge and address the specific mental health needs of neurodivergent individuals, ensuring that interventions are both affirming and effective.

The Role of Education: Inclusion or Assimilation?

Another point of divergence emerges in the discussions surrounding education and the role of schools in supporting neurodivergent learners. The chapter on mental health in schools stresses the importance of multi-component, preventative, and inclusive approaches to mental health support. It advocates for frameworks like the Continuum of Support, which recognises the varying needs of neurodivergent learners and provides a flexible approach to intervention. However, the chapter also warns against "neurodiversity-lite" – a diluted version of the neurodiversity paradigm that reduces neurodivergence to a set of 'superpowers' without truly addressing the systemic and institutional barriers that neurodivergent learners face.

This cautionary note points to a key divergence in how the neurodiversity paradigm is applied in education. While many advocate for full inclusion and systemic changes to support neurodivergent students, others argue that the emphasis on inclusion must be carefully considered. Is inclusion about assimilating neurodivergent individuals into a system that is fundamentally not designed for them, or is it about redesigning that system to better meet their needs? Here, the neurodiversity paradigm provides a critique of traditional educational practices, but it also faces challenges in reconciling the ideal of inclusion with the practical realities of an education system that has historically marginalised neurodivergent students.

This divergence points to a critical question within the neurodiversity movement: Should the goal be to transform existing systems to be more accommodating, or should the focus shift to creating entirely new models of support that centre on neurodivergent ways of learning and interacting? This question underscores the tension between reformist and radical approaches within the neurodiversity paradigm, as discussed in the chapters on higher education systems and mental health support.

Engaging with Competing Ideas: Moving beyond the Binary

These tensions, the balancing act between affirming neurodivergence while addressing co-occurring mental health issues, and the debate between inclusion and assimilation in education, are not easily resolved. They reflect the complexity of the neurodiversity paradigm itself. However, rather than detracting from the paradigm, these competing ideas enrich it by pushing us to think critically about its application in real-world settings.

As this volume has shown, neurodiversity is not a monolithic concept but a fluid, evolving framework that must continue to be critically engaged with as new insights emerge. The challenges and tensions identified within these chapters are not obstacles to the progress of the neurodiversity movement, but rather opportunities for deeper engagement and growth. By continuing to explore these complexities, we can further develop a neurodiversity paradigm that is inclusive, responsive, and capable of meeting the diverse needs of neurodivergent individuals across all aspects of society.

Moving Forward: Embracing Complexity

The future of the neurodiversity paradigm is one that embraces complexity. As we continue to learn, adapt, and evolve within this paradigm shift, we must remain open to dialogue, critique, and revision. The discussions in this book reflect the diverse and sometimes competing ideas that are part of this ongoing conversation. They also highlight the importance of flexibility, as we cannot afford to treat neurodivergence as a static or one-size-fits-all concept.

By embracing this complexity, we will move closer to the ultimate goal of creating a society in which neurodivergent individuals are not just accepted but celebrated. This requires not only changing the way we think about neurodivergence, but also the way we structure our systems of support, from mental health care to education and beyond. The journey is ongoing, and as we continue to listen to and learn from neurodivergent voices, we can shape a more inclusive, equitable future for all.

One critical dimension that must be addressed in greater detail is the relationship between neurodiversity and global perspectives, particularly from non-Western contexts. While the neurodiversity paradigm has made significant strides in advocating for a more inclusive, affirming approach to neurological differences, it is essential to recognise that much of the discourse around neurodivergence has been shaped by Western frameworks. This is especially evident in the fields of mental health, education, and social policy, where neurodivergent experiences and perspectives from the Global South, home to diverse cultures, histories, and systems, have been largely overlooked.

The neurodiversity paradigm, which champions the natural variation of human cognition and promotes inclusion, has evolved within a predominantly Western context. This cultural lens, while undeniably important in advancing neurodivergent rights in the Global North, risks marginalising the voices, practices, and experiences of neurodivergent individuals in the Global South. As the chapters in this volume have demonstrated, neurodivergent individuals across the world face common challenges such as societal stigma, exclusion, and lack of support. However, the ways in which these challenges manifest and the strategies employed to address them are deeply influenced by local cultural, political, and economic contexts.

The Need for a Global Neurodiversity Perspective

The Global South, comprising regions in Africa, Asia, Latin America, and the Pacific, has a rich diversity of cultural perspectives, medical traditions, and social structures that shape the way neurodivergence is understood and addressed. In these regions, neurodivergence is often viewed through lenses that are different from the individualistic, medicalised frameworks commonly seen in Western discourse. In many cases, traditional healing practices, communal forms of care, and collective responsibility for well-being may be the primary modes of support for neurodivergent individuals. However, the growing influence of Western models of disability and mental health, often driven by global institutions and international policy frameworks, threatens to overshadow these local, culturally specific approaches to neurodivergence.

Currently, the intersection between neurodiversity and the Global South is an under-researched area that requires urgent attention. As highlighted in Chapter 9, the neurodiversity movement, in its current form, risks imposing Western-centric ideas of neurodivergence onto contexts that may not share the same historical, cultural, or epistemological foundations. For example, neurodivergent conditions such as autism or ADHD, which are increasingly diagnosed and understood through medical models in Western countries, may not be recognised in the same way, or at all, in non-Western societies. Furthermore, these conditions may be conceptualised differently, framed in terms of spiritual or social rather than psychological or medical factors.

Thus, the neurodiversity paradigm must engage critically with the complexities of cultural difference. As it expands globally, it must be attuned to the risk of inadvertently imposing Western notions of neurological difference as the universal standard. Again, as highlighted in Chapter 9, caution is required to ensure that neurodiversity does not unintentionally reinforce a colonial mindset that views non-Western ideas and practices as inferior or lacking in sophistication. Instead, there must be a recognition of the value of diverse cultural understandings of neurodivergence and an openness to learning from these perspectives.

The Danger of Universalising the Western Neurodiversity Model

The challenge of expanding the neurodiversity paradigm beyond the West is not only academic; it is also deeply political and ethical. The universalisation of Western models of neurodivergence risks perpetuating a form of epistemic hegemony, where the knowledge systems, practices, and lived experiences of people in the Global South are marginalised, rendered invisible, or dismissed. The risk here is twofold. Firstly, it can lead to the imposition of a one-size-fits-all model of neurodivergence that fails to take into account the diverse ways in which different societies interpret and respond to neurological differences. Secondly, it can further entrench existing inequalities by disregarding the lived experiences of neurodivergent individuals from non-Western cultures and ignoring their agency in shaping their own support systems.

In light of this, it is essential that the neurodiversity paradigm adopts a more pluralistic, inclusive approach that values non-Western perspectives. This means recognising the limitations of the Western model and being open to alternative ways of understanding neurodivergence. For example, in many Indigenous cultures, differences in cognition, behaviour, or social interaction may be understood as part of a larger spiritual or cosmological order, rather than framed as medical or psychological conditions. In other contexts, such as in parts of Africa or South Asia, neurodivergence may be linked to social roles or familial obligations, with the emphasis placed on communal care and responsibility rather than individual therapy or diagnosis. These perspectives are not only valid but also offer important insights into how societies can be more inclusive of neurodivergent individuals without resorting to the pathologising tendencies that often characterise Western mental health models.

Moving beyond Western Hegemony: A Call for Interdisciplinary and Cross-Cultural Research

To avoid the unintentional discrimination of non-Western ideas and perspectives, the neurodiversity paradigm must undergo a process of decolonisation. This involves recognising the intellectual traditions, healing practices, and community-based approaches that have existed long before Western medical models of neurodivergence were introduced. It also requires a shift in how research is conducted, ensuring that scholars from the Global South are given the platform and recognition they deserve in shaping the future of neurodiversity discourse. There must be a concerted effort to engage with Indigenous knowledge systems, local mental health traditions, and community-based practices that offer alternative models of neurodivergence and disability.

Moreover, as scholars and practitioners in the Global North begin to engage with these non-Western ideas, it is essential that the research be collaborative, involving neurodivergent individuals from the Global South in the design, implementation, and dissemination of studies. This will not only ensure that the research is culturally appropriate and sensitive but also empower local communities to shape the discourse on neurodiversity in ways that are meaningful and relevant to their contexts.

There is an urgent need for interdisciplinary and cross-cultural research that examines how the neurodiversity paradigm can be adapted and applied in the Global South. This research should focus on understanding how neurodivergence is conceptualised across different cultures, how mental health challenges are addressed in non-Western contexts, and what best practices can be shared between regions. Furthermore, this research must be underpinned by a commitment to anti-colonial, anti-racist, and intersectional principles, recognising the ways in which systems of oppression – whether racial, economic, or cultural – impact neurodivergent individuals differently across the globe.

Toward a Truly Global Neurodiversity Paradigm

While the neurodiversity paradigm has made significant strides in advocating for the rights, dignity, and inclusion of neurodivergent individuals, its global application remains an under-researched and critically important area. The expanding discourse on neurodiversity must move beyond the limitations of Western frameworks and engage deeply with non-Western perspectives. This process of globalising the neurodiversity paradigm is not without its challenges, but it is essential for ensuring that neurodivergent individuals worldwide can benefit from inclusive, affirming, and culturally relevant support systems.

As we continue to develop the neurodiversity paradigm, we must ensure that it does not inadvertently discriminate against or exclude non-Western ideas. This requires careful attention to the risks of imposing a universal Western model on diverse cultural contexts and an active effort to centre the voices and experiences of neurodivergent individuals from the Global South. Only through a truly global, interdisciplinary, and culturally attuned approach can we build a neurodiversity movement that is inclusive, equitable, and empowering for all neurodivergent individuals, regardless of their geographic, cultural, or social background.

Conclusion

In conclusion, this volume has illuminated the multifaceted and evolving nature of neurodiversity, showcasing its intersections with mental health, education, and social structures across both Western and non-Western contexts. Through an exploration of lived experiences, the book has made clear that neurodivergent individuals face unique challenges that require systemic change and a fundamental rethinking of how we conceptualise neurological differences. By embracing a neurodiversity-affirming framework, we have the opportunity to foster a society that values diversity in cognition and experience, moving beyond outdated medicalised models that pathologise difference. However, this shift cannot occur in isolation – it requires a commitment to empirical, lived experience work that prioritises the voices of neurodivergent individuals and advocates for their active involvement in shaping the policies and practices that affect their lives. This approach must be inclusive, culturally sensitive, and grounded in the principles of justice and equity, ensuring that no one is left behind, whether in the Global North or Global South. As we continue to learn and evolve within the neurodiversity paradigm, we must collectively say goodbye to exclusion and non-acceptance, forging a future where all neurodivergent individuals are not only accepted but celebrated for the unique perspectives they bring to the world.

Index

Note: Page numbers in *italic* indicate a figure on the corresponding page.

142; disability in higher education 144–145; mental health 146–147; recommendations 147–148, 149–150; reforming the systems 148–149; reframing mental health 146–147; student development theory 144; theoretical background 141–142
urominority 4, 131
urotypical 18–23, 27–30, 42–46, 71–72
ew Zealand 155–157, 165–166; accessing services 163–165; complexity 159; diverse understandings 159–161; intersectionality 158–159; language 161; neurodiversity and mental illness nexus 157–158; racism and marginalisation 161–163

perationalising neurodiversity 128–129
utcomes, adverse 66–68
verly dominant psychological theories 12–14

artnerships 132–133
ersistent depressive disorder (PDD)/ dysthymia 102–103
lanning 133
olicy 81–88, 133, 173–174, 178
olitical ideologies 14–15
remenstrual dysphoric disorder (PMDD) 104–105
providers, healthcare: communication with 64–66
pseudoscientific medical practices 11–12
psychological theories, overly dominant 12–14

racism 161–163
reform 148–149
relationships 132–133
research 179–180
resilience 43–44

school-age learners 126–128; iatrogenic harm to 128–131
screening scales 98

self-harm/suicidal ideation 4, 27, 146, 176
sensation 120; role in emotional experience 118–120
sensory processing differences 37, 122
service provision see mental health service provision
services, access to 163–165
setting, impact of 98–99
social anxiety disorder (SAD) 107–109
social inclusion/exclusion 2
social model 19–22
social stigma 40–42
societal factors 40–42, 176
SPACE framework 74–75, 75
stigma 1–4, 7–8, 40–47, 141–142, 146–150, 157–159, 173, 176–178
Street-Level Bureaucracy 81
strengths-based approach 21
stress 5–7, 28–35, 44–47, 81–85, 106–107, 116–118, 175–176
Student Development Theory (SDT) 7, 142, 144
students see college students; school-age learners
support, continuum of 127–128
survey: development of 62–63; respondents to 63; results 63–70
systems, reform of 148–149

theories: comorbidity 95–97; co-occurrence 97; Critical Disability Theory (CDT) 142; Neurodiversity Paradigm 141–143; overly dominant psychological theories 12–14; Student Development Theory (SDT) 144
thought patterns, negative 35–36
Tourette's syndrome 6, 17, 114–115
trauma 28–35, 173–176
triple empathy problem 71–74

uncertainty, intolerance of 36–38
universalisation 179

Western hegemony 179–180
Western neurodiversity model 179

For Product Safety Concerns and Information please contact our EU
representative GPSR@taylorandfrancis.com
Taylor & Francis Verlag GmbH, Kaufingerstraße 24, 80331 München, Germany